THE SUPERMARINE
SPITFIRE

Supermarine Spitfire VB

1 Aerial stub attachment
2 Rudder upper hinge
3 Fabric-covered rudder
4 Rudder tab
5 Sternpost
6 Rudder tab hinge
7 Rear navigation light
8 Starboard elevator tab
9 Starboard elevator structure
10 Elevator balance
11 Tailplane front spar
12 IFF aerial
13 Castoring non-retractable
   tailwheel
14 Tailwheel strut
15 Fuselage double frame
16 Elevator control lever
17 Tailplane spar/
   fuselage attachment

18 Fin rear spar
   (fuselage frame
   extension)
19 Fin front spar
   (fuselage frame
   extension)
20 Port elevator tab hinge
21 Port elevator
22 IFF aerial
23 Port tailplane
24 Rudder control lever
25 Cross shaft
26 Tailwheel oleo access place
27 Tailwheel oleo shock-absorber
28 Fuselage angled frame
29 Battery compartment
30 Lower longeron
31 Elevator control cables
32 Fuselage construction
33 Rudder control cables
34 Radio compartment
35 Radio support tray
36 Flare chute
37 Oxygen bottle
38 Auxiliary long-range fuel tank
   (29gal/132l)
39 Dorsal formation light
40 Aerial lead-in
41 HF aerial
42 Aerial mast
43 Cockpit aft glazing
44 Voltage regulator
45 Canopy track
46 Structural bulkhead
47 Headrest
48 Plexiglass canopy
49 Rear-view mirror
50 Entry flap (port)

51 Air bottles (alternative rear
   fuselage stowage)
52 Sutton harness
53 Pilot's seat (moulded Bakelite)
54 Datum longeron
55 Seat support frame
56 Wingroot fillet
57 Seat adjustment lever
58 Rudder pedal frame
59 Elevator control connecting tube
60 Control column spade grip
61 Trim wheel
62 Reflector gunsight
63 External windscreen armour
64 Instrument panel
65 Main fuselage fuel tank
   (48gal/218l)
66 Fuel tank/longeron
   attachment fittings

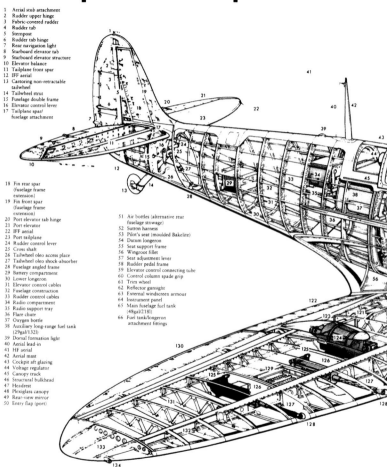

4

GREAT AIRCRAFT OF WWII

This edition printed in 2009

© 2002 Bookmart Limited

ISBN: 978-1-86147-300-4

1 3 5 7 9 10 8 6 4 2

Published by Abbeydale Press
An imprint of Bookmart Ltd
Registered Number 2372865
Blaby Road, Wigston,
Leicester, LE18 4SE
United Kingdom

Originally published by Bookmart Ltd as part of
Great Aircraft of WWII (hardback).

Printed in Thailand

67 Rudder pedals
68 Rudder bar
69 King post
70 Fuselage lower fuel tank (37gal/168l)
71 Firewall/bulkhead
72 Engine bearer attachment
73 Steel tube bearers
74 Magneto
75 'Fishtail'/exhaust manifold
76 Gun heating 'intensifier'
77 Hydraulic tank
78 Fuel filler cap
79 Air compressor intake
80 Air compressor
81 Rolls-Royce Merlin 45 engine
82 Coolant piping
83 Port cannon wing fairing
84 Flaps
85 Aileron control cables
86 Aileron push tube
87 Bellcrank

88 Aileron hinge
89 Port aileron
90 Machine-gun access panels
91 Port wingtip
92 Port navigation light
93 Leading-edge skinning
94 Machine-gun ports (protected)
95 20mm cannon muzzle
96 Three-blade constant-speed propeller
97 Spinner
98 Propeller hub
99 Coolant tank
100 Cowling fastening
101 Engine anti-vibration mounting pad
102 Engine accessories
103 Engine bearers
104 Main engine support member
105 Coolant pipe
106 Exposed oil tank
107 Port mainwheel

108 Mainwheel fairing
109 Carburettor air intake
110 Stub/spar attachment
111 Mainwheel leg pivot point
112 Main spar
113 Leading-edge ribs (diagonals deleted for clarity)
114 Mainwheel leg shock-absorber
115 Mainwheel fairing
116 Starboard mainwheel
117 Angled axle
118 Cannon barrel support fairing
119 Spar cut-out
120 Mainwheel well
121 Flap structure
122 Flap structure
123 Cannon wing fairing
124 Cannon magazine drum (120 rounds)

125 Machine-gun support brackets
126 Gun access panels
127 .303in machine-gun barrels
128 Machine-gun ports
129 Ammunition boxes (350rpg)
130 Starboard aileron construction
131 Wing ribs
132 Single-tube outer spar section
133 Wingtip structure
134 Starboard navigation light

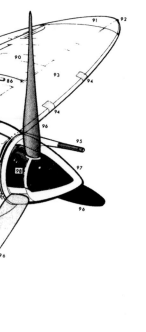

A FIGHTER IS BORN

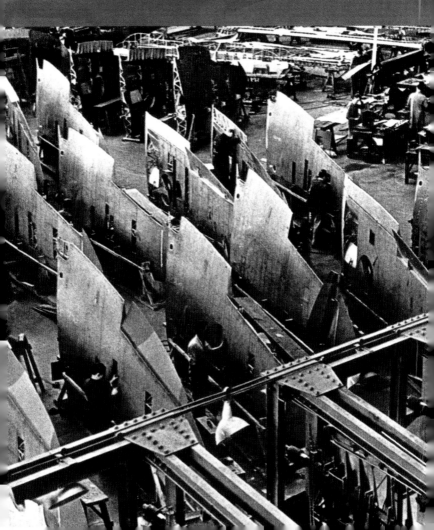

The story of the Spitfire began almost ten years before Dick Audet's famous action, in December 1934. Then, at the Supermarine Aviation Company's works at Southampton, Reginald Mitchell and his team finalized the layout of their new high-speed fighter for the RAF.

Mitchell had established his name as a highly successful designer of racing floatplanes for the Schneider Trophy competition. One of his designs – the Supermarine S.5 – had won the Schneider Trophy competition in 1927. The S.6 won it two years later in 1929. After another two-year gap the Supermarine S.6B won the trophy outright for Britain in 1931 and later went on to raise the World Air Speed record to 407mph (655km/hr).

These had been magnificent achievements but the market for high-speed racing seaplanes was extremely limited. The Supermarine company's main 'bread and butter' products were its big Southampton and Scapa flying boats which now equipped seven RAF maritime patrol squadrons.

In 1934 the fastest fighter in the Royal Air Force was the Hawker Fury, which had a maximum speed of 207mph at 14,000 ft (333km/hr at 4,270m). At that time, Air Vice Marshal Hugh Dowding was responsible for issuing to manufacturers the specifications for new aircraft required for the Royal Air Force. Dowding was what we would now call a 'technocrat'. He saw the vital need for a new fighter to bridge the huge gap in performance between the Schneider Trophy racers and the biplanes that were then in service.

MITCHELL'S FIRST FIGHTER

In February 1934 Reginald Mitchell's first fighter design appeared, the Supermarine Type 224.

Far left: Production of wings at Woolston, early in 1939.

THE SCHNEIDER TROPHY AND THE SPITFIRE

The Supermarine S.6B, Reginald Mitchell's final racing floatplane design, gained the Schneider Trophy outright for Great Britain in 1931. Later that year it raised the world absolute speed record to 407mph (655km/hr). One common myth about the Spitfire is that it was 'developed from' the Supermarine S.6B. This is simply not true. The two aircraft were quite different designs, intended for quite different roles.

Type Single-seat racing floatplane.
Power Plant One Rolls-Royce 'R' engine developing 2,350hp.
Dimensions Span 30ft 0in (9.14m), length 28ft 10in (8.79m).
Weight Maximum loaded weight 6,086lb (2760kg).
Performance Maximum speed 407mph at 245 ft (655km/hr at 75m), a World record.

Right: The Supermarine S.6 racing floatplane won the Schneider Trophy for Great Britain in 1931. Later that year it captured the world absolute speed record at 407mph (655km/hr).

THE SUPERMARINE TYPE 224

REGINALD MITCHELL'S FIRST FIGHTER DESIGN

This single-seat interceptor fighter used a novel type of evaporative cooling for the engine, employing a steam condenser built into the leading edge of each wing. The system gave continual trouble and would probably have precluded the fighter being ordered for the RAF even if its performance had been more impressive.

Type Single-seat interceptor fighter.
Armament Four Vickers 0.303in (7.7mm) machine guns synchronized to fire through the propeller arc.
Power Plant One Rolls-Royce Goshawk developing 680hp.
Dimensions Span 45ft 10in (13.97m)

length 29ft 5$\frac{1}{4}$in (8.97m).
Weight Maximum loaded weight 4,743lb (2,151kg).
Performance Maximum speed 228mph at 15,000ft (367km/hr at 4,575m); time to climb to 15,000ft, 9$\frac{1}{2}$ minutes.

Above: The Supermarine Type 224, Reginald Mitchell's unsuccessful first attempt at designing a fighter aircraft.

Right: The Hawker Fury, the fastest fighter type in the RAF in 1934, had a maximum speed of 207mph (333km/hr).

The aircraft took part in a competition to select a new fighter type for the Royal Air Force. The Type 224 proved a flop. Its maximum speed was only 228mph (367km/hr) and it took 9$\frac{1}{2}$ minutes to reach 15,000 ft (4,575m). The cooling system for the engine, gave continual trouble. The winner of the competition, the Gloster entrant later named the Gladiator, had a maximum speed of 242mph (390km/hr) and it climbed to 15,000 ft in 6$\frac{1}{2}$ minutes.

Having learned that painful lesson, Reginald Mitchell persuaded the company to allow him to design a smaller, and more streamlined fighter. This time he would use the new 1,000 horse power V-12 engine, later named the Merlin, then under test at the Rolls-Royce company in Derby. When Air Vice Marshal Dowding saw details of the proposed new fighter he gave it his full support, and issued an official Royal Air Force specification so that the government would meet most of the cost of building a proto-type.

The new fighter made its maiden flight on 5 March 1936, with Chief Test Pilot 'Mutt' Summers at the controls. the Air Ministry allocated a name to the new fighter – 'Spitfire'.

FASTEST FIGHTER

'It is claimed that the Spitfire is the fastest military aeroplane in the world. It is small and light for a machine of its calibre (the structural weight is said to have been brought down to a level never before attained in the single-seat fighter class), and its speed and manoeuvrability are something to marvel at.

'Tight turns were made at high speed after dives, and the control at low speeds was amply demonstrated. The demonstration was cramped by low clouds, but after the main flying display the machine was taken up again and gave one of the smoothest displays of high-speed aerobatics ever seen in this country.'

FLIGHT MAGAZINE 3 JULY 1936

Above: The prototype Supermarine F.37/34, serial number K 5054, pictured at Eastleigh shortly before its maiden flight. The metal parts of the aircraft were unpainted, the aircraft carried no armament and the undercarriage was locked in the down position.

When Mitchell learned of the official choice of name, he was heard to comment: 'It's the sort of bloody-silly name they would give it!'

During flight tests the new fighter attained a maximum speed of 349mph at 16,800 ft (562km/hr at 5,122m), and in the climb it reached 30,000 ft (9,145m) in 17 minutes. It was one of the most heavily armed, fighters, designed to carry eight Browning .303in (7.7mm) machine guns in the wings.

LARGE ORDER

The Spitfire became available at exactly the right time for the Royal Air Force. In Germany the Luftwaffe was building up its strength rapidly. Its new monoplane fighter type, the Messerschmitt 109, was on the point of entering large-scale production. To meet the mounting threat, in June 1936 the British Government signed a contract for 310 Spitfires.

The Spitfire first appeared on 18 June 1936, at Eastleigh. With press photographers snapping away, Jeffrey Quill started the Spitfire's engine and taxied to one end of the runway. As he pushed open the throttle to begin his take-off run, the pilot made a brief scan of his instruments, and noticed the needle of the oil pressure gauge suddenly drop to zero. That left him in an unenviable position. He had no room to stop before reaching the airfield boundary. The pilot eased the aircraft into the air and reduced power. He eased open the throttle for one last burst of power, the engine responded and he made a safe landing.

PROTOTYPE SPITFIRE

Type Single-seat interceptor fighter.
Armament Eight-.303in (7.7mm) Browning machine guns with 350 rounds per gun.
Power Plant One Rolls-Royce Merlin Type C liquid cooled V-12 engine with single-speed supercharger developing 990hp.
Dimensions Span 40ft (12.1m); length 29ft 11in (9.17m).
Weight Maximum loaded weight 5,395lb (2,446kg).
Performance Maximum speed 349 mph at 16,800 ft (562 km/hr at 5,122 m). Service ceiling 35,400ft (10,790m).

Below: The Supermarine works at Woolston near Southampton.
Above: Close to disaster! Jeffrey Quill taking off in the prototype Spitfire at Eastleigh on 18 June 1936. A few seconds before this photograph was taken, an oil pipe had come adrift. In the background is the Southern Railway works over which the aircraft had to pass before it returned to the airfield. By skilful flying, Quill landed before the engine seized. Had the prototype been lost that day, it is possible that the RAF might have cancelled its order in which case the Spitfire would not have gone into production.

Examination of the engine revealed that an oil pipe had come adrift, allowing the lubrication system to run dry. The engine was changed and sent to Rolls Royce for examination, but it had suffered remarkably little damage. Had the prototype been lost during its first air display, the consequences to the nation hardly bear thinking about. Only the one Spitfire existed and it had not completed its initial performance trials with the Royal Air Force. If it had crashed the Royal Air Force would probably have cancelled the contract and ordered other fighters instead. That would have had a disastrous effect on the capability of Fighter Command during the Battle of Britain, four years later.

Five days later the Spitfire resumed flying with a new engine. On 27 June Flight Lieutenant Hugh Edwardes-Jones demonstrated the aircraft at the Royal Air Force Pageant at Hendon. Two days later 'Mutt' Summers flew it at the Society of British Aircraft Constructors' air display at Hatfield. The demonstrations aroused enormous public interest in the fighter, and drew lyrical descriptions in the press.

ON DISPLAY

The prototype completed its initial service trials at Martlesham Heath in July 1936, and returned to Eastleigh for modification. The fighter received a newer version of the Merlin, giving slightly greater power, and eight machine guns were fitted in the wings.

One of the most serious problems was that the fighter's guns did not work reliably at high altitude. During the initial firing trials in March 1937, all eight guns fired perfectly at 4,000 ft (1,220m). A few days later, when an RAF pilot climbed the Spitfire to 32,000 ft (9,755m) over the North Sea for the first high-altitude firing, it nearly ended in tragedy. One gun fired 171 rounds before it failed, another fired 8 rounds, one fired 4 rounds and the remaining five guns failed to fire at all. When the Spitfire touched down at Martlesham Heath after the test the shock of the landing released the previously frozen-up breech blocks. Three of the weapons loosed off a round in the general direction of Felixstowe, fortunately without hitting anyone.

'...the Spitfires will be useless as fighting aircraft...'

During the next 18 months Supermarine engineers tried various schemes to solve the problem of gun freezing, but the guns were still not function-

MY GOD, IT'S MADE OF TIN

Whenever the prototype Spitfire landed away from its base, it was the subject of great interest. At that time most airframes comprised a wood or light metal framework with a covering of linen fabric. The streamlined all-metal monoplane Spitfire with its enclosed cockpit and retractable undercarriage made every other aircraft in the Royal Air Force look positively prehistoric!

During a test flight in December 1936 Jeffrey Quill ran short of fuel, and landed his Spitfire near Chichester. As he taxied in, a crowd of RAF ground crewmen gathered to meet it. Then, Quill recalled:

'I taxied to a standstill and shut down, and could hear a tapping sound. I checked I had shut everything down, but the tapping sound continued. Then as I climbed out I saw the reason. Several mechanics were standing around the rear fuselage, tapping it with their knuckles disbelievingly. "My God, one of them exclaimed, It's made of tin!"'

ing reliably in July 1938 when the first Spitfires were delivered to the Royal Air Force.

It took until October 1938 to resolve the problem. Then on the 14th, a service pilot took the prototype to high altitude and fired off the entire contents of the ammunition boxes. The gun-heating modification was then incorporated in all Spitfires on the production line.

During the test programme the prototype Spitfire survived two serious accidents. During March 1937, it made an emergency landing with engine failure.

Later it suffered an undercarriage collapse, after a fatigue fracture in one of the main wheel legs. On 4 September 1939, the aircraft suffered serious damage in a fatal landing accident. Since there was no further use for it the machine was scrapped.

The prototype Spitfire had cost the public purse a mere £15,776.

Below: The prototype Spitfire wearing military camouflage, in 1938. The muzzles of the two outer machine guns can be seen protruding from the wing.

SPITFIRE IN ACTION

The initial order for 310 Spitfires placed the Supermarine Company in a difficult position. They had previously built small batches of flying boats for the Royal Air Force and its work force numbered only about 500. The new all-metal fighter required specialized manufacturing techniques, and at a time when the aircraft industry was expanding it was difficult to recruit workers with the necessary skills. As a result there were delays in getting the fighter into production.

In August 1938, No. 19 Squadron at Duxford received the first Spitfires. It took until December for the unit to get its full complement of aircraft, then other squadrons began to re-equip. By this time Hugh Dowding had been promoted to Air Chief Marshal and held the post of Commander-in-Chief RAF Fighter Command. By a quirk of history, the man who had done so much to bring the Spitfire into being was now to direct these fighters into action.

When Great Britain declared war on Germany in September 1939, RAF Fighter Command possessed 187 Spitfires in front-line units.

Spitfires first saw action on 6 September 1939, during the so-called 'Battle of Barking Creek'.

Because of a technical fault at the radar station at Canewdon in Essex, aircraft flying west of the station appeared on the screen as if their position

Left: Cockpit of early Spitfire I.
Inset: Spitfires of No. 19 Squadron.

SPITFIRE I

Type: Single-seat interceptor fighter.
Armament: Eight Browning .303in (7.7mm) machine guns with 350 rounds per gun.
Power Plant: One Rolls-Royce Merlin II liquid cooled V-12 engine with single-speed supercharger developing 1030 horse power.
Dimensions: Span 36ft 10in (10.98m); length 29ft 11in (9.11m).
Weight: Maximum loaded weight 5,819lb (2,639kg).
Performance: Maximum speed 362mph at 18,500ft (583km/hr at 5,640m).

Top and overleaf: The 600th production Spitfire during its testing in April 1940. During the Battle of Britain this aircraft served with No.64 Squadron.
Above: Spitfires and Hurricanes from several squadrons lined up at Digby in Lincolnshire. The aircaft had assembled there prior to a massed flypast over cities in the Midlands to mark Empire Air Day on 20 May 1939. (No. 72 Squadron Archive)

Spitfires first saw action on 6 September 1939, during the so-called 'Battle of Barking Creek'

was east of the radar. It looked as if the Luftwaffe was about to launch an onslaught on the capital. The operators at Canewdon reported 20 unidentified aircraft heading towards London from the east.

> ### For the next hour chaos, utter and complete, reigned over the Thames estuary

Within minutes the formations being tracked on the radar, all of them now designated as 'hostile', increased to twelve.

A GERMAN PILOT'S OPINION OF THE SPITFIRE

Below: Spitfires in captivity: by the beginning of the Battle of Britain the Germans had captured four Spitfires in flying or repairable condition.
Bottom: A captured Spitfire painted in bogus British markings and used in propaganda photographs.

'I was able to fly a captured Spitfire at Jever. My first impression was that it had a beautiful engine. It purred. The engine of the Messerschmitt 109 was very loud. Also the Spitfire was easier to fly, and to land, than the Me 109. The 109 was unforgiving of any inattention. I felt familiar with the Spitfire from the very start. That was my first and lasting impression. But with my experience with the 109, I personally would not have

traded it for a Spitfire. I had the impression, though I did not fly the Spitfire long enough to prove it, that the 109 was the faster, especially in the dive. Also, I think the pilot's view was better from the 109. In the Spitfire one flew further back, a bit more over the wing.'

OBERLEUTNANT HANS SCHMOLLER-HALDY, MESSERSCHMITT 109 PILOT, FIGHTER GESCHWADER 54

Soon afterwards an anti-aircraft gun battery opened fire at 'twin-engined bombers' passing overhead. Shortly after that, the leader of a Spitfire squadron broadcast a 'Tally Ho!' call, to indicate that he had enemy planes in sight and was about to engage. For the next hour chaos, utter and complete, reigned over the Thames Estuary. Squadrons of fighters cruised between the banks of cloud, seeking enemy planes

but finding only friendly ones. There were several brief fire fights, each one broken off when it became evident that the 'opponents' were 'friendly ones'. The shortage of fuel forced the Spitfires and Hurricanes to return to their airfields. There had never been any German aircraft in the area. The fiasco cost the RAF three aircraft destroyed; two Hurricanes shot down by Spitfires of No. 74 Squadron and a Blenheim shot down by anti-aircraft fire. One RAF pilot was killed.

Following the action Fighter Command launched an official inquiry to determine what had gone wrong and prevent a recurrence. One lesson, which has to be re-learned for each war, was the folly of opening

Top: Spitfires of No. 41 Squadron photographed during the Battle of Britain.
Above: Spitfires of Nos 222 and 603 Squadrons at Hornchurch at the time of the Battle of Britain.

Note the steam roller in the background, to roll flat the filled-in bomb craters on the airfield.
Below: The Messerschmitt 109E was the most formidable opponent facing RAF Fighter Command.

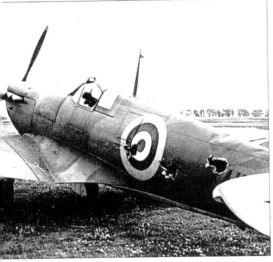

Left: *Spitfire X4110 had a service life of only 15 minutes! On the morning of 18 August 1940 this brand new aircraft arrived at No.602 Squadron at Westhampnett as a replacement. Before there was time to paint on the squadron markings Flight Lieutenant Dunlop Urie took it into action and in an encounter with Me 109s the fighter suffered severe damage.*

Spitfires and Hurricanes flew large numbers of sorties to cover the evacuation of Dunkirk

fire on aircraft that had not been positively identified as 'hostile'. Another was the looking at the reports from one radar in isolation (stations had reported seeing no aircraft, but the absence of plots had been ignored). A further lesson was the need to fit IFF (identification friend or foe) radar equipment in all RAF fighters, and the programme to build and install this equipment received top priority.

The Spitfires first encountered German aircraft en masse on on 21 May 1940, when rapid advance of the German army

into Belgium and France brought the war to within reach of RAF fighters operating from airfields in Kent. During the following weeks, Spitfires and Hurricanes flew large numbers of sorties to cover the evacuation of Allied troops from Dunkirk.

BATTLE OF BRITAIN

By July 1940 RAF Fighter Command possessed fifty squadrons of single-seat fighters, thirty-one with Hurricanes and nineteen with Spitfires. The Battle of Britain opened with

Above: Pilot Officer Robert Doe of No. 234 Squadron was credited with eleven enemy aircraft destroyed and two shared destroyed. He then moved to a Hurricane squadron and shot down three more. Doe suffered serious injuries during a crash landing in January 1941, and these prevented him flying for several months.
Above right: Dunlop Urie, his feet bandaged, waiting to be taken to hospital.
Right: Squadron Leader Donald MacDonell commanded No. 64 Squadron during the Battle and was credited with nine enemy aircraft destroyed and one shared destroyed.

WAITING AT READINESS

During the Battle of Britain RAF fighter squadrons waiting to go into action were held on the ground at what was known as Readiness 5 Minutes. The fighters sat in their earth-and-brick revetments around the perimeter of the airfield, and from time to time the ground crews would run the engines to warm the oil and ensure the planes could take off immediately. Squadron Leader Don MacDonell, commander of No. 64 Squadron during the Battle, explained what it was like.

'When we were at Readiness the pilots would be relaxing at the dispersal area – reading, chatting, playing cards. Each Flight had a separate crew room, so no pilot was too far from his Spitfire. I would be out of my office, wearing flying kit and Mae West, with the Flight I was to lead on that day. Each pilot's parachute was laid out on the seat of his aircraft, with the straps laid over the armour plating at the back of the cockpit.

Every time the telephone rang there would be a ghastly silence. The orderly would answer it and often hear something like: "Yes, Sir... yes Sir...Sergeant Smith wanted on the phone." And everyone would breath again.'

Luftwaffe attacks on convoys of shipping passing through the English Channel, in an effort to disrupt the coastal traffic and also to force the RAF into action.

Above left: Flying Officer Leonard Haines of No. 19 Squadron was credited with eight enemy 'kills' and four shared destroyed. He died in a flying accident in April 1941.

Above right: Squadron Leader Derek Boitel-Gill commanding No. 152 Squadron was credited with eight aircraft destroyed. He died in a flying accident in September 1941.

There were repeated attacks on Fighter Command airfields in the south of England

These actions were a prelude to the main Luftwaffe campaign, which began on 13 August, aimed at destroying Fighter Command. That day German aircraft launched multi-pronged attacks on the Royal Navy bases at Portland and Southampton and on the airfields at Detling and Eastchurch.

Every major airfield in the No. 11 Group area took hard knocks. However, there was an efficient damage-repair organisation and in the event only

'SCRAMBLE'

In Fighter Command the code-word 'Scramble' meant 'get airborne as soon as possible'. When pilots received the order they ran as if their lives depended on it. Each 30-second delay in getting airborne meant 1,000 feet (305m) less altitude they had when they met the enemy. Everyone knew that a Spitfire caught in the climb was easy meat for a Messerschmitt attacking in a dive. Squadron Leader Donald MacDonell explained the procedure for getting airborne:

'The orderly answering the telephone would shout "SCRAMBLE!" and each pilot would dash for his aircraft. One mechanic would already have started the engine; the other would be holding the parachute up and help me strap it on. Then I would climb into the cockpit and he would pass my seat straps over my shoulders and help me fasten them. When I gave the thumbs-up he would slam shut the side door and I would pull tight the various straps. I would pull on my helmet, plug in the R/T lead and check that the engine was running properly. If all was well I would wave to the groundcrew to pull away the chocks, open the throttle, and move forward across the grass to the take-off position. There I would line up, open the throttle wide and begin my take-off run with the rest of my pilots following as fast as they could. The whole thing, from the scramble order to the last aircraft leaving the ground, took about a minute and a half.'

SPITFIRE DEPLOYMENT, SEPTEMBER 1940

Spitfire units, at 14th September, before the Battle of Britain on the next day. First figure aircraft serviceable, in brackets aircraft unserviceable.

No. 10 GROUP, HQ BOX, WILTSHIRE
Middle Wallop Sector
No. 152 Squadron 17 (2) Warmwell
No. 609 Squadron 15 (3) Middle Wallop
St Eval Sector
No. 234 Squadron 16 (1) St Eval
Group Total **48 (6)**

No. 11 GROUP, HQ UXBRIDGE, MIDDLESEX
Biggin Hill Sector
No. 72 Squadron 10 (7) Biggin Hill
No. 92 Squadron 16 (1) Biggin Hill
No. 66 Squadron 14 (2) Gravesend
Hornchurch Sector
No. 603 Squadron 14 (5) Hornchurch
No. 41 Squadron 12 (6) Rochford
No. 222 Squadron 11 (3) Rochford
Tangmere Sector
No. 602 Squadron 15 (4) Westhampnett
Group Total **92 (28)**

No. 12 GROUP, HQ WATNALL, NOTTINGHAMSHIRE
Duxford Sector
No. 19 Squadron 14 (0) Fowlmere
Coltishall Sector
No. 74 Squadron 14 (8) Coltishall
Wittering Sector
No. 266 Squadron 14 (5) Wittering
Digby Sector
No. 611 Squadron 17 (1) Digby
Kirton-in-Lindsey Sector
No. 616 Squadron 14 (4) Kirton-in-Lindsey
No. 64 Squadron 7 (3) Leconfield
6 (3) Ringway
Group Total **86 (24)**

No. 13 GROUP, HQ NEWCASTLE, NORTHUMBERLAND
Catterick Sector
No. 54 Squadron 15 (2) Catterick
Usworth Sector
No. 610 Squadron 14 (5) Acklington
Turnhouse Sector
No. 65 Squadron 15 (5) Turnhouse
Group Total **44 (12)**

Spitfires at Operational Training Units 26 (24)

Spitfire Production During Week Prior to 14 September 38

Replacement Spitfires held at Maintenance Units, 14 September 1940
Ready for immediate issue to units 47
Ready for issue within four days 10

Below left: Sergeant Basil Whall flew with No.602 Squadron and was credited with seven enemy aircraft destroyed and two shared destroyed. In October 1940 he suffered fatal injuries when he tried to land his damaged aircraft after a combat sortie.
Below right: Lieutenant Arthur 'Admiral' Blake, a Fleet Air Arm pilot loaned to RAF Fighter Command, flew with No.19 Squadron. Credited with four enemy aircraft destroyed, he was shot down and killed in October 1940.

one airfield, that at Manston in Kent, was put out of action for more than a few hours. Only in rare instances were the raiders able to catch RAF fighters on the ground. By the time the German bombers arrived to deliver their attack on an airfield, the Spitfires and Hurricanes based there were usually airborne and well clear. Fighters able to fly but not fight took off on 'survival scrambles' with orders to keep clear of the area until the threat had passed. Aircraft unable to fly were wheeled into the protective revetments, or dispersed around the airfield where they were difficult to hit. As a result, the frontline fighter units lost less than twenty fighters destroyed on the ground, despite the almost daily attacks on airfields.

On 7 September the Luftwaffe shifted its attack to London, concentrating its main effort against the sprawling dock area to the east of the city. During the following week there were three further attacks on the capital. Then on 15 September, Battle of Britain Day, the Luftwaffe mounted two separate raids on London.

'IT DEMONSTRATED THE DETERMINATION AND BRAVERY WITH WHICH THE TOMMIES WERE FIGHTING OVER THEIR OWN COUNTRY'

Early on the afternoon of 15 September 1940, as the Heinkel 111s of Bomber Geschwader 26 were passing Maidstone on their way home, the formation suddenly came under attack from Spitfires. Leutnant Roderich Cescotti, one of the German pilots, recalled:

'A few Tommies succeeded in penetrating our fighter escort. I saw a Spitfire dive steeply through our escort, level out and close rapidly on our formation. It opened fire, from ahead and to the right, and its tracers streaked towards us. At that moment a Bf 109, which we had not seen before, appeared behind the Spitfire and we saw its rounds striking the Spitfire's tail. But the Tommy continued his attack, coming straight for us, and his rounds slashed into our aircraft. We could not return the fire for fear of hitting the Messerschmitt. I put my left arm across my face to protect it from the plexiglass splinters flying around the cockpit, holding the controls with my right hand. With only the thin plexiglass between us, we were eye-to-eye with the enemy's eight machine guns. At the last moment the Spitfire pulled up and passed very close over though out of control, and went down steeply trailing black smoke. Waggling its wings, the Messerschmitt swept past us and curved in for another attack. The action lasted only a few seconds, but it demonstrated the determination and bravery with which the Tommies were fighting over their own country.'

Cescotti's Heinkel had taken several hits, but he was able to hold position in formation. He made a normal landing at his base at Wevelghem in Belgium.

Almost certainly the courageous Spitfire pilot was Flying Officer Peter Pease of No.603 Squadron, who was shot down at the time, the place, and in the manner described by Cescotti. When the blazing fighter smashed into the ground a few miles southeast of Maidstone, Pease was still in the cockpit.

The son of Sir Richard Pease, Arthur Peter Pease studied at Eton and Cambridge University before joining the Royal Air Force at the beginning of the war. In July 1940 he was posted to No 603 Squadron based at Dyce airfield near Aberdeen and later that month he shared in the destruction of a Heinkel 111. Early in August the Squadron moved to Hornchurch, north-east of London, to take part in the defence of southern England. On 3 September Pease was credited with shooting down a Messerschmitt 109, and four days later his Spitfire suffered battle damage and he made a crash landing at Hornchurch. Just over a week later, on 15 September Peter Pease died in action.

Above: *Flying Officer Peter Pease of No.603 Squadron.*

'I FELT JOLLY GLAD TO BE DOWN ON THE GROUND WITHOUT HAVING CAUGHT FIRE'

'We were just going in to attack when somebody yelled 'Messerschmitts' over the R.T and the whole squadron spilt up. Actually it was a false alarm. The bombers were my object, so I snooped in under the 110s and attacked the bombers (about 40–50 Heinkel 111s) from the starboard beam.

'I got in a burst of about three seconds when – Crash! and the whole World seemed to be tumbling in on me. I pushed the stick forward hard, went into a vertical dive and held it until I was below cloud. The chief trouble was petrol gushing into the cockpit at the rate of gallons all over my feet, and a sort of lake of petrol in the bottom of the cockpit. My knee and leg were tingling all over as if I had pushed them into a bed of nettles. There was a bullet hole in my windscreen where a bullet had come in and entered the dashboard, knocking away the starter button. Another bullet, I think an explosive one, had knocked away one of my petrol taps in front of the joystick, spattering my leg with little splinters and sending a chunk of something through the back-side of my petrol tank near the bottom. I made for home at top speed to get there before all my petrol ran out. I was about 15 miles from the aerodrome and it was a heart-rending business with all that petrol gushing over my legs and the constant danger of fire. About five miles from the 'drome smoke began to come from under my dashboard. I thought the whole thing might blow up at any minute, so I switched off my engine. The smoke stopped. I glided towards the 'drome and tried putting my wheels down. One came down and the other remained stuck up. There was nothing for it but to make a one-wheel landing. I switched on my engine again to make the aerodrome. It took me some way and then began to smoke again, so I hastily switched off. I was now near enough and made a normal approach and held off. I made a good landing, touching down lightly. The unsupported wing slowly began to drop. I was able to hold it up for some time and then down came the wing tip on the ground. I began to slew round and counteracted as much as possible with the brake on the wheel which was down. I ended up going sideways on one wheel, a tail wheel and a wing tip. Luckily, the good tyre held out and the only damage to the aeroplane, apart from that done by the bullets, was a wing tip that is easily replaceable.

'I hopped out and went off to the M.O. to get a lot of metal splinters picked out of my leg and wrist. I felt jolly glad to be down on the ground without having caught fire.'

PILOT OFFICER ERIC MARRS of No.152 Squadron describing his action on 30 September 1940

BATTLE OF BRITAIN DAY

The first attack took place shortly before noon in a force comprised of twenty-one Messerschmitt 109 fighter-bombers and twenty-seven Dornier 17 bombers, with an escort of about a hundred and eighty Me 109s. The fighter-bombers were to attack rail targets throughout the London area, while the Dorniers were to hit the concentration of rail lines and junctions at Battersea.

Left: A pilot of No. 313 (Czech) Squadron running to his Spitfire during a scramble take off.

Two hours later there was a heavier attack on a series of targets in the London dock area.

No. 11 Group of Fighter Command, possessed 310 serviceable single-seat fighters. Of that total 218 were Hurricanes, and 92 were Spitfires. About one third of the available squadrons, Hurricanes and Spitfires, engaged the raiding forces as they made their way across Kent to the capital. The main body of defending fighters assembled over the outskirts of London. It was there that the two great clashes occurred and most of the aircraft were shot down.

Above: WAAF mechanics helping the pilot strap into a Spitfire Mark II of No.411 (Canadian) Squadron, at Digby in Lincolnshire in 1941.
Right: A few Mark II Spitfires were modified for the Air Sea Rescue role, carrying two cylindrical drums in parachutes in the rear fuselage holding an inflatable rubber dinghy and ration packs for survivors.

During the afternoon of the 15th, the Luftwaffe also launched smaller attacks on targets on the south coast. Twenty-six Heinkels bombed the Royal Navy base at Portland, and a small force of Messerschmitt 109 and 110 fighter-bombers tried unsuccessfully to hit the Supermarine plant at Southampton.

That day fifty-five German aircraft were destroyed, most of them falling to fighter attack. The RAF lost eight Spitfires and twenty-one Hurricanes. The Spitfire force suffered a loss rate of 4.2 per hundred sorties, while the Hurricane force suffered a loss rate of 6.4 per hundred sorties. In

action the Spitfire's superior performance meant it had a 50 per cent better chance of survival compared with the Hurricane. The German losses on 15 September fell far short of the 185 aircraft the defenders claimed as destroyed. Yet the action is rightly deemed to mark the climax of the Battle. Two days later Adolf Hitler ordered an indefinite postponement of Operation Sealion, the planned invasion of Britain. The ships and barges concentrated at ports along the Channel coast returned to their normal tasks and it was clear that the threat of invasion had passed.

THE MARK II

Near the end of the Battle of Britain the Spitfire Mark II entered service. Similar to the Mark I, it was powered by the Merlin 12 engine giving an additional 110 hp. With its armour protection and additional equipment, the Mark II weighed 350lb (159kg) more than the early Mark I. The Spitfire emerged from the Battle of Britain with a proven record of success in the limited role of home-defence fighter. If the Spitfire was to play a major part in the war, it would have to modify its role.

MAINTAINING SPITFIRE PRODUCTION

On 26 September 1940 a raiding force of fifty-nine Heinkel 111s mounted a devastating attack on the two main Supermarine factories at Woolston and Itchen. The bombers wrecked most of the factory buildings at both sites, striking a body blow at Spitfire production.

On the day following the attack Lord Beaverbrook, Winston Churchill's tireless Minister of Aircraft Production, visited Southampton to inspect the damage. On his decision the two wrecked factories were abandoned. Production of Spitfires was to be dispersed into several smaller units in towns and cities. Fortuitously most of the machine tools and production jigs at Woolston and Itchen had survived the attack. Also, the final assembly hangers at Eastleigh airfield had not been touched. Supermarine executives toured Southampton, Winchester, Salisbury, Trowbridge, Reading and Newbury and the surrounding areas, looking at every large open building. Motor repair garages, laundries and bus stations were the obvious choices. Accompanying each Supermarine executive was a policeman who carried a letter of introduction from the Chief Constable of the area, requesting cooperation but giving no reason for the visit. Where a building was considered suitable for use in the dispersed production scheme, the not-always-delighted owner received official papers requisitioning the building. As each new site was acquired, the Spitfire production jigs and tools were brought in and set up.

Never again would Spitfire production be as vulnerable to air attack as it had been in September 1940.

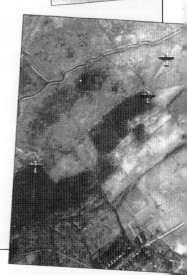

Above right and below: *Following the attack on the Supermarine factories, Spitfire production was dispersed into several small units in the surrounding towns and cities. These photographs show Spitfire wing leading edges being manufactured at the requisitioned garage of Anna Valley Motors Ltd at Salisbury.*

Far right, below: *A remarkable photograph taken from a Messerschmitt 110 reconnaissance aircraft over Snodland, Kent, showing Spitfires of No. 64 Squadron climbing into position to intercept the aircraft. The Messerschmitt suffered severe damage in the ensuing engagement and the radio operator was killed.*

SPITFIRE SKYPLANES

In time of war it is difficult to exaggerate the importance of aerial reconnaissance. To plan effective air attacks, staff officers require the best possible information on each target. They need to know where bombs should be aimed to cause maximum damage. They also need to know the layout of the defences around each target, so they can route the bombers to avoid the worst of them. Without such information, attacking forces will inflict less damage, and suffer heavier losses. The best source of such information is aerial photography.

Today the idea of using an unarmed reconnaissance aircraft, is well accepted. It was not always so. Before the Second World War most air forces employed modified bombers to fly long-range reconnaissance missions. These machines had to carry guns and gunners to fight their way through to targets.

Shortly before the outbreak of war, Flying Officer Maurice 'Shorty' Longbottom, suggested a better means of securing reconnaissance photographs. In a memo he set down his views on the future of strategic aerial reconnaissance. Longbottom

suggested that reconnaissance should be done 'by the use of a single small machine, relying solely on its speed, climb and ceiling to avoid detection.' Longbottom believed the ideal aircraft would be a Spitfire with the guns, ammunition, radio and other unnecessary equipment removed.

The Air Ministry greeted Longbottom's memorandum with polite interest, but initially the paper was pigeon-holed.

Main left: *Compare the 1939 inset photograph with the main one, of Bullinghen, taken in April 1944 from a Spitfire at the same altitude, with a camera fitted with a 36in lens. Far more ground detail is visible.*

Top: *Spitfire PR IC used for high-altitude photographic missions. This aircraft carried its vertically mounted cameras in a blister under the starboard wing, seen in the open position for the removal of the film magazines.*

Middle: *Spitfire PR IF. This aircraft carried its vertically mounted cameras in the rear fuselage. Blister fuel tanks under the wings gave it increased range.*

Above: *Spitfire PR IG used for low-altitude photograph targets beneath cloud. These aircraft wore a very pale shade of pink the same as clouds on an overcast day.*

RECONNAISSANCE VARIANTS

PR IA Original PR variant, one 5in (12.7cm) lens camera mounted in each wing. No additional fuel.

PR IB One 8in (20.3cm) lens camera in each wing. Additional fuel: 29-gallon (132l) tank in the rear fuselage.

PR IC As PR IB, but with the two 8in lens cameras mounted in tandem in a blister fairing under the starboard wing. Additional fuel: 29-gallon (132l) tank in the rear fuselage, 30-gallon (136.5l) blister tank under the port wing.

PR ID First major re-design of the Spitfire for the reconnaissance role. Carried two 8in or two 20in (50.8cm) lens cameras in the rear fuselage. Additional fuel: large fuel tank built integrally with the leading edge of the wing, capacity 114 gal (518l); 29-gallon (132l) tank in the rear fuselage. This variant replaced the Marks IA, IB, IC and IF in front-line service during 1941. When fitted with the Merlin 45 engine it became the PR 5D, then it was redesignated as the PR Mark 4.

PR IE Designed for the low-altitude

reconnaissance role; only one example produced. Oblique camera under each wing, pointing at right angles to the line of flight. Additional fuel: 29-gallon (132l) tank in rear fuselage.

PR IF Carried two 8in or two 20in (50.8cm) lens cameras in the rear fuselage. Additional fuel: 30-gallon (136.5l) blister tank under each wing, 29-gallon (132l) tank in the rear fuselage.

PR IG Designed for low-altitude reconnaissance role. One oblique camera mounted in the rear fuselage,

Above: A reconnaisance Spitfire at high altitude. The pilots avoided leaving condensation trails, as these betrayed their positions, making them vulnerable to fighter interception.

could point either to port or to starboard. In addition there was one 14in (36.5cm) and one 5in (12.7cm) mounted vertically in the rear fuselage. Additional fuel: 29-gallon (132l) tank in the rear fuselage.

The RAF was desperately short of modern reconnaisance aircraft fighters, needing every available Spitfire for the defence of Great Britain. Air Chief Marshal Dowding was unwilling to release these aircraft for other roles, no matter how persuasive the arguments might appear.

It took only six weeks of war to change people's minds. The main RAF reconnaissance aircraft then in use, the low performance Blenheim, was quite inadequate for the task. Rarely could they photograph targets any distance inside enemy territory, and they suffered heavy losses whenever they tried.

SECRET NEW UNIT

Air Chief Marshal Dowding reluctantly agreed to release a couple of Spitfires for the reconnaissance role. The aircraft went to a highly secret new unit based at Heston north of London, headed by Wing Commander Sidney Cotton. One of the officers who helped him set up the unit was 'Shorty' Longbottom himself.

Cotton's first step was to modify the Spitfires for the new role and commence operations over enemy territory. Each aircraft was fitted with a pair of cameras, mounted in each wing in the space previously occupied by the guns and ammunition boxes. Metal plates sealed off

Far right: Interior of the huge Spitfire production facility at Castle Bromwich, Birmingham. Morris Motors Ltd built the factory, under contract to the British Government. The plant produced some twelve thousand Spitfires, over half of the total. At its peak it turned out 320 Spitfires a month.

Below: Dramatic low-altitude shot of the German cruiser Hopper in dry dock, at heavily defended Brest.

SKYPLANE PILOT

'During the early [photographic reconnaissance] missions there was no heating in our Spitfires. For the high altitude missions we wore thick suits with electrical heating. Trussed up in our Mae West and parachute, one could scarcely move in the narrow cockpit of the Spitfire. When flying over enemy territory one had to be searching the sky the whole time for enemy fighters. On more than one occasion I started violent evasive action to shake off a suspected enemy fighter, only to discover that it was a small speck of dirt on the inside of my perspex canopy!

'A big worry over enemy territory was that one might start leaving a condensation trail without knowing it, thus pointing out one's position to the enemy. To avoid that we had small mirrors fitted in the blisters on each side of the canopy, so that one could see the trail as soon as it started to form. When that happened one could either climb or descend until the trail ceased. If possible, we liked to climb above the trail's layer because then fighters trying to intercept us had first to climb through the trail's layer themselves and could be seen in good time.'

PILOT OFFICER GORDON GREEN, SPITFIRE PILOT,
PHOTOGRAPHIC RECONNAISSANCE UNIT

the empty gun ports, and groundcrewmen applied plaster of Paris to fill the joints in the skinning. Then each aircraft received a coat of polish to give it a smooth, high gloss, finish. With these changes the maximum speed of the reconnaissance Spitfires was about 12mph (20km/hr) faster than the fighter version.

In November 1939 the Spitfire reconnaissance unit under the cover-designation 'No. 2 Camouflage Unit', moved to Seclin in France to begin operational trials. On the 18th, Longbottom, now a Flight Lieutenant, took off to photograph the German city of Aachen. Flying at 33,000ft (10,000m), he found navigation difficult. When his films were developed, they showed a strip of Belgian territory to the south of Aachen. Longbottom learned the lesson well, and when he returned to the area four days later, he made a successful photographic run over the German border defences.

During the next few weeks, Spitfires photographed several targets in western Germany, including the Ruhr industrial area. Significantly, and in distinct contrast to the Blenheims, the Spitfires flew their missions without loss or serious interference from the German defences. Photographs taken from 33,000 ft (10,000m) with 5in (12.7cm) focal-length cameras produced very small-scale pictures, however. The interpreters could pick out roads, railways, villages and major fortifications. But even with prints enlarged as

much as the grain of the film allowed, it was not possible to see troop positions or individual vehicles. If the Spitfire's capabilities were to be fully exploited, longer lens cameras would be needed. Apart from that proviso, the flights proved the essential soundness of Longbottom's proposals. As a result Air Chief Marshal Dowding agreed to release a dozen more Spitfires for the reconnaissance role.

In January 1940 an improved photographic reconnaissance Spitfire was ready for operations, the PR IB (for details of this and other reconnaissance variants, see opposite; the earlier variant became known as the PR IA). In February, Longbottom demonstrated the usefulness of the PR IB's additional range capability when he photographed the important German naval bases at Wilhelmshaven and Emden.

Cotton's unit was renamed the Photographic Development Unit, the new title revealing its true role for the first time. In 1940 the operations in France were reorganized and a further unit, No. 212 Squadron, formed at Seclin to conduct the

Left: Seamstresses applying the fabric covering to Spitfire rudders, at Castle Bromwich. The Spitfire's rudder weighed only 18lb (8kg), but was strong enough to withstand manoeuvring at high speed.

Spitfire reconnaisance missions from there.

LONG-RANGE VISION

In March 1940 a so-called 'long-range' reconnaisance version of the Spitfire appeared, the PR IC, with a further fuel tank to increase its reach. On 7 April Longbottom took this aircraft to Kiel, the first RAF aircraft to photograph the important naval base since the outbreak of war.

Little over a month later, on 10 May 1940, German forces launched their powerful Blitzkrieg attack on France, Holland and Belgium. During the hectic weeks that followed No. 212 Squadron photographed

Below: A showpiece of the British aircraft industry, the Castle Bromwich plant had a constant stream of important visitors. Here Winston Churchill is seen chatting with Alex Henshaw, Chief Test Pilot at the factory.

each stage of the advance of the German Panzer columns. The squadron then withdrew to England, where its aircraft and personnel were incorporated in the PDU at Heston.

Thus far the reconnaissance Spitfires had flown their missions at medium or high altitude, and photographed their targets from directly above. Most of the RAF's aerial photography would continue to be done that way. A few Spitfires were fitted with the so-called oblique camera installation, with a camera pointing at right angles to the line of flight and a few degrees below the horizontal. On 7 July 1940 Flying Officer Alistair Taylor proved the value of the new installation. Despite a 700ft (213m) cloud base and heavy rain, he took good photographs of shipping inside Boulogne harbour as he flew past the outer mole. From then on low-altitude photography, nicknamed 'dicing' because of the risks involved, became an important additional role for the reconnaissance Spitfires.

Also in July 1940, the Photographic Development Unit underwent yet another name change. It became the Photographic Reconnaissance Unit (PRU) and Wing Commander Geoffrey Tuttle replaced Sidney Cotton as its commander. The changes of name and commander made no difference to the way the unit operated, however.

Longbottom took the PR IC to Kiel, the first RAF aircraft to photograph the important naval base

---

At the end of July a further Spitfire reconnaissance variant appeared, the 'super-long-range' PR IF. This variant had a radius of action about 100 miles (160 km) greater than the Type IC. Operating from airfields in East Anglia, it could photograph targets as far afield as Berlin.

Throughout the summer of 1940, reconnaissance Spitfires kept a daily watch on the German preparations for the invasion of Britain. Each day they sallied forth to photograph each of the ports along the Channel coast, observing the growing assemblies of barges and shipping at each. Then on 20 September, three days after Adolf Hitler's order to postpone the invasion, a reconnaissance Spitfire returned bearing the first hard evidence of the change in German plans. Its photographs of Cherbourg harbour showed that five destroyers and a torpedo boat had left the port since the previous reconnaissance. In the weeks that followed, almost every

'IT WAS ALL RATHER LIKE A FOX HUNT...'

'During the early [photographic reconnaissance] missions to cover Brest [in 1941] we lost about five pilots fairly quickly. After the first couple had failed to return the Flight Commander, Flight Lieutenant Keith Arnold, asked Benson [the headquarters of the reconnaissance units] to send some reserve pilots. They duly arrived. Both took off for Brest that evening and neither came back. That was a very sobering incident.

'The important thing with any photographic mission was to take the photos if one could, and get them back to base. As the "boss" of PRU, Wing Commander Geoffrey Tuttle, often used to say, "I want you to get home safely not just because I like your faces, but because if you don't the whole sortie will be a waste of time!" So it was no use trying to play hide and seek with the Luftwaffe. If one had lost surprise during the approach to a heavily defended target, the best thing was to abandon the mission. One could go back another time when things might be better. Looking back at my time with the PRU, I get a lot of satisfaction from the knowledge that although I played my part in the war, I never had to fire a shot in anger. In one sense we in the reconnaissance business had things easy. All the time it was impressed on us: bring back the photographs or, if you can't, bring back the aeroplane. An infantryman taking part in the Battle of Alamein could not suddenly decide "This is ridiculous, I'm going home!" He just had to go on. But if we thought we had lost the element of surprise we were not only permitted to turn back, we were expected to do so. On the other hand there were times when I knew real fear. When one was 15 minutes out from Brest on a low altitude sortie, one's heart was beating away and as the target got nearer one's mouth got completely dry. Anyone who was not frightened at the thought of going in to photograph one of the most heavily defended targets in Europe, was not human.'

PILOT OFFICER GORDON GREEN, SPITFIRE PILOT, PHOTOGRAPHIC RECONNAISSANCE UNIT

successive reconnaissance flight revealed fewer ships and barges in each port as the vessels resumed their normal tasks. The threat to Great Britain had passed.

TO STETTIN

The 'long range' and 'extra long range' versions of the Spitfire opened new vistas for photographic reconnaissance and the targets it could cover. Yet in terms of range, the modified fighter could do even better. Supermarine redesigned the wing to take a huge additional fuel tank that took up almost the entire leading edge back to the main spar. In October 1940 the first Spitfires modified in this way, the PR ID, became available for operations.

When carrying its full load of fuel the PR ID was difficult to handle, as Flight Lieutenant

Neil Wheeler explained. 'You could not fly it straight and level for the first half hour or hour after take off. Until you had emptied the rear tank, the aircraft hunted the whole time. The centre of gravity was so far back that you couldn't control it.' Once part of the fuel load had been consumed, however, the Type D handled well and its extra range gave it a dramatic extension of reconnaissance cover. On 29 October 1940 one of these aircraft photographed the port of Stettin on the Baltic (now Sczecin in Poland) and returned after 5 hours and 20 minutes airborne.

The final reconnaissance variant of the Spitfire I was the Type G, optimized for the low-altitude photographic role with an oblique camera mounted in the rear fuselage. This version retained the fighter's standard

armament of eight .303in (7.7mm) machine guns to enable it to defend itself against enemy fighters.

By 1941 the reconnaissance Spitfires possessed the range to photograph targets almost anywhere in western Europe.

Above: Test pilots striding out to fly brand new Spitfires off the production line at Castle Bromwich.

THE SPITFIRE
SPREADS ITS WINGS

In the spring of 1941 a new production version of the Spitfire appeared, the Mark V. This was fitted with the Merlin 45 engine which gave increases of, respectively, 440 and 330 horse power over the versions fitted to the Marks I and II. The main production version of the Spitfire V carried an armament of a 20mm cannon and four .303in (7.7mm) machine guns.

SPITFIRE V

Type Single-seat general purpose fighter.
Armament Four Hispano 20 mm cannon with 120 rounds per gun, or two Hispano 20 mm cannon with 120 rounds per gun and four Browning .303in (7.7mm) machine guns with 350 rounds per gun, or eight .303in (7.7mm) Browning machine guns with 350 rounds per gun. Maximum bomb load two 250lb (113kg) bombs.
Power Plant One Rolls-Royce Merlin 45 liquid cooled V-12 engine developing 1,470hp.
Dimensions Span 36ft 10in (10.98m), 32ft 6in (9.9m, clipped wings); length 29ft 11in (9.11m).
Weight Maximum loaded weight 6,070lb (2,752kg).
Performance Maximum speed 371mph at 20,000ft (597km/hr at 6,100m). Service ceiling 38,000ft (11,585m).

Left and inset: Spitfire VC fitted with four 20mm cannon, being loaded on the aircraft carrier USS Wasp docked at Glasgow in April 1942. The wingtips had been removed and placed in the cockpit.
Right, top: The Daimler-Benz company at Stuttgart fitted a DB605 engine into a captured Mark V.
Right, below: Spitfire in trouble: a still from a combat film taken by the Luftwaffe fighter ace Major Gerhard Schoepfel of Fighter Geschwader 26, showing cannon shells bursting on the fuselage.

In 1941 Fighter Command moved from the defensive to the offensive. Simultaneously Spitfire production rose to a point where it exceeded losses. During the Battle of Britain nineteen squadrons had operated Spitfires. By September 1941 there were twenty-seven and by the end of 1941 Fighter Command had forty-six squadrons equipped with Spitfires.

The Mark V had a performance significantly better than the earlier variants of the Spitfire, yet it was not good enough. In the summer of 1941 the Luftwaffe introduced a new, more effective fighter into service: the Focke Wulf 190.

The Focke Wulf was 25-30mph (40-48km/hr) faster than the Spitfire V at most altitudes and it could out-climb, out-dive and out-roll the British fighter. The Spitfire V's only advantage over its new opponent was that it could turn tighter.

Fortunately for the RAF, the Luftwaffe was heavily committed to supporting the campaign in Russia. As a result the size of the fighter force retained in the west, would remain relatively small.

SPITFIRES TO MALTA

The next major challenge to face the Spitfire came early in 1942. Malta was the cornerstone of Britain's strategy in the

Left: In September 1942 the US manned 'Eagle' Squadrons of the RAF were officially transferred to the US Army Air Force with their aircraft. This aircraft went with No.121 Squadron to become part of the 335th Fighter Squadron of the 4th Fighter Group.

Mediterranean. Torpedo-bombers operating from the island took a steady toll of ships carrying supplies and reinforcements to sustain the Axis ground forces in North Africa. The island lay within 100 miles (160km) of Axis airfields in Sicily and suffered frequent and destructive air attacks. Malta's survival depended on her air defences, but the Hurricanes based on the island were outclassed by the Messerschmitt 109Fs opposing them.

Only the Spitfire V could engage the Me 109F on equal terms, but the distance from Gibraltar to Malta was far beyond the Spitfire's normal

Right: US Army Air Force mechanics carry out an engine change on a spare. *Below:* Armourers of No. 72 Squadron cleaning the barrel and removing the ammunition drum from the Hispano 20mm cannon.

When the new German fighter first appeared, it came as a severe shock to Fighter Command

ferry range. The strength of the Axis naval and air forces besieging the island precluded any large delivery of fighters by sea. The Hurricanes already on Malta had been transported half way by aircraft carrier, which launched them to fly the rest of the way to the island. The Spitfires needed to use the same method; from fly-off point to Malta was approximately 660 miles (1,062km). Engineers at Supermarine designed a 90-gallon (409l) drop tank. The first delivery of Spitfires took place on 7 March 1942, fifteen taking off from HMS *Eagle*.

Above: The flight deck of Wasp pictured late on the afternoon of 19 April, as the carrier prepared to fly off her brood of Spitfires soon after first light the following morning. Ranged in front and to the left of them are the carrier's own Wildcat fighters.
Left: The Focke Wulf 190 fighter was a formidable opponent for the Spitfire Mark V.

SPITFIRE V VERSUS FOCKE WULF 190A

In July 1942, a comparative trial between a Spitfire V and a captured Focke Wulf 190 fighter took place. These trials revealed just how formidable a foe they were. Excerpts from the official RAF report on the trials are given below:

The FW 190 was compared with a Spitfire VB from an operational squadron for speed and all-round manoeuvrability at heights up to 25,000ft (7,620m). The FW 190 is superior in speed at all heights, and the approximate differences are as follows:

At 2,000ft (610m) the FW 190 is 25–30mph (40–48km/hr) faster than the Spitfire 5B
At 3,000ft (915m) the FW 190 is 30–35mph (48–56km/hr) faster than the Spitfire 5B
At 5,000ft (1,525m) the FW 190 is 25mph (40km/hr) faster than the Spitfire VB
At 9,000ft (2,744m) the FW 190 is 25–30 mph faster than the Spitfire 5B
At 15,000ft (4573m) the FW 190 is 20mph (32km/hr) faster than the Spitfire 5B
At 18,000ft (5,488m) the FW 190 is 20mph (32km/hr) faster than the Spitfire VB
At 21,000ft (6,400m) the FW 190 is 20–25mph (32–40km/hr) faster than the Spitfire VB

Climb: The climb of the FW 190 is superior to that of the Spitfire VB at all heights. The best speeds for climbing are approximately the same, but the angle of the FW 190 is considerably steeper. Under maximum continuous climbing conditions the climb of the FW 190 is about 450ft/min (137m/min) better up to 25,000ft (7,620m).
Dive: Comparative dives between the two aircraft have shown that the FW 190 can leave the Spitfire with ease, particularly during the initial stages.
Manoeuvrability: The manoeuvrability of the FW 190 is better than that of the Spitfire VB except in turning circles. The FW 190 has better acceleration under all conditions of flight and this must obviously be most useful during combat.

When the FW 190 was in a turn and was attacked by the Spitfire, the superior rate of roll enabled it to flick into a diving turn in the opposite direction. The pilot of the Spitfire found great difficulty in following this manoeuvre and even when prepared for it, was seldom able to allow the correct deflection. A dive from this manoeuvre enabled the FW 190 to draw away from the Spitfire which was then forced to break off the attack.

The above trials have shown that the Spitfire VB must cruise at high speed when in an area where enemy fighters can be expected.

Left: After each launch of Spitfires on deck, those in the hangar were brought up by lift. This required slick timing. A Spitfire is about to begin its takeoff; the aircraft ahead of it can be seen climbing away, just above the starboard wing. Meanwhile, the lift is already on the way to the hangar to pick up the next aircraft.

Middle: Scene on the flight deck of USS Wasp on the morning of 9 May 1942, as the carrier prepares to launch her aircraft for the largest resupply of aircraft to Malta. In the background, preparing to launch her Spitfires also, is HMS Eagle.

Above: A soldier, a sailor and an airman carry out refuelling and rearming of a Spitfire of No. 603 Squadron at Takali, Malta, In the spring of 1942. The blast pen was constructed from empty petrol tins filled with sand.

AMERICAN HELP

The Spitfires arrived just in time. The defending fighter units were heavily outnumbered. On 1 April Winston Churchill sent a personal telegram to President Roosevelt asking for help:

'Air attack on Malta is very heavy. There are now in Sicily about 400 German and 200 Italian fighters. Malta can only now muster 20 to 30 serviceable fighters. We keep feeding Malta with Spitfires in packets of 16 loosed from EAGLE carrier.

'This has worked quite well but EAGLE is now laid up for a month by defects in her steering gear. Would you be willing to allow your carrier WASP to do one of these trips provided details are satisfactorily agreed between the Navy Staffs? We estimate that WASP could take 50 or more Spitfires . . .'

Within three days of receiving the telegram the US President agreed to the request. Six days after that *Wasp* docked at Port Glasgow to load 47 Spitfires for the island. On the 20th April, the carrier began launching the Spitfires. Forty-six of the 47 fighters that took off reached Malta safely. These Spitfires, however, were to be destroyed in the air or on the ground, in the following days.

Right and below: Spitfire Vs of the No. 54 Squadron based at Darwin, Australia, early in 1943 providing air defence for the Northern Territory. (Australian War Memorial)

Again Malta was in crisis, and again Mr Churchill asked the US President to help. The American carrier returned to Glasgow on 29 April and took on a further forty-seven Spitfires. By then HMS *Eagle* at Gibraltar had completed her repairs, and she took on a further seventeen fighters.

MALTA SAVED

As *Wasp* entered the Mediterranean a second time, *Eagle* set sail from Gibraltar to join her. The two carriers and their escorts headed east together and shortly after dawn on 9 May they launched their Spitfires. Sixty of the 64 fighters that set out reached Malta. It was sufficient to change the course of the battle. The island's air defences were now strong enough to resist Axis air attacks, and could be topped up with 'penny packets' of Spitfires from the smaller carriers.

By late 1942 the RAF possessed a more cost-effective method of delivering Spitfires to Malta from Gibraltar. Supermarine engineers had modified the Mark V to fly the distance non-stop, by fitting a 170 gallon (772l) drop tank under the fuselage and a 29 gallon (132l) auxiliary tank in the rear fuselage. The modified Spitfire could now fly the 1,100 mile (1,770km) distance in a single hop.

During October and November 1942 seventeen Spitfires took off from Gibraltar to fly to Malta. All except one of them made it.

The Allied victory at El Alamein, and the subsequent expulsion of Axis forces from Libya, lifted the siege of Malta.

BY SPITFIRE TO MALTA

Pilot Officer Michael Le Bas of No. 601 Squadron described his take off in a Spitfire from the deck of USS *Wasp*. His heavily loaded aircraft carried a 90-gallon (409l) drop tank under the fuselage. Ahead lay a flight of 660 miles (1,062km), about as far as from London to Prague.

'The deck officer began rotating his checkered flag and I pushed forward the throttle to emergency override to get the last ounce of power out of my Merlin. The Spitfire picked up speed rapidly in its headlong charge down the deck, but not rapidly enough. The ship's bows got closer and closer and still I had insufficient airspeed and suddenly – I was off the end. With only 60 feet to play with before I hit the water, I retracted the undercarriage and eased forward on the stick to build up speed. Down and down went the Spitfire until, about fifteen feet above the waves, it reached flying speed and I was able to level out. After what seemed an age, my speed built up and I was able to climb away. It had been a hairy introduction to flying off an aircraft carrier. Things had happened so quickly that there was no time to think.'

After the initial encounters with Focke Wulf 190s, Fighter Command made strong demands for an improved fighter with the performance to meet the new challenge. There could be no question of designing, building and bringing into service a completely new aircraft; on the most optimistic time scale that would have taken at least four years. Fighter Command could not wait that long.

Rolls-Royce already had the answer to the problem in a new version of the Merlin. Previous versions of the engine used a single-stage supercharger. The new engine employed a two-stage supercharger, in which the output from the first blower fed into the second to compress the charge of air further before it entered the carburettor. The two-stage supercharger gave a spectacular improvement in high-altitude performance. At 30,000ft (9,145m) the Merlin 45 was a engine with a single-stage supercharger developed about 720 horse power. At the same altitude the same basic engine fitted with a two-stage supercharger developed about 1,020 horse power, an increase of more than 40 per cent. The extra plumbing added about 200 pounds (90kg) to the weight of the engine and increased its length by 9 inches (23cm).

In September 1941, an experimental Spitfire incorporating the two-stage supercharger began flight testing.

> ### *There could be no question of designing, building and bringing into service a brand new aircraft*

Far Left: A Spitfire VII, the high-altitude Interceptor version of the famous fighter. Note the distinctive long-span wing with pointed tips.

SPITFIRE MARK IX

Type Single-seat general purpose fighter and fighter-bomber.
Armament Two Hispano 20mm cannon with 120 rounds per gun, four Browning .303in (7.7mm) machine guns with 350 rounds per gun; or two Hispano 20mm cannon with 120 rounds per gun and two Browning .5in (12.7mm) machine guns with 250 rounds per gun. Maximum bomb load one 50-pound (226kg) bomb and two 250 pounders (113kg).
Power Plant One Rolls-Royce Merlin 61, 63 or 70 liquid cooled V-12 engine with two-stage supercharger. Merlin 65 developed 1,565 hp.
Dimensions Span 40ft 2in (12.85, pointed wing tips), 36ft 10in (10.98m, normal wing tips) or 32ft 6in (9.9m, clipped wings); length 30ft 0in (9.14m).
Weight Maximum loaded weight 7,500lb (3,400kg).
Performance Maximum speed 400mph at 25,000ft (657km/hr at 7,622m); service ceiling 43,000ft (13,110m).

Below: Spitfire IX of No. 402 (Canadian) Squadron.

TURNING POINT IN AN AIR WAR

On the afternoon of 30 July 1942 Flight Lieutenant Donald Kingaby of No. 64 Squadron scored his 16th aerial victory. Afterwards he reported:

'I sighted approximately 12 FW 190s 2,000ft [610m] below us at 12,000ft [3,658m] just off Boulogne proceeding towards French coast. We dived down on them and I attacked a FW 190 from astern and below giving a very short burst, about half a second, from 300yd. I was forced to break away as I was crowded out by other Spits. I broke down and right and caught another FW as he commenced to dive away. At 14,000ft [4,268m] approx. I gave a burst of cannon and M/G, 400 yd range hitting E/A along fuselage. Pieces fell off and E/A continued in straight dive nearly vertical It followed E/A down to 5,000ft [1,525m] over Boulogne and saw him hit the deck just outside the town of Boulogne and explode and burn up. Returned to base at Oft.'

The combat report was little different from many others in the summer of 1942, yet this air combat marked a significant turning point in the air war over Europe. It was the first time the Spitfire Mark IX had encountered the Focke Wulf 190 in action. The latest variant of the British fighter showed that it could take on its once-feared opponent on equal terms. The Luftwaffe would never regain their superiority in the skies.

The Merlin 61 Spitfire was considerably faster than any previous version, with a maximum speed of 414mph at 27,200ft (667km/hr at 8,300m). Its service ceiling was over 41,000 ft (12,500m).

THREE NEW VARIANTS

The Spitfire VII was a high-altitude interceptor version, with a pressurized cabin and a longer wingspan giving increased area. Its airframe was redesigned and strengthened to compensate for the increases in engine power and weight the fighter had incurred previously. The second of the new variants, the Spitfire VIII, was similar to the Mark VII but lacked the pressurized cabin of that type.

These two versions required a large amount of re-design as well as retooling of the production lines. Neither version would be available in quantity until the spring of 1943.

In the meantime Fighter Command quickly needed a fighter to counter the FW 190. The solution was the Spitfire IX, which was essentially a Mark V with the minimum of modification necessary to take the Merlin 61 engine.

The Mark V was not really strong enough to accept the additional engine power. In wartime, however, the RAF was prepared to accept this deficiency in the name of operational expediency.

Left and above: A damaged aircraft repaired and returned to service was as valuable as a new aircraft, and the RAF salvage teams and repair organization played a valuable role. This Spitfire of No. 403 (Canadian) Squadron crash-landed in a minefield in Normandy. After a sweep of the area to ensure that it was safe, the fighter was dismantled and loaded on to a transporter.

The first production Spitfire IXs arrived at No. 64 Squadron at Hornchurch during June 1942, and the unit resumed operations with the new variant at the end of July. The new Spitfire quickly demonstrated that it was the equal of the Focke Wulf 190 in combat. Proof of this came, when a German pilot inadvertently landed his FW 190 at Pembrey in South Wales. The RAF carried out detailed flight tests with

SPITFIRE IX VERSUS FOCKE WULF 190A

In July 1942 a Spitfire IX was flown in a comparative trial against a captured Focke Wulf 190. The similarities in performances were remarkable. Excerpts from the official trials report are given below:

Comparative Speeds: The FW 190 was compared with a fully operational Spitfire IX for speed and manoeuvrability at heights up to 25,000ft (7,620m). The Spitfire IX at most heights is slightly superior in speed to the FW 190 and the approximate differences in speeds at various heights are as follows:

At 2,000ft (610m) the FW 190 is 7–8mph (11–13km/hr) faster than the Spitfire IX

At 5,000ft (1,524m) the FW 190 and the Spitfire IX are approximately the same

At 8,000ft (2,44m) the Spitfire IX is 8mph (13km/hr) faster than the FW 190

At 15,000ft (4,573m) the Spitfire IX is 5mph (8km/hr) faster than the FW 190

At 18,000ft (5,488m) the FW 190 is 3mph (5km/hr) faster than the Spitfire IX

At 21,000ft (6,400m) the FW 190 and the Spitfire IX are approximately the same

At 25,000ft (7,622m) the Spitfire IX is 5–7mph (8–11km/hr) faster than the FW 190

Climb: During comparative climbs at various heights up to 23,000ft (7,012m), with both aircraft flying under maximum continuous climbing conditions, little difference was found between the two aircraft although on the whole the Spitfire IX was slightly better. Above 22,000ft (6,707m) the climb of the FW 190 is falling off rapidly, whereas the climb of the Spitfire IX is increasing.

Dive: The FW 190 is faster than the Spitfire IX in a dive, particularly during the initial stage. This superiority is not as marked as with the Spitfire VB.

Manoeuvrability: The FW 190 is more manoeuvrable than the Spitfire IX except in turning circles. The superior rate of roll of the FW 190 enabled it to avoid the Spitfire IX, by flicking over into a diving turn in the opposition direction.

The Spitfire IX's worst heights for fighting the FW 190 were between 18,000 and 22,000ft (5,486m and 6,707m) and below 3,000ft (914m).

The initial acceleration of the FW 190 is better than the Spitfire IX under all conditions of flight, except in level flight at such altitudes where the Spitfire has a speed advantage.

The general impression of the pilots in the trials is that the Spitfire IX compares well with the FW 190. Provided the Spitfire has the initiative, it undoubtedly has a good chance of shooting down the FW 190.

the captured aircraft to determine its exact performance and then had it fly mock combats with each of the main Allied fighters.

MARK IX IN SERVICE

The new variant had an immediate impact on the air situation. In combat it was impossible to distinguish it from the Mark V, and FW 190 pilots could never be certain which Spitfire variant they faced. The German fighters became markedly less aggressive and RAF fighter losses fell appreciably.

The first major action involving Spitfire IXs was on 19 August 1942, on the French coast. Four squadrons flew the new variant that day and they mounted 14 squadron-sized missions comprising about 150 sorties.

By the spring of 1943 the Spitfire IX equipped most of the RAF's single-seat fighter squadrons based in Great Britain. The re-engineered variants of the Spitfire intended to replace

---

MARK VII

Type Single-seat high-altitude interceptor fighter with pressurized cabin.

Armament Two Hispano 20mm cannon with 120 rounds per gun, four Browning .303in (7.7mm) machine guns with 350 rounds per gun. Aircraft assigned to ultra high-altitude interception duties sometimes carried only the four .303 in machine guns.

Power Plant One Rolls-Royce Merlin 61, 64 or 71 liquid cooled V-12 engine with two-stage supercharger. Merlin 61 developed 1,565hp.

Dimensions: Span 40ft 2in (12.85m, pointed wing tips) or 36ft 10in (10.98m normal wing tips); length 30ft (9.15m).

Weight Maximum loaded weight 8,000lb (3,628kg).

Performance (Rolls-Royce Merlin 71 engine) maximum speed 424mph at 29,500ft (682km/hr at 8,994m); service ceiling 45,100ft (13.750m).

---

the Mark IX saw rather less use.

By the time the Mark VIII became available in quantity, in the spring of 1943, the FW 190 menace over north west Europe had been contained. The entire

Left: The Spitfire Mark XVI was similar to the Mark IX but was powered by the version of the Merlin engine built under licence by the American Packard Company. Late production Spitfire IXs and XVIs featured cut-down fuselages and bubble canopies.
Bottom left: Floatplane conversion of the Spitfire. A small number of aircraft were modified in this way but none saw action.

BUBBLE CANOPY

In most cases where Spitfires were shot down by enemy fighters, the victim never saw his assailant in time to take effective evasive action. Most such attacks were mounted from the fighter's blind zone, below and behind. Any modification that reduced the likelihood of a surprise attack would increase the fighter's chances of survival in combat.

The answer was to cutback the rear fuselage behind the cockpit, and fit the fighter with a bubble canopy. The first modified Spitfire flew in the summer of 1943. Manufacturer's trials showed little significant deterioration in the aircraft's handling. Experienced service pilots were impressed with the improvement in view from the bubble canopy. Their report stated:

'This is an enormous improvement. The pilot can see quite easily round to his fin and past it, almost to the further edge of the tailplane.

By banking the aircraft slightly during weaving action, the downward view to the rear is opened up well.'

Modified Spitfires began to reach the operational squadrons early in 1945.

entire 1,658-aircraft production run of this variant went overseas to units operating in the Middle East, the Far East and Australia.

The Mark IX, continued in production a lot longer than anyone had expected. The Supermarine and Castle Bromwich plants together turned out nearly six thousand of them.

The Spitfire XVI airframe was almost identical to that of the Mark IX, but it was powered by a version of the Merlin built by the American Packard Company. Late production Spitfire IXs and XVIs featured cut-down fuselages and bubble canopies, features which gave the pilot greatly improved vision behind and below the fighter.

The introduction of the Merlin 60 series improved the performance of the Spitfire to the point where it could fight the FW 190 on equal terms. Yet engineers at Rolls-Royce were not content to rest on their laurels. As we shall observe in the next chapter, they had something even better on offer.

ENTER THE GRIFFON

Mark XIV Spitfire of No. 402 (Canadian) Squadron. This version was the most effective variant to operate in the air superiority role during the Second World War.

In 1939 Rolls-Royce had begun development of a larger engine, later named the Griffon. With a cubic capacity of 65 gallons (36.75l), the new engine was one-third larger than its predecessor. The initial production version, with a single-stage supercharger, developed 1,735 hp. By clever positioning of components, the designers kept the length of the Griffon to within 3 inches (7.5cm), and the weight to within 600 pounds (272kg), of the equivalent figures for the Merlin. The new engine's frontal area was little greater than that of its predecessor.

In November 1941 an experimental Griffon prototype, the Mark IV, began flight testing. The aircraft had a maximum speed of 372mph at 5,700ft (600km/hr at 1,740m) which increased to 397mph at 18,000ft (640km/hr at 5,500m).

To counter the threat the RAF issued a requirement for a low-altitude interceptor

At about this time the Luftwaffe commenced tip-and-run attacks on towns on the south and east coasts of England. Small forces of fighter-bombers ran in at low altitude to avoid radar detection. To counter the threat the RAF issued a requirement for a low-altitude interceptor. The Griffon Spitfire offered the best in performance at low altitude, and this became the prototype for the Mark XII fighter.

SPITFIRE XII

Type Single-seat fighter optimized for operations at low and medium altitudes.
Armament Two Hispano 20mm cannon with 120 rounds per gun, four Browning .303in (7.7mm) machine guns with 350 rounds per gun.
Power Plant One Rolls-Royce Griffon 4 liquid cooled V-12 engine with single-stage supercharger developing 1,735 horse power.
Dimensions Span 32ft 7in (9.93m); length 30ft 9in (9.37m).
Weight Maximum loaded weight 7,400lb (3,356kg).
Performance Maximum speed 389mph at 12,500ft (626km/hr at 3,810m); service ceiling 37,350ft (11,387m).

Below: The first Griffon-powered Spitfire, pictured after the aircraft had been modified to become the prototype Mark XII low-altitude fighter.

SPITFIRE XIV

Type Single-seat fighter and fighter reconnaissance aircraft.
Armament Two Hispano 20mm cannon with 120 rounds per gun, four Browning .303in (7.7mm) machine guns with 350 rounds per gun; or two Hispano 20mm cannon with 120 rounds per gun and two Browning .5in (12.7mm) machine guns with 250 rounds per gun. Fighter reconnaissance version carried an oblique-mounted camera in the rear fuselage.
Power Plant One Rolls-Royce Griffon 65 liquid cooled V-12 engine with two-stage supercharger developing 2,035hp.
Dimensions Span 36ft 1in (10.98m normal wing tips) or 32ft 7in (9.93m, clipped wings); length 32ft 8in (9.96m).
Weight Maximum loaded weight 10,065 pounds (4,565kg).
Performance Maximum speed 439mph at 24,500ft (707km/hr); service ceiling 43,000ft (13,110m).

Supermarine got a production order to build one hundred examples.

Like the Mark IX, the early production Mark XIIs used Mark V airframes with the minimum of modification necessary to take the new engine. Production Mark XIIs all had clipped wings. Compared with the Mark IX, the Mark XII was 14mph (22km/hr) faster at sea level and 8mph faster at 10,000 ft. But above 20,000ft (6,100m) performance fell away rapidly and the Mark XII became progressively slower than the Mark IX.

In the spring of 1943 Nos 41 and 91 Squadrons commenced operations with Mark XIIs from Hawkinge airfield near Folkestone. The units flew standing patrols against enemy fighter-bombers attacking coastal targets. On 25 May, No. 91 Squadron scrambled six fighters to engage FW 190 fighter-bombers attacking Folkestone. The Spitfires claimed the destruction of six raiders, without loss to themselves.

Although the Mark XII, was faster than the opposing fighter types at low and medium altitudes, this was of little value during offensive sweeps over France. German fighter pilots preferred to remain at altitude, coming down only to deliver high-speed diving attacks before making zoom climbs back to altitude. Rarely would they let themselves be drawn into turning fights with Spitfires below 20,000 ft.

An obvious next step for the Spitfire was to fit it with a Griffon with a two-stage supercharger. The new engine, the Griffon 65, appeared in the spring of 1943 and developed an impressive 1,540hp for take-off and 2,035hp at 7,000 ft (2,134m). Six Spitfire VIIIs were modified to take the new engine and became prototypes for the Mark XIV.

Flight tests with pre-production Mark XIVs revealed it to be an extremely effective fighter, giving a huge improvement in performance over the Mark IX. During comparative trials against a captured FW 190 and a Messerschmitt 109G, the Spitfire XIV showed itself to be superior to the German fighters in almost every respect.

The new variant went into production in the autumn of 1943. In the spring of 1944, Nos 91, 322 and 610 Squadrons received Mark XIVs. All three units were fully operational in June when the V.1 flying bomb attacks on London commenced.

SPITFIRE v FLYING BOMB

Although the V.ls flew a straight and predictable path, usually they were not easy targets. The majority flew at speeds around 350mph (563km/hr) and heights of between 3,000 and 4,000ft (915 and 1,220m).The highest came in at around 8,000 ft (2,440m) and the lowest flew at treetop height – which often led to their early demise!

> *Although the V.1s flew a straight and predictable path, usually they were not easy targets*

Protecting the capital were four separate layers of defences. The first layer, extending from mid-Channel to about 10 miles (16km) short of the south coast, was the Outer Fighter Patrol Area where Spitfires and other fighters could engage the flying bombs. Next came the Gun Belt, with more than 2,500 AA guns of all calibres positioned along the strip of coast between Beachy Head and Dover; this was off-limits to fighters, allowing gunners freedom to shoot at anything that came within range. From 10 miles (16km) inland to 10 miles (16km) short of London was the Inner Fighter Area where

---

SPITFIRE XIV COMPARED WITH FOCKE WULF 190A

Early in 1944 the Air Fighting Development Unit at Duxford flew a Spitfire XIV in a comparative trial against a captured Focke Wulf 190A. Excerpts from the official trials report are given below:

Maximum Speeds: From 0–5,000ft (0–1,525m) and 15,000–20,000ft (4,573–6,100m) the Spitfire XIV is only 20mph (32km/hr) faster; at all other heights it is up to 60mph (97km/hr) faster.

Maximum Climb: The Spitfire XIV has a considerably greater rate of climb than the FW 190 A at all altitudes.

Dive: After the initial part of the dive, during which the FW 190 gains slightly, the Spitfire XIV has a slight advantage.

Turning Circle: The Spitfire XIV can easily turn inside the FW 190. In the case of a right-hand turn, this difference is not quite so pronounced.

Rate of Roll: The FW 190 is very much better.

Conclusions: In defence, the Spitfire XIV should use its remarkable maximum climb and turning circle against any enemy aircraft. In the attack it can afford to 'mix it' but should beware of the quick roll and dive. If this manoeuvre is used by an FW 190 and the Spitfire XIV follows, it will probably not be able to close the range until the FW 190 has pulled out of its dive.

SPITFIRE XIV COMPARED WITH ME109G

Early in 1944 the Air Fighting Development Unit at Duxford flew a Spitfire XIV in a comparative trial against a captured Messerschmitt 109G, the latest sub-type of the famous German fighter. Excerpts from the official trials report are given below:

Maximum Speed: The Spitfire XIV is 40mph (64km/hr) faster at all heights except near 16,000ft (4,878m), where it is only 10mph (16km/hr) faster.

Maximum Climb: The same result: at 16,000ft (4,877m) the two aircraft are identical, otherwise the Spitfire XIV out-climbs the Me 109G. The zoom climb is practically identical when the climb is made without opening the throttle. Climbing at full throttle, the Spitfire XIV draws away from the Me 109G quite easily.

Dive: During the initial part of the dive, the Me 109G pulls away slightly, but when a speed of 380mph (611 km/hr) is reached, the Spitfire XIV begins to gain on the Me 109G.

Turning Circle: The Spitfire XIV easily out-turns the Me 109G in either direction.

Rate of Roll: The Spitfire XIV rolls much more quickly in either direction.

Conclusion: The Spitfire XIV is superior to the Me 109G in every respect.

Below: During mock combats the Me 109G was no match for the Spitfire XIV.

more fighters engaged the V.1s. The final layer, was the barrage balloon zone consisting of over a thousand balloons, which began 10 miles short of the London built-up area and ended at its outskirts.

All available squadrons with Mark XIVs redeployed to the Kent area to defend the capital.

AIR SUPERIORITY FIGHTER

At the end of August 1944, Allied ground forces advancing along the north coast of France overran the last of the V.1 launching sites in the Pas de Calais. The 8,617th and last fly-ing bomb launched from that area crossed the south coast of England on the morning of 1 September.

Following the capture of the V.1 sites, the Spitfire XIV squadrons redeployed to airfields in Belgium, to resume operations against conventional enemy aircraft. Four further squadrons joined them soon afterwards, Nos 41, 130, 350 and 403 Squadrons.

The Mark XXI was intended as the 'definitive' fighter variant of the Spitfire. Powered by the Griffon 65 engine, it featured a completely redesigned wing with a much-strengthened internal structure. It carried the four 20mm cannon armament as standard. Early production machines had unpleasant handling characteristics. It took a few months to iron out these bugs and as a result the variant entered service only during the final few weeks of the war.

The delay in bringing the Mark XXI into action had no effect on the air war in Europe, for the Allied Air Forces defeated the Luftwaffe with the fighter types in service.

In the next chapter we shall observe the work done to improve the effectiveness of reconnaissance variants.

As the war progressed, the Royal Air Force faced increasing demands to provide reconnaissance photographs of targets deep inside occupied territory in Europe. Yet, by the summer of 1942, the improving German air defences inflicted mounting losses on the reconnaissance Spitfires. The obvious answer was to produce a higher performance reconnaissance aircraft powered by the Merlin 61 engine. The new variant, the Spitfire PR XI, combined the strengthened airframe of the Mark VIII fighter with the integral wing fuel tank and rear fuselage camera installation of the PR Marks ID and VD.

Left: Spitfire PR XI in invasion markings. Note the ports in the rear fuselage for the two vertical cameras.

Until the PR XI became available, fifteen Mark IX fighters underwent modification for the reconnaissance role. Designated PR IXs, these aircraft had the armament removed and a pair of vertical cameras installed in the rear fuselage. The version had no extra internal fuel tankage, and during operations it usually flew with a 90 gallon (409l) drop tank under the fuselage. No. 541 Squadron at Benson received the first PR Mark IXs in November 1942. Although the limited tankage confined the PR IX to operations over western Europe, it restored the ability to photograph defended targets without incurring serious losses.

In December 1942 the first Spitfire PR XIs began coming off the production line. The new variant could operate at altitudes above 42,000ft (12,800m), some 10,000ft

SPITFIRE MK XI

Type Single-seat long range reconnaissance aircraft.

War Load Two vertically mounted reconnaissance cameras, could also carry one oblique mounted camera. No armament.

Power Plant One Rolls-Royce Merlin 63 liquid cooled V-12 engine with two-stage supercharger developing 1,650hp.

Dimensions Span 36ft 10in (10.98m); length 31ft 1in (9.47m).

Weight Maximum loaded weight 8,519lb (3,863kg).

Performance Maximum speed 417mph at 24,000ft (671km/hr at 7317m); service ceiling 44,000ft (13,415m).

(3,000m) higher than previous reconnaissance versions. The

Below and overleaf: Spitfire XIs of the 10th Photo Group, US Army Air Force. The unit operated this variant on photographic reconnaissance missions over occupied Europe.

47

SPITFIRE XIX

Type Single-seat long-range reconnaissance aircraft.
War Load Two vertically mounted reconnaissance cameras, could also carry one oblique mounted camera. No armament.
Power Plant One Rolls-Royce Griffon 66 liquid cooled V-12 engine with two-stage super-charger developing 2,035hp.
Dimensions Span 36ft 10in (10.98m normal wing tips); length 32ft 8in (9.96m).
Weight Maximum loaded weight 10,450lb (4,739kg) .
Performance Maximum speed 445mph at 26,000ft (716km/hr at 7,927m); operational ceiling in excess of 49,000ft (14,940m).

Above: PR XI of US 10th Photo Group.

Below: German pilots clamber over a captured PR XI.

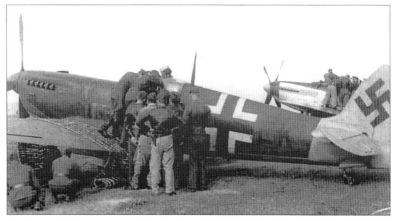

Mark XI replaced all other unarmed versions of the Spitfire in front-line reconnaissance units, and 471 examples were built. For more than a year after the variant entered service, it was almost immune to fighter interception while flying at high altitude.

In the autumn of 1943 the US 8th Air Force in Great Britain received a dozen Mark XIs. These formed the 14th Photo Squadron, 10th Photographic Group, based at Mount Farm near Oxford. The unit's role was to take pre-strike and post-strike photographs of tar-

gets attacked by the US heavy bombers. Major Walt Weitner, commander of the 14th, described his impressions of flying this version on operations:

'With all the extra clothing, the parachute, dinghy, life jacket and oxygen mask, the narrow cockpit of a Spitfire was no place for the claustrophobic! With a full load of fuel, the Spit would "lean" disconcertingly during turns when one taxied. Once the gear was up and you pulled up the nose, boy would she climb!'

The Mark XI cruised at altitudes around 39,000ft, ascending above that altitude if enemy fighters tried to intercept it. Weitner found the Spitfire easy to handle at very high altitude:

'For high altitude work the Spit was unequalled. One had always to have hold of the stick, but it needed little pressure. In the reconnaissance business you were continually banking to search the sky all around for enemy fighters and to check the navigation.'

NEW VARIANTS

The system of allocating Spitfire numbers was anything but methodical, and the PR Mark X entered service more than a year later than the PR XI. The Mark X was similar to the Mark XI, but it was fitted with a pressurized cabin. Only sixteen examples were built, however, and the variant

entered service with Nos 541 and 542 Squadrons in May 1944. The commander of the latter unit, Squadron Leader Alfred Ball, remembered the PR X with no great affection:

'I flew the PR X a few times on operations. They were not popular because of the poor visibility out of the very thick perspex canopy. Outside everything looked a slightly discoloured yellow, the perspex was not as clear as on an ordinary Spitfire. The extra weight of the pressure cabin led the Mark X to feel much heavier than the Mark XI. We preferred the unpressurized Mark XI to the Mark X.'

'Once the gear was up and you pulled up the nose, boy would she climb!'

The Mark XI's near-immunity from fighter interception lasted until the spring of 1944. Then the Luftwaffe deployed its first jet fighter types, the rocket-propelled Me 163 and the turbojet powered Me 262. High flying Allied reconnaissance aircraft, unarmed and alone, offered perfect targets on which the German jet pilots could make practice interceptions.

A fighter-reconnaissance

version of the Spitfire XIV entered service in small numbers, fitted with an oblique camera in the rear fuselage.

THE MARK XIX

With the increasing threat of interception from German jet fighters, there was a requirement for a Griffon-powered long-range unarmed reconnaissance variant. This became the PR Mark XIX, with integral wing fuel tanks as fitted to the PR XI and its predecessors.

The new variant entered service in May 1944 and gave a huge advance in performance over the PR XI. Later production Mark XIXs had pressurized cabins, built to an improved design. Comfortably ensconced in their pressurized cabins, pilots often took this variant above 49,000ft (above 15,000m).

Altogether 225 examples of the PR XIX were built, before production of this version ended in the spring of 1946.

Photographic reconnaissance was one role that the Spitfire's designer had not envisaged. Another was that of fighter-bomber.

Below: The Mark XIX was the final reconnaissance version of the Spitfire, and remained in front-line service in this role until 1954. This example carries a 170-gallon (773l) ferry tank under the fuselage.

SPITFIRE
FIGHTER-BOMBER

Winston Churchill once commented that 'Air power is the most difficult of all forms of military force to measure, or even to express in precise terms.' One can apply those same words to air superiority. Certainly, once the enemy air force is driven from the skies, the side with air superiority possesses a great advantage. However, to exploit this advantage types of aircraft other than the pure fighter must be brought into play. Bombers, transports and reconnaissance aircraft can then capitalize on the situation and mount effective operations to support the land battle. To assist with this, part of the fighter force will relinquish air-to-air operations and join in the attack on ground targets.

By June 1944, the Luftwaffe had been so weakened that it was rarely able to operate over northern France. Having secured air superiority, many Spitfire units switched to the fighter-bomber role. They were the bane of the German ground troops, as they bombed and strafed anything that moved in the rear areas.

TARGET ROMMEL

An action by Spitfire fighter-bombers that had far-reaching consequences for the land battle occurred on 17 July 1944. That day Field Marshal Erwin Rommel, commander of German ground forces in Normandy, needed to travel urgently to a sector of the front where an Allied breakthrough seemed imminent. A flight of Mustangs on low-level reconnaissance observed the staff car speeding along a road near Lisieux, and reported their find. Spitfires of No. 602 Squadron, flying an armed reconnaissance over the area, were immediately ordered to investigate the sighting.

Squadron Leader Chris Le Roux, the formation leader, spotted the car and carried out a low altitude strafing attack with cannon and machine guns. He scored several hits and, its driver dead at the wheel, the car ran off the road and crashed into a tree. Rommel suffered a fractured skull and severe concussion, and was replaced at a critical stage in the land battle.

Far left: Spitfire IX fighter-bombers of No. 601 Squadron about to take off from Fano, Italy. **Below and overleaf:** Mark IXs fitted with two 250lb (113kg) bombs under the wings.

'THE EFFECT OF AIR SUPERIORITY'

'... we always knew when we were flying over the front line either when starting out on a reconnaissance mission or when returning: the contrast was astonishing, for in German occupied territory not a thing moved; perhaps a solitary vehicle would be observed, but as soon as the driver or look-out saw an aeroplane the vehicle stopped. Over our own territory masses of tents and convoys were to be seen, and that was the effect that air superiority, or the complete lack of it, had on land forces and their everyday existence.'

GROUP CAPTAIN G. MILLINGTON, COMMANDER NO. 285 (RECONNAISSANCE) WING IN ITALY, 1944, IN HIS BOOK THE UNSEEN EYE

BOMB LOADS CARRIED

The bomb loads carried by Spitfires depended on the nature of the target and its distance from base. The greater the distance the aircraft had to fly, the smaller the bomb load it could carry. Normally the Spitfires carried two 250 pound (113kg) bombs under the wings or a 500 pounder (226kg) under the fuselage. However, if the target was relatively close to base, the aircraft might carry the 500 pounder as well as two 250 pounders. Once the bombs had been dropped, the fighter could switch to the ground-attack role. When operating in the fighter-bomber role, Spitfires usually flew in sections of four or six, depending on the type of target and the weight of attack required.

Once the bombs had dropped, the fighter's powerful gun armament made it an effective ground-strafing aircraft

Flying Officer David Green flew Spitfires with No. 73 Squadron over Italy and Yugoslavia. He describes the normal tactics for a dive-bombing attack in a Spitfire:

'Carrying two 250lb bombs, the Spitfire made a very fine dive bomber. It could attack accurately and didn't need a fighter escort because as soon as the bombs had been released it was a fighter. The briefing beforehand had to be good enough for us to be able to fly right up to the target identify it and bomb it.

AIR SUPPORT FOR THE ARMY, 10 NOV 1944

SQUADRON	AIRCRAFT	TIME UP	REMARKS
No. 7 SAAF	6 Spitfire	0945	Bombed medium gun position.
No. 1 SAAF	6 Spitfire	1000	Bombed field guns near Forli.
No. 601	6 Spitfire	1015	Bombed field guns near Forli. Light AA fire. One aircraft failed to pull out of dive possible due to flak hit, pilot killed.
No. 2 SAAF	6 Spitfire	1020	Two aircraft returned early. Rest bombed gun position and carried out strafing attacks. Heavy AA from target, no losses.
No. 92	6 Spitfire	1025	Bombed gun positions S. Faenza.
No. 92	6 Spitfire	1030	Bombed and strafed gun and mortar positions near S. Faenza.
No. 4 SAAF	6 Spitfire	1040	Dive-bombed gun positions.
No. 2 SAAF	6 Spitfire	1105	Bombed 3 gun positions, target well strafed. Light AA from target.
No. 4 SAAF	6 Spitfire	1135	Bombed gun positions.

We normally operated in sections of four, and would fly to the target at 10,000 feet in finger-four battle formation.

'As the target came into view I would position it so that it appeared to be running down the line of my port cannon. When the target emerged from under the trailing edge I would pull the aircraft up, roll it over on its back and let the nose drop until the target was lined up in the gunsight graticule. That way, one got the Spitfire to go down in the correct angle of dive of 60 degrees. The other aircraft in the section, Nos 2, 3, and 4, would be following me down still in echelon.'

When the leader's dive took him to an altitude of 4,000 feet (1,219m) above the ground, he released his bombs.

'It was a pretty steep dive, it felt as if one was going down vertically.'

'I would let go my bombs and call "Bombs gone!"; the other chaps in the section would then release theirs. If there had been little flak, I would pull hard on the stick to bring the aircraft out of the dive and into a slight climb, so that I could look over my shoulder to see where the bombs had gone. But if we were being fired at, we would use our high forward speed to get us down to ground level where there was cover.'

During the final months of the war almost every attack launched by the British army

received strong fighter bomber support. The example above shows the scale of air support for the British advance on the Montone River in Italy, on 10 November 1944, over a two hour period.

VERSATILITY

Given the ability of the Spitfire in the fighter-bomber role, the reader should remember that attacks on ground targets were far from everyone's thoughts when the Spitfire was conceived.

The Spitfire remained in front-line service in the RAF for nearly a decade after the end of the war. In the next chapter we shall observe the final stages of its lengthy career in that service and also in foreign air forces.

THE AVRO LANCASTER

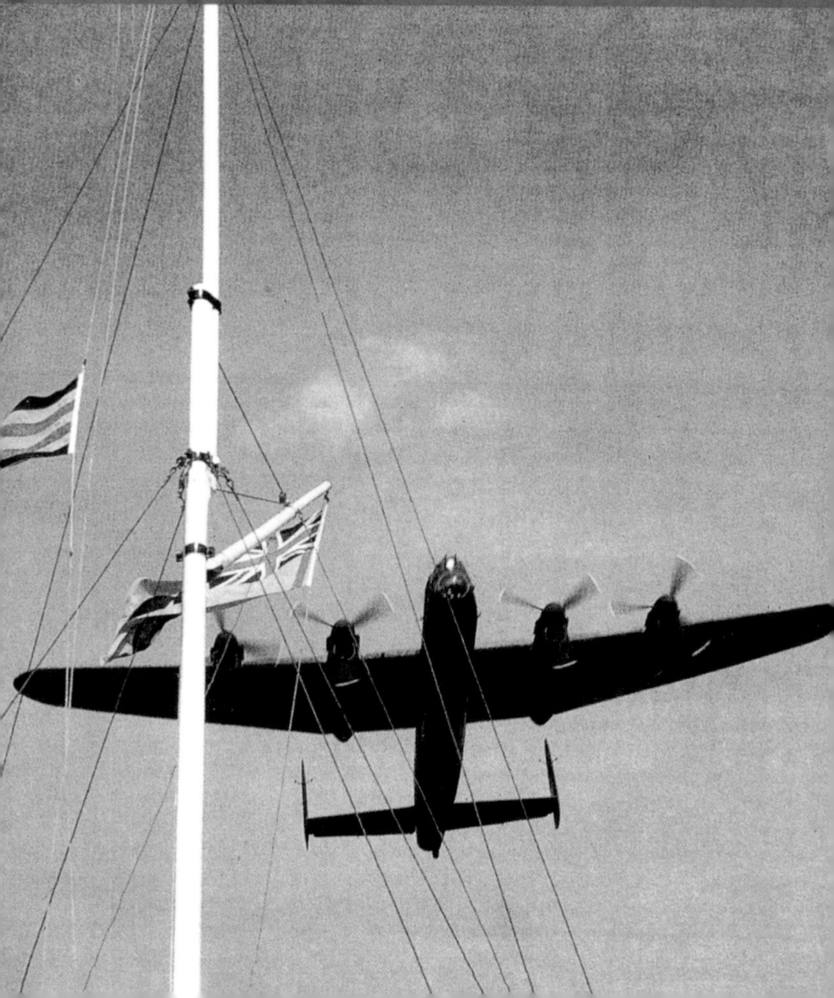

1 Two .303in (7.7mm) Browning machine guns
2 Frazer-Nash power-operated nose turret
3 Nose blister
4 Bomb-aimer's panel (optically flat)
5 Bomb-aimer's control panel
6 Side windows
7 External air temperature thermometer
8 Pitot head
9 Bomb-aimer's chest support
10 Fire extinguisher
11 Parachute emergency exit
12 F-24 camera
13 Glycol tank/step
14 Ventilator fairing
15 Bomb-bay doors forward actuating jacks
16 Bomb-bay doors forward actuating jacks
17 Control linkage
18 Rudder panels
19 Instrument panel
20 Windscreen sprays
21 Windscreen
22 Dimmer switches
23 Flight-engineer's folding seat
24 Flight-engineer's control panel
25 Pilot's seat
26 Flight-deck floor level
27 Elevator and rudder control rods (underfloor)
28 Trim tab control cables
29 Main floor/bomb-bay support longeron
30 Fire extinguisher
31 Wireless installation
32 Navigator's seat
33 Canopy rear/down-view blister
34 Pilot's head armour
35 Cockpit canopy emergency escape hatch
36 D/F loop
37 Aerial mast support
38 Electrical services panel
39 Navigator's compartment window
40 Navigator's desk
41 Aircraft and radio compass receiver
42 Wireless-operator's desk
43 Wireless-operator's seat
44 Wireless-operator's compartment window
45 Front spar carry-through/ fuselage frame
46 Astrodome
47 Inboard section wing ribs
48 Spar join
49 Aerial mast
50 Starboard inboard engine nacelle
51 Spinner
52 Three-blade de Havilland constant-speed propellers
53 Oil cooler intake
54 Oil cooler radiator
55 Carburettor air intake
56 Radiator shutter
57 Engine bearer frame
58 Exhaust flame-damper shroud
59 Packard-built Rolls-Royce Merlin 28 liquid-cooled engine
60 Nacelle/wing fairing
61 Fuel tank bearer ribs
62 Intermediate ribs
63 Leading-edge structure
64 Wing stringers
65 Wingtip skinning
66 Starboard navigation light
67 Starboard formation light
68 Aileron hinge fairings
69 Wing rear spar
70 Starboard aileron
71 Aileron balance tab

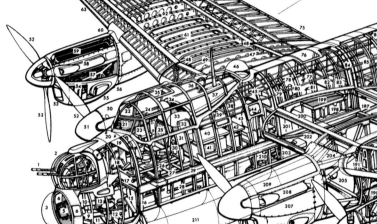

72 Balance tab control rod
73 Aileron trim tab
74 HF aerial
75 Split trailing-edge flap (outboard section)
76 Emergency (ditching) exit
77 Crash axe stowage
78 Fire extinguisher
79 Hydraulic reservoir
80 Signal/flare pistol stowage
81 Parachute stowage box/spar step
82 Rear spar carry-through
83 Bunk backrest
84 Rear spar fuselage frame
85 Emergency packs
86 Roof light
87 Dinghy manual release cable (dinghy stowage in starboard wingroot)
88 Mid-gunner's parachute stowage

89 Tail turret ammunition box
90 Ammunition feed track
91 Emergency (ditching) exit
92 Flame floats stowage
93 Sea markers stowage
94 Roof light
95 Dorsal turret fairing
96 Frazer-Nash power-operated dorsal turret

Avro Lancaster Mk III

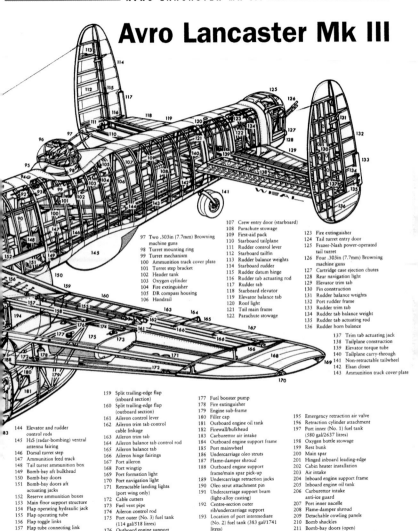

97 Two .303in (7.7mm) Browning machine guns
98 Turret mounting ring
99 Turret mechanism
100 Ammunition track cover plate
101 Turret step bracket
102 Header tank
103 Oxygen cylinder
104 Fire extinguisher
105 DR compass housing
106 Handrail
107 Crew entry door (starboard)
108 Parachute stowage
109 First-aid pack
110 Starboard tailplane
111 Rudder control lever
112 Starboard tailfin
113 Rudder balance weights
114 Starboard rudder
115 Rudder datum hinge
116 Rudder tab actuating rod
117 Rudder tab
118 Starboard elevator
119 Elevator balance tab
120 Roof light
121 Tail main frame
122 Parachute stowage
123 Fire extinguisher
124 Tail turret entry door
125 Frazer-Nash power-operated tail turret
126 Four .303in (7.7mm) Browning machine guns
127 Cartridge case ejection chutes
128 Rear navigation light
129 Elevator trim tab
130 Fin construction
131 Rudder balance weights
132 Port rudder frame
133 Rudder trim tab
134 Rudder tab balance weight
135 Rudder tab actuating rod
136 Rudder horn balance
137 Trim tab actuating jack
138 Tailplane construction
139 Elevator torque tube
140 Tailplane carry-through
141 Non-retractable tailwheel
142 Elsan closet
143 Ammunition track cover plate
144 Elevator and rudder control rods
145 H₂S (radar-bombing) ventral antenna fairing
146 Dorsal turret step
147 Ammunition feed track
148 Tail turret ammunition box
149 Bomb-bay aft bulkhead
150 Bomb-bay doors
151 Bomb-bay doors aft actuating jacks
152 Reserve ammunition boxes
153 Main floor support structure
154 Flap operating hydraulic jack
155 Flap operating tube
156 Flap toggle links
157 Flap tube connecting link
158 Rear spar
159 Split trailing-edge flap (inboard section)
160 Split trailing-edge flap (outboard section)
161 Aileron control lever
162 Aileron trim tab control cable linkage
163 Aileron trim tab
164 Aileron balance tab control rod
165 Aileron balance tab
166 Aileron hinge fairings
167 Port aileron
168 Port heater tank
169 Port formation light
170 Port navigation light
171 Retractable landing lights (port wing only)
172 Cable cutters
173 Fuel vent pipe
174 Aileron control rod
175 Port outer (No. 3) fuel tank (114 gal/518 litres)
176 Outboard engine support frame/rear spar pick-up
177 Fuel booster pump
178 Fire extinguisher
179 Engine sub-frame
180 Filler cap
181 Outboard engine oil tank
182 Firewall/bulkhead
183 Carburettor air intake
184 Outboard engine support frame
185 Port mainwheel
186 Undercarriage oleo struts
187 Flame-damper shroud
188 Outboard engine support frame/main spar pick-up
189 Undercarriage retraction jacks
190 Oleo strut attachment pin
191 Undercarriage support beam (light-alloy casting)
192 Centre-section outer rib/undercarriage support
193 Location of port intermediate (No. 2) fuel tank (383 gal/1741 litres)
194 Mainwheel well
195 Emergency retraction air valve
196 Retraction cylinder attachment
197 Port inner (No. 1) fuel tank (580 gal/2637 litres)
198 Oxygen bottle stowage
199 Rest bunk
200 Main spar
201 Hinged inboard leading-edge
202 Cabin heater installation
203 Air intake
204 Inboard engine support frame
205 Inboard engine oil tank
206 Carburettor intake anti-ice guard
207 Port inner nacelle
208 Flame-damper shroud
209 Detachable cowling panels
210 Bomb shackles
211 Bomb-bay doors (open)
212 8000lb (2532kg) bomb

THE MANCHESTER

The origins of the Lancaster lay in Air Ministry Specification P13/36, issued in September 1936, but it was some time before the definitive aircraft emerged. The requirements included a maximum bomb load of 8,000lb (3.63 tonnes), a six-man crew, which included a ventral gunner, and the ability to operate from existing 4,500ft (1,375m) long grass strips. Power was to be provided by two Rolls-Royce Vultures, a 24 cylinder liquid-cooled engine which was expected to develop about 2,000hp.

The Handley Page Company had early doubts about the Vulture, and switched to the proven Merlin, for what was to become the Halifax. At A. V. Roe, chief designer Roy Chadwick persevered with the bomber, with Napier's Sabre as a fall-back engine.

Two prototypes of the Avro Type 679, later to be named the Manchester, were ordered with-

Left: The Lancaster Mk I, originally known as the Manchester III, was developed around the Manchester fuselage and wing centre section.

AVRO 679

Dimensions
Wing span 80ft 2in (24.43m)
Tailplane span 22ft 0in (6.70m)
Length 70ft 0in (21.33m)
Height 19ft 6in (5.94m)

Weights
Maximum take-off 45,000lb (20,400kg)
Maximum bomb load 10,000lb (4,500kg)

Power
Two Rolls-Royce 24 cylinder Vulture I liquid-cooled engines rated at 1,720hp each.

Performance
Maximum speed 256mph (412km/hr) at 12,500ft (3,800m)
Range with maximum bomb load c1,200 miles (1,930km) Service ceiling c18,000ft (5,500m)

Armament
Two .303 Browning machine guns in each of three Nash and Thompson power-operated turrets, nose, tail, and a retractable ventral 'dustbin'. None fitted on first flight.

in a week of Specification P13/36 being issued, and the first flight took place at Ringway Airport on 25 July 1939. It was a large aircraft, with the wing in the mid position, and with twin fins and rudders. Handling problems were immediately apparent; the

controls were heavy, and lateral stability left much to be desired. The take-off run was far longer than anticipated, with no bomb load, with the gun turrets omitted and their positions faired over. Meanwhile the second prototype, already well advanced, was modified to try to cure these faults. The outer wing sections were redesigned, extending the span to 90ft 1in (27.46m); the control surfaces (ailerons and elevators) were improved, and larger fins and rudders fitted.

In the expectation that the faults of the first prototype would soon be overcome, contracts were placed for the production of 1,200 Manchesters. The first flight of the second prototype took place on 26 May 1940, handling had improved but directional stability, especially at low airspeeds, was still far from adequate. It was then decided to fit a central fin, which went some way towards improving matters.

Below: The twin-engined Manchester was the forerunner of the Lancaster. This No.61 Squadron aircraft failed to return from a raid on Hamburg in April 1942.

Above: The Manchester IA left off the central fin, but the span of the tailplane was greatly increased.

There were problems with the Vulture whose design had been started in 1935. It had two V-12 engines on a common crankcase, one upright, with the other inverted beneath it. With a capacity of 42.48 litres, it was expected to deliver over 2,000hp at 3,000rpm for take-off, and 1,710hp at an altitude of 15,000ft (4,570m).

The Vulture was just that bit too clever for the time

Lubrication, excessive wear, metal fatigue and overheating all gave cause for concern. But with the build-up of RAF Bomber Command, it was decided to continue with the Manchester, in the hope that the problems would be solved.

DEFENSIVE

The gun turrets were installed in the second prototype; two .303 Brownings in the nose, tail, and in a retractable ventral 'dustbin' arrangement. These also gave rise to handling problems. When rotated, they interfered with the slipstream. The nose turret caused the aircraft to veer to one side, while the rear turret caused vibration in the elevators.

Battle experience in 1939 led to a rethinking of the defensive armament for bombers. The ventral turret was deleted and a twin-gun mid-upper turret installed. The armament of the tail turret was to be doubled to four machine guns, but various weight restrictions prevented this being put into practice for some considerable time.

Despite the problems, the Manchester had many good points. The layout of the spacious cabin was highly praised, while the bomb bay could hold either four 2,000 pounders (900kg) or four sea mines; or one of the new 4,000lb (1,800kg) bombs together with six 1,000 pounders (450kg). The structure was sturdy, and adjustments to the flight control system resulted in an aircraft that was quite pleasant to fly.

Continuing problems with the Vulture engines limited it to 52,000lb (23.59 tonnes)and to 12,000ft (3,660m) with maximum bomb load and 50 per cent fuel.

STOP GAP

Further testing revealed an average of only 76 flying hours between engine failures, and generally the Manchester was only able to maintain height on one engine at fairly light all-up weights. The Manchester was rushed into service even though it would be only an interim type with Bomber Command.

The first operational Manchester squadron was No. 207, formed at Waddington late in 1940. Composed mainly of experienced crews, conversion onto type proceeded, and the Manchester was released for short-range operations with a reduced bomb load.

The target was the German cruiser Admiral Hipper

The first operation was flown by six aircraft on the night of 24/25 February 1941 with six aircraft. The target was the German cruiser *Admiral Hipper*, which was in the French port of Brest. None of these early aircraft were fitted with the mid-upper gun turret, and the ventral dustbin

MANCHESTER SQUADRONS

Sqn No.	Bases	1st Operation	Last Operation
207	Waddington Bottesford	24 Feb 1941	11/12 March 1942
97	Waddington Coningsby	8/9 April 1941	9/10 Jan 1942
61	N. Luffenham Syerston	14/15 Aug 1941	1/2 June 1942
83	Scampton	28 Jan 1942	1/2 June 1942
106	Coningsby	20 March 1942	25/26 June 1942
50	Skellingthorpe Swinderby	8/9 April 1942	25/26 June 1942
49	Scampton	2/3 May 1942	25/26 June 1942

The operational careers of the last four squadrons listed were very short, partly due to the fact that the similarities between the Lancaster and the Manchester allowed for an easy switch over.

remained unmanned for the raid. The bomb load consisted of twelve 500lb (225kg) semi-armour piercing bombs. Only moderate flak was encountered, and all aircraft returned safely. *Admiral Hipper* was not hit, which was only to be expected in those early days of the night-bombing war.

The first Manchester lost to enemy action came over England on 13 March, when a No. 207 Squadron aircraft was caught shortly after take-off.

The Vultures claimed their first victim exactly a week later, when a Manchester crashed shortly after take-off following an engine fire. On 13 April, all Manchesters were grounded for engine changes. Several aircraft were now entering service with the mid-upper turret, while the grounding period allowed others to have this fitted.

The Manchester still continued to be plagued by engine problems. The summer of 1941 saw the introduction of the Manchester 1A, which had a tailplane of increased span, taller twin fins and rudders, and no central fin.

LANCASTERS

The Manchester was being overtaken by events. The first Lancasters reached the squadrons late in 1941, and the fate of the twin-engined aircraft was sealed. It was finally withdrawn from Bomber Command operations after a raid on Bremen on 25/26 June 1942.

MANCHESTER 1A

Dimensions
Wingspan 90ft 1in (27.46m); Tailplane span 33ft 0in (10.06m); Length 70ft 0in (21.33m); Height 19ft 6in (9.54m).

Weights
Maximum take-off 56,000lb (25,400kg);
Maximum bomb load 10,350lb (4,700kg).

Power
Two Rolls-Royce 24 cylinder Vulture II liquid-cooled engines rated at 1,845hp each.

Performance
Maximum speed 265mph (426km/hr) at 17,000ft (5,200km/hr);
Range with maximum bomb load 1,200 miles (1,930km); Service ceiling 19,200ft (5,850m).

Armament
Two Browning .303 machine guns in nose and dorsal turrets; four .303 Browning machine guns in tail turret.

THE LANCASTER
DESCRIBED

It has been said that the Lancaster arose from the failure of the Manchester but in the autumn of 1938, long before the first flight of the Manchester prototype, A.V. Roe's design office considered the possibility of a four-engined variant of the Type 679. But only the most basic work was done at this stage on what was to become the Avro Type 683.

Early in the following year, a new specification was issued; B.1/39. Its ultimate purpose was to produce a heavy bomber which would start to replace the four-engined Stirlings and Halifaxes (neither of which had yet flown), and the Manchester itself in four to five years' time.

The requirements were stringent; a cruising speed of 280mph (450km/hr) at 15,000ft (4,570m) while carrying a bomb load of 9,000lb (4.08 tonnes); only slightly

Left: As a safeguard against a shortage of Merlins, the Mk II Lancaster was powered by Bristol Hercules radial engines.

Above: The first four-engined bomber to enter service with Bomber Command was the Short Stirling. It was inferior to the Lancaster in both performance and load-carrying.

less than the maximum of 10,000lb (4.54 tonnes) specified. Range under these conditions was to be a minimum of 2,500 miles (4,000km). This was pushing the state of the art very hard, with the requirement for defensive armament, which was to consist of tail and ventral turrets each carrying four 20mm cannon. These turrets did not even exist at that time, and the complexity, weight and drag of such planes ensured that they never would. Prototype aircraft were ordered from both Handley Page and Bristol, but neither got past the mock-up stage. The Air Ministry

was however interested in A.V. Roe's proposal for a four-engined bomber developed from the Manchester. Initial progress with the four-engined machine was slow. Not until the production Manchester could be finalized could serious work start on its derivative.

The advantages of four-engined bombers seem glaringly obvious. Because they were

BRITISH BOMBER COMPARISONS 1941

A/C type	Cruise Speed at Altitude	Bomb Load for Max Radius	Radius with Max Bomb
Wellington	170mph (273km/hr) at 11,300ft (3,450m)	2,500lb (1,130kg) for 1,100 miles (1,770km)	560 miles (900km) with a 4,500lb (2,040kg)
Stirling	208mph (335km/hr) at 13,800ft (4,200m)	3,500lb (1,590kg) for 855 miles (1,37km)	285 miles (460km) with (6,350kg)
Halifax	203mph (327km/hr) 15,100ft (4,600m)	5,800lb (2,630kg) for 910 miles (1,465km)	580 miles (930km) with 8,000lb (3,630kg)
Manchester	205mph (330km/hr) 13,650ft (4,160m)	8,100lb (3,675kg) for 885 miles (1,425km)	500 miles (805km) with 10,350lb (4,700kg)

From the above table it can be seen that the payload/range of the twin-engined Manchester was significantly better than either of its four-engined contemporaries. It totally outclassed the Wellington.

Above: The Rolls-Royce Merlin XX engine installation package for the Beaufighter IIF was adapted for the Lancaster.

bigger than their twin-engined counterparts, they could carry heavier loads of fuel and weaponry. In 1939, the twin-engined Manchester could carry a 40 per cent greater bomb load than the four-engined Halifax over a comparable distance. Two engines required fewer systems, less weight, less maintenance, and lower costs for spares and replacements. Aerodynamically, with only two engines instead of four, there was less drag to overcome in flight. The difficulty was producing an engine of sufficient power to do the job. The Napier Sabre was scheduled to power the Manchester II, but delays ensured this leading variant was never built.

The Merlin was the obvious choice for the Type 683, but

The overall wingspan was increased to accommodate engines

demand for this engine for Spitfires and Hurricanes was high. As a backup, the more powerful but heavier and draggier Bristol Hercules radial was selected. Increased demand for the Hercules caused by Stirling production eventually led to the IIF variant. Rolls-Royce had developed an engine installation package, which, with minor changes, proved eminently suitable for the new bomber.

Type 683, known in the design office as the Lancaster from a very early stage, was developed around the Manchester fuselage and wing centre section. The cavernous bomb bay met all current requirements. The overall wingspan was substantially increased to accommodate the outboard engines, which also had the effect of improving take-off performance.

FOUR ENGINES

At the end of August 1940, the decision was taken that Bomber Command's strategic force would be entirely equipped as soon as possible with four-engined bombers. In retrospect this decision seems extraordinary. The four-engined heavy bomber had yet to prove itself, but there remained one sound operational reason for the decision. Even reliable engines

Left: The Avro Type 683 prototype was initially known as the Manchester III, and only later renamed the Lancaster I.

Above: The second Lancaster prototype introduced a ventral turret that was fitted to early production aircraft.

Trials at Boscombe Down showed good handling qualities although, directional stability was lacking. With the new Merlin XXs fitted, the prototype reached a maximum speed of 310mph (500km/hr) at 21,000ft (6,400m) – an outstanding performance for a heavy bomber of that era. The use of Manchester sub-assemblies speeded up the output.

SECOND PROTOTYPE M

The second Lancaster prototype, which made its maiden flight on 13 May 1941, was rather nearer to the production

failed occasionally, and all were vulnerable to flak and fighters. The failure of one engine in a four-engined type was much less serious than the same case in a twin, in which a full 50 per cent of the available power was lost, and asymmetric handling problems, with all the remaining power on one side, were far more extreme.

> **Trials at Boscombe Down showed good handling qualities but directional stability was lacking**

The decision to proceed with the four-engined Avro bomber was taken, although as a security measure the name Lancaster was dropped and the Type 683 became known as the Manchester Mark III, the Mark II designation having been reserved for the Napier Sabre-powered aircraft, which in fact was never built. The prototype used a Manchester I airframe

powered by Merlin Xs, and retained the short-span tailplane and triple fin layout of that aircraft. The first flight took place on 9 January 1941.

LANCASTER

Dimensions
Wingspan 102ft 0in (31.09m); Length (tail up) 69ft 6in (21.18m); Height (tail up) 20ft 6in (6.25m); Wing area 1,297 sq ft (120.45m²)

Weights
Empty 36,900lb (16,740kg); Normal loaded 53,000lb (24,040kg); Maximum overload 65,000lb (29,480kg); B.I Special with 22,000lb (9,980kg); Grand Slam 70,000lb (31,750kg); Maximum internal bomb load 14,000lb (6,350kg).

Power
Four Rolls-Royce Merlin 12 cylinder liquid-cooled engines each rated at 1,460hp (variable depending on type) driving a three-bladed variable-pitch, constant-speed propeller. Lancaster B.III powered by four Bristol Hercules 14 cylinder air-cooled radial engines each rated at 1,650hp.

Fuel and Oil
Total fuel 2,154gal (9,790 litres) in six wing tanks. 580gal (2,637 litres) in each inboard wing tank; 383gal (740 litres) in each intermediate wing tank, and 114gal (518 litres) in each outboard wing tank. One or two overload 400gal (1,818 litre) tanks could be mounted in the bomb bay. Oil tank capacity 150gal (682 litres) carried in four wing tanks.

Performance
Maximum speed 270mph (434km/hr) at 19,000ft (5,800m); Cruise speed 210mph (338km/hr); 19.3 min to 11,000ft (3,350m); 43.5min to 20,000ft (6,100m); Service ceiling 21,500ft (6,550m); Range with 14,000lb (6,350kg) bomb load 1,160 miles (1,870km); with 7,000lb (1,795kg) bomb load and one overload fuel tank 2,230 miles (3,590km).

Armament
Two .303 Browning machine guns with 1,000rpg in a Frazer-Nash power-operated turret in the nose; ditto in the mid-upper position, and four Browning machine guns with 2,500 rpg in a Frazer-Nash power-operated turret in the tail. A few aircraft retained the ventral gun position, while many others had the mid-upper turret removed. Others were fitted with two .50 Browning heavy machine guns.

---

machine standard, stressed for an all-up weight of 60,000lb (27.22 tonnes), and with a dorsal gun turret fitted. It retained the ventral turret for the time being. The third prototype followed on 26 November of that year, which was powered by Hercules VI radials, and became the prototype Lancaster Mark II. But long before the radial-engined machine took to the air, production Mark Is were rolling off the lines.

All-up weight had been increased to 65,000lb (29.48 tonnes) maximum; maximum bomb load had been increased to 14,000lb (6.35 tonnes); two extra fuel tanks had been fitted in the wings, and the ventral turret had been removed. A collar fairing had been added around the mid-upper turret to stop the guns being depressed enough to damage the aircraft, and a four-gun turret was standard in the tail position. The crew consisted of seven men; the pilot, who was also the aircraft captain, regardless of rank; a second pilot, who was quickly replaced by the new category of flight engineer; a bomb-aimer, who also manned the front

Above: The standard camouflage scheme was dark green and dark earth disruptive pattern above and matt black below.

turret; a navigator; a wireless operator, and mid-upper and tail gunners.

THE LANCASTER CLOSE UP

The Lancaster is a lady, and for that reason is never described as 'it', but always as 'she'. Very much the grand dame, the indomitable dowager, yet with a twinkle in her eye to hint at a racy past in her younger days. Her attire is sombre, a staid dull black on undersides of wings and tail and fuselage sides complemented by a tasteful camouflage scheme on top. Guns protrude from turrets in

her nose and tail and mid-way down her upper fuselage. The first impression is that she is big. Her huge main wheels, suspended on sturdy legs beneath the inboard engine nacelles, are almost shoulder-height, while the front fuselage towers high above us. Her mid-mounted wings spread 50ft (15m) to either side, carrying the four sleek cowlings which house the Rolls-Royce Merlin engines with their shrouded exhausts, fronted by large three-bladed propellors.

In the front of her nose is a hemispherical transparent dome, with a round optically flat panel

Below: Figures on the ground give scale to the first production Lancaster, seen prior to delivery to Boscombe Down for type testing.

LANCASTER GUN TURRET

Type	FN 5	FN 50	FN 20	FN 64
Position	Nose	Mid-upper	Tail	Ventral
Guns	2 x .303 Browning Mk II	2 x .303 Browning Mk II	4 x .303 Browning Mk II	2 x .303 Browning Mk II
Rounds	1,000	1,000	2,500	500
Gunsight	Mk III Reflector	Mk IIIA Reflector	Mk III Reflector or Gyro Mk IIc	Periscopic
Traverse	+/-95°	360°	+/-94°	+/-90°
Elevation	60°	20°	60°	0°
Depression	45°	2°	45°	60°

looking downwards. Above is a turret from which project two .303 Browning machine guns. Immediately behind the turret is a glazed cabin for the pilot and his flight engineer, but we see little of this as we walk beneath the giant bird.

What we do see is the huge bomb bay, which starts almost immediately beneath the front of the cabin and reaches back to a point almost level with the dorsal turret. As is usual before engine start-up, the bomb bay doors are open, revealing the sinister outlines of the contents. In the centre is a large, dark green cylinder, a 4,000lb (1,800kg) high explosive 'cookie'. It is surrounded by twelve SBCs (Small Bomb Containers) filled with incendiaries. This is the most usual Lancaster bomb load.

We climb up and in, then it's down onto the central catwalk

Astern of the bomb bay is a teardrop-shaped fairing. This houses the scanner for H2S, the latest radar bombing and navi-gational aid. We enter the Lancaster through a small hatch in the starboard side. A short metal ladder hooks onto the sill, and we climb up and in, onto an inner step, then it's down onto the central catwalk.

REAR GUNNER

Once inside, the interior of a Lancaster is bleak indeed. The structure, fuselage formers and longerons are bare, showing the metal skin. Running the length of the fuselage walls are pipes, rods, all manner of plumbing and wiring. These are for carrying hydraulic fluid and power to where it is needed.

At this point, the first member of the crew leaves us. He passes the primitive Elsan toilet to his right, scrambles over the tailplane spar structure, pauses to stow his parachute, then squeezes into his cold and cramped position, shutting the armoured doors behind him. He is the rear gunner, and his job is arguably the most danger-ous, and certainly the coldest, the most lonely and isolated, of any Lancaster crewman.

From now until the end of the mission, his only human contact will be the disembodied voices of other crew members over the intercom. The German night fighters almost always attack from astern. If he is given the opportunity to use his skills, his four rifle-calibre machine guns are far outranged by the cannon of the German night fighters which, if visibility is good enough, can stand off and shoot at him. They can also slip below, where they are difficult to see, and pick off the bomber with their upward-firing guns.

Even in defeat, the rear gun-ner's fate is a lonely one.

Below: The open doors give some idea of the vast size of the bomb bay. The bombs were released in a preset sequence.

Above: Up the ladder and in. A crew from No. 9 Squadron board their Lancaster ready for a mission.

stowing his parachute in its place high on the right, he climbs into his turret via a step on the left of the fuselage.

The mid-upper gunner has only two machine guns. His field of fire is obstructed, however, to the rear by the tailplane and fins on each side, and straight ahead by the navigator's astrodome. The turret is surrounded by a fairing which contains a cam track. By restricting the movement of the guns, this ensures that he cannot damage his own aircraft when firing. When the guns are elevated at 20 degrees or more, turret traverse is fast and smooth, but below this it is much slower. This is to avoid damage to the

The call to bale out is 'Abracadabra Jump, Jump! Abracadabra Jump, Jump!'. It sounds silly, but it has one advantage. It cannot possibly be misunderstood but was seldom used, and the order given in plain language. On hearing the command to bale out, the rear gunner opens his armoured doors at the rear of his turret, reaches back for his parachute and clips it onto his chest harness. He swivels his turret right round until the open doors are facing outwards, then does a backward roll out into the night sky above a hostile country. This is of course presupposing that his parachute has not been burnt or shot to pieces, that he is still able to turn his turret to the escape position, and that his out-of-control bomber will allow him to make these necessary moves.

The rest of the crew turn to the right along the catwalk. On the far wall is a handrail, very necessary for moving about in flight. Next to reach his station is the mid-upper gunner. After

LANCASTER BOMB LOADS

Bombing, and especially night bombing, was a very imprecise art in the Second World War. Even finding the target was difficult enough; hitting it often seemed next to impossible. The solution adopted was to saturate the target area with bombs; high explosive to demolish buildings and incendiaries to set the ruins on fire. It was crude, but it was the only practicable means available to Bomber Command. There were of course specialized weapons called for greater accuracy, but these were less common.

Blast and demolition
1) 1 x 8,000lb (3,630kg) HE plus 6 (max) 500lb (225kg) HE.
2) 14 x 1,000lb (450kg) HE.

Blast, demolition and fire
3) 1 x 4,000lb (1,800kg) HE plus 3 x 1,000lb HE plus up to 6 SBCs (Small Bomb Containers) each holding either 236 4lb (2kg) or 24 x 30lb (14kg) incendiaries.
4) 1 x 4,000lb (1,800kg) HE plus up to 12 SBCs.

Maximum incendiary
5) 14 SBCs.

Deployed tactical targets
6) 1 x 4,000lb (1,800kg) HE plus up to 18,500lb (225kg) HE.

Low-level attacks
7) 6 x 1,000lb (450kg) HE with delayed action fuses.

Hardened targets, naval installations, ships etc.
8) 6 x 2,000lb (900kg) armour piercing with very short delay fuses.

Minelaying
9) Up to six 1,500lb (680kg) or 1,850lb (840kg) mines.

Above: Emergency escape from the rear turret was made by turning it sideways as seen here, then rolling out backwards.
Left: The mid-upper turret, showing the fairing which prevented the gunner from damaging his own aircraft.
Below: H2S position in the Lancaster. Top left is the curtain which shuts out light; to the right is the flight engineer's position, with his seat folded. (Alfred Price)

turret fairing at full depression, but in action, it is a serious disadvantage as it makes tracking a fast-moving enemy fighter very difficult.

In an emergency the mid-upper gunner must get out of the turret, retrieve his parachute, and depart through the door by which he entered. Just ahead of the mid-upper turret is an escape hatch in the fuselage roof, which is used in the event of a crash landing or a ditching at sea. In the latter event, a dinghy is housed in the upper surface of the starboard wing-root, which hopefully can be released manually from inside the aircraft, and which should then inflate automatically if the Lancaster comes down in the 'drink', as it is generally known.

The walls in this area of the fuselage are cluttered with fire extinguishers and flame float and sea marker canisters.

Further up the fuselage is the rear wing spar carry-through, with a step on the far side which contains more parachute stowage. To the left of this is the rest bunk, which is normally used only for casualties.

A few feet along is yet another obstacle, the main wing spar

carry-through. We arrive at the main crew positions through a 7mm-thick armoured door. Situated on the left is the wireless operator's small table and radio. There is a small window which is level with the leading edge of the wing, but at night a curtain is drawn across it. This is mainly because he needs artificial light by which to work, and this must not be allowed to betray the presence of the bomber to any roving fighters which might be in the area. The wireless operator has the warmest place in the aircraft; often he is overheated while other crew members are freezing.

H2S, a blind bombing aid which shows a radar picture of the ground

In front of the wireless operator sits the navigator, sideways on. He also has a table on which he spreads out charts and a computer. Above him is an astrodome, through which the navigator can estimate a very approximate position. There is also another piece of equipment.

This is H2S, a blind bombing aid which shows a radar picture of the ground below on a television-type screen. It needs good interpretation to get good results, and like all electronic aids of this era, it can be temperamental. But it helps.

THE PILOT

Up front, his seat on a raised floor section to the left of the main cabin, is the pilot, who is also the aircraft captain.

Above left: The H2S scanner housing supplanted the ventral turret position on many aircraft. This is a late war model.
Above right: Lancaster pilot's position, showing the sliding hatch through which escape was barely possible. However, the extensively glazed cabin gave a good all-round view.

He has a good all-round view through the canopy. There is a direct-vision panel on either side of the windshield, and in the canopy roof is an escape hatch. Behind him is a 4mm-thick sheet of armour.

In front of the pilot is the control column which directs the elevators in the tail, causing the aircraft to climb or dive. A wheel-type yoke moves like a car steering wheel, controlling the ailerons in the wings to make the aircraft bank to left or right. At his feet are the rudder pedals, which are used for flat turns to either side.

Low to the pilot's left is the compass, but for convenience a compass repeater is mounted on the divided windshield. The dash contains many dials and switches, while the throttle levers and propellor speed con-

trols are mounted on a central console where they can be reached by both the pilot and the flight engineer.

The flight engineer sits to the right of the pilot on a folding seat, allowing access to the bomb aimer's and front gunner's positions. His task is to look after the engines, throttle settings and propellor pitch settings, fuel flow, and also act as the pilot's assistant.

He has two panels to monitor. One, on the starboard side, contains oil and fuel gauges, booster pump switches, fuel pressure warning lights, and fuel tank selector cocks. The other is part of the main dash, and contains revolution counters, boost gauges, ignition switches, engine fire extinguisher buttons and propellor feathering buttons.

BOMB AIMER

Squeezing past the flight engineer's station, we clamber down into the nose. This is the territory of the bomb aimer, who usually mans the nose turret when not actually on the bombing run, although he can also be called upon to assist the naviga-

tor by map-reading.

The bomb aimer lies prone, his chest propped on an adjustable support. Beneath him is the forward escape hatch. which may also be used by the flight engineer and the pilot.

To the right of the bomb aimer is the bomb fusing and selection panel. It is essential that the bombs are released in a predetermined order from the long bay. For this, a selector box is used. Also featured are camera controls and photo-flares which enable a picture to be taken of the aim point.

BOMBS GONE

The bomb sight is of the vector type, into which the aircraft speed and altitude are set, together with the ballistic data, and the estimated wind speed and direction. The sight is gyro-stabilized, which allows banked turns to be made during the run up to the target. Two lines of light on a reflecting screen form a cross which indicates where the bomb will drop. Over the intercom the bomb aimer guides the pilot to a position where the extension of the

Left: Bomb release switch in hand, the bomb aimer lies prone facing his Mk XIV vector sight.
Above: All late-production Lancasters, regardless of mark, were fitted with an enlarged nose transparency.

vertical line passes through the aim point. When the bomber is lined up correctly, the aim point appears to slide gradually down the vertical line. Then when the cross touches the target, the bomb aimer presses the button and down go the bombs, bringing destruction to the target below. When not engaged in dropping bombs, the bomb aimer occupies the nose turret, with its two machine guns. At night he will probably have little to do; rarely is visibility clear enough to allow the night fighters to attack from head-on. In daylight or at low level the situation could be different, and the turret might be occupied even on the bombing run. The gunner had no footrest, and in moments of excitement may well have tread on the bomb aimer's head, to say nothing of showering him with hot 'empties' when he fires.

This then is the Lancaster, a bomber in which many thousands of men went to war, and for which many thousands of crewmen had affection, and faith that she was the best.

Below: When not actually on the bombing run, the bomb aimer normally manned the front gun turret. This Lancaster was visiting the USA on a goodwill mission in 1942.

INTO SERVICE

The first unit to receive the Lancaster was No. 44 (Rhodesia) Squadron at Waddington. The first Lancaster prototype arrived in mid September 1941, while several Manchester pilots were transferred to the squadron to ease the task of conversion. Not until Christmas Eve did the first three operational aircraft arrive, followed by four more on 28 December.

No. 44 Squadron had flown Hampdens, but as from January 1942, seven of the Manchester squadrons were progressively re-equipped with the Lancaster. Brand new Manchesters were still coming off the production lines, and Lancaster production was not yet in full swing. Also, the similarities of the two aircraft made it relatively easy to convert Manchester crews to the Lancaster; the latter could therefore be introduced into service faster by bringing more Manchesters on stream. The first Lancasters reached No. 97 Squadron in January, and No. 207 Squadron in March 1942.

The first Lancaster operation took place on the night of 3/4 March 1942. Four Lancasters

Above: This former No. 44 Squadron aircraft flew the Atlantic to Canada to serve as a pattern aircraft for Lancaster production. Far left: Fitters swarm all over the port inner engine of this Lancaster Mk 11 of No. 408 'Goose' Squadron, RCAF.

of No. 44 Squadron laid mines (an operation codenamed 'Gardening') off the German coast. All returned safely. In the first excursion over Germany, two aircraft of the same squadron joined a raid on Essen, again without loss. The first Lancaster to be lost in action failed to return from another Gardening sortie on 24/25 March.

THE AUGSBURG RAID

In the Spring of 1942 U-boat production facilities became priority targets, and one of the most important was the MAN works at Augsburg, where their diesel engines were made. Augsburg was not far from Munich, a round trip of some 1,250 miles (2,000km), mostly over enemy territory.

On the afternoon of 17 April, 12 Lancasters took off for Augsburg. The first wave of six, flying in two Vics of three, was from No. 44 Squadron, led by Squadron leader John Nettleton. Two miles (3km) astern and about 3 miles (5km) to starboard was the second wave, six Lancasters from No. 97

AUSBERG RAID REPORT, EXTRACT

Aircraft Attacking	Bombs Dropped	Release Height	Time at Target	Results observed
8	14.3 tons	50/400ft	1955/2015	Huge red flames seen. One a/c claimed hits on main building, two others claim bombs in target area.

Owing to poor light and low altitude, photographs lacked all essential detail. No bomb bursts are shown, but a large fire is seen probably in the city of Augsburg, and it is clear that at least one and probably all the aircraft passed directly over the target. A PR photograph taken on 25/4 reveals severe damage chiefly to the S end of the works. The main Diesel Assembly Shop has suffered heavy damage.

Above: Squadron Leader John Nettleton led the daring daylight raid on the U-boat engine factory at Augsburg, for which he was awarded the Victoria Cross.

LANCASTER SQUADRONS, OPERATION MILLENNIUM

Sqn No.	Base	Date of 1st Op.
144	Waddington	3 March 1942
97	Woodhall Spa	20/21 March 1942
207	Bottesford	24/25 April 1942
83	Coningsby	29/30 April 1942
61	Syerston	5/6 May 1942
106	Coningsby	30/31 May 1942
50	Skellingthorpe	30/31 May 1942
		(one a/c only)

Squadron, led by Squadron leader John Sherwood. Each aircraft carried four 1,000lb (450kg) bombs with 11-second delayed action fuses.

Diversionary attacks were planned to keep German fighters occupied, but these miscarried. Between 20 and 30 Messerschmitt 109s of JG.2 returning to base encountered the rear Vic of Nettleton's wave. They shot down all three before turning their attention to the leading trio. One more Lancaster went down and the others were damaged before the Germans, by now low on fuel and ammunition, broke off the running battle. The second wave, although only a few miles away, was not spotted.

Nettleton and Flying Officer J. Garwell, the other survivor of the first wave, bored eastwards on track for Munich until over the Ammer lake they swung north towards Augsburg, followed at a distance of about 10 miles (16km) by the No. 97 Squadron formation.

Augsburg finally came into sight, and the two remaining Lancasters of No. 44 Squadron detoured around some tall factory chimneys and commenced their bombing run. At this point Garwell's aircraft was hit by flak and, shortly after releasing his bombs, he had to slide the burning Lancaster onto the ground. Four of the seven crewmen aboard survived, to be taken prisoner. Nettleton's Lancaster alone escaped into the gathering gloom.

Minutes later, the first Vic of the second wave from 97 Squadron arrived to find a thoroughly alerted defence. Unlike Nettleton, Sherwood did not attempt to dodge around the factory chimneys, but climbed above them. All three aircraft bombed accurately, but Sherwood's Lancaster was mortally hit by ground fire, and crashed in flames shortly after. By some miracle, Sherwood

Below: Wellingtons were the most numerous bombers participating in Operation Millennium. However, they were soon to be phased out in favour of the Avro Lancaster. (via Flypast)

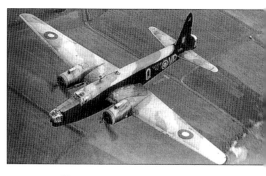

Above: No. 83 Squadron Lancasters took part in the 1,000 bomber raid on Cologne. This unit was also the first Lancaster Pathfinder squadron.

Right: Cologne at the end of the war, showing the devastation around the cathedral. Wrecked bridges block the Rhine.

himself survived with only minor injuries.

Meanwhile the final Vic, now came racing in from the south. They were met by a storm of anti-aircraft fire, and all three were badly damaged. One blew up just as its bombs fell clear, but the other two got through.

Seventeen bombs hit the factory buildings, causing extensive damage. Nettleton was awarded the Victoria Cross for his exploit, and many other survivors were decorated for this, the first Lancaster raid to be made public. But with a loss rate exceeding 50 per cent it was not repeatable.

OPERATION MILLENNIUM

By the end of May 1942, seven squadrons had Lancasters. This

was just in time for them to take part in a raid which for Bomber Command was a turning point in the night air offensive.

The strategic bombing of the Third Reich was, in its early days, an haphazard affair, with individual crews plotting their own courses and timings. Navigation was inexact, and only one crew in three managed to place their bombs within 5 miles (8km) of the target. To make matters worse, the German night fighter defences had taken the measure of this form of attack, and losses were steadily increasing. The future of Bomber Command looked increasingly uncertain. This was the situation when Air Marshal Arthur Harris assumed command in February 1942.

Harris realized that a raid by 1,000 bombers would be the biggest raid ever; the magic number of 1,000 would attract interest and demonstrate that RAF Bomber Command was truly a force to be reckoned with.

> **All aircraft would follow the same route from a merge point off the coast**

The target chosen was Cologne. The city was within range of a new radio navigational device called Gee, and on a moonlit night the Rhine was easily identifiable from the air. All aircraft would follow the same route from a merge point off the coast. The entire attack was to

Above: Mk I R5609 flew with No. 97 Squadron on the Cologne and Essen thousand-bomber raids. Later it took part in the Battles of the Ruhr, Berlin, Hamburg and Peenemunde. It survived the war. (Alfred Price)

last just 90 minutes, an average of more than 11 aircraft bombing every minute! The German defences would be saturated by weight of numbers, minimizing losses.

The Cologne raid took place on the night of 30/31 May, 1942. The attack was in three waves, the first consisting of Gee-equipped Wellingtons and Stirlings with selected crews. The second wave consisted of the remaining Stirlings and Wellingtons, and the other twin-engined types; Hampdens, Whitleys and Manchesters. The third wave consisted of more than 125 Halifaxes and about 75 Lancasters which were scheduled to be over the target during the final 15 minutes of the attack. As the fastest and most heavily armed aircraft in the force, they were the least vulnerable to German night fighters. Losses to the third wave

amounted to a mere 1.9 per cent, compared with 4.8 per cent to the first wave and 4.1 per cent to the second.

For Bomber Command, it opened a new era in strategic bombing. Within three years, Lancasters would make up virtually the whole of the raiding force, and the damage they wrought upon German industry and communications was incalculable.

The secret of success for Operation Millennium had been the ability to find the target and mark it for the following crews. Gee was a useful navigation aid, but it not only lacked accuracy but was too short-ranged to cover many important targets. A special target-finding force was eventually formed in July 1942.

THE PATHFINDERS

Bomber Command introduced a competition to promote increased efficiency in the form of a photographic ladder. It became standard procedure for each bomber to photograph its aim point, and each squadron's position on the ladder was

determined by the accuracy of these. The ladder indicated which squadrons (and also which crews) were consistently finding their targets.

The first loads to go down contained a high proportion of incendiaries

Path Finder Force (PFF) was formed, commanded by Group Captain Don Bennett, an Australian navigation expert and prewar trail-blazer.

Bomber Command was divided into operational areas called Groups. The squadron heading the photographic ladder in each of the four Bomber Groups was transferred to the newly formed No. 8 Pathfinder Group, based in Huntingdon. By the end of the war, there were 14 Lancaster-equipped PFF Squadrons.

Regrettably PFF did not manage to bring about an instant improvement in bombing effectiveness. This had to wait for new navigational devices, for special pyrotechnic markers, and the development of methods which made the best use of them.

The former duly arrived in the shape of Oboe, an accurate but range-limited radio bombing device carried by Mosquitos. Dependent on signals from ground transmitters in England, it took in the highly industrialized Ruhr area but not much else.

The heavy bombers had H2S a radar navigation and blind bombing aid, but it was much less accurate than Oboe.

Above: Flak bursts punctuate the night sky over Germany as Pathfinder markers go down on a target in Germany. Two other bombers are just visible.

Parachute flares had long been used as an aid to target finding. They had however two drawbacks. Unless visibility was good, they would not light up the ground sufficiently well for crews to visually identify a target, or even pinpoint their own location. Then, of course, unless the flares were released in the right area, they simply illuminated a strange and often unrecognisable area of Germany, which was not a lot of help. Used in conjunction with Oboe or H2S, flares became far more effective.

In Operation Millennium, the first loads to go down contained a high proportion of incendiaries, to start fires which would lead the following bombers to the target area. Something more accurate was needed, and this duly arrived in the form of markers, known as Target Indicators, or TIs.

Each TI contained 60 pyrotechnic candles. A barometric fuse preset to operate at low altitude blew the TI open, cascading the candles onto the ground, igniting as they went. Seen from above, the contents of each TI would appear as an intense pool of light, about 900ft (275m) in diameter. Burning time was about three minutes, so they needed to be replenished at frequent intervals.

By now the Germans had started to produce dummy targets to mislead the bombers. Their obvious reaction to TIs was to copy them and, when a raid was imminent, set them off on a dummy target. To circumvent this, TIs were produced in a combination of colours; red, yellow, green, etc., and used in a predetermined order which varied from raid to raid.

When cloud covered the target, sky markers were used. These were parachute flares in a variety of colours. Dropped by Oboe or H2S aircraft, they demanded a complicated offset bomber technique.

Skymarking gave accuracy far superior to the early years of the war, when 'agricultural bombing' – the accidental bombing of fields – was a common occurrence.

With the new equipment available, all that remained was to find the best methods of employing it. Oboe Mosquitos were used for the initial marking of all targets within its range. Outside Oboe 1 reach, H2S was used. Tactics were roughly as follows. The first aircraft to arrive, typically five minutes before the main attack was scheduled to start, were the Finders, backed by a few Supporters. The Finders dropped flares where they thought that the aiming points were likely to be. Having visually identified the aim point, they would drop further flares directly above it.

The Finders would be followed by the Illuminators, who would drop sticks of flares directly across the aim point. Then would come the Primary Markers, to put TIs on the aim point itself. Backers-Up would continue to drop TIs at intervals, to give the Main Force an aiming point throughout the attack.

This form of visual marking was codenamed Newhaven. When, due to poor visibility or broken cloud, the marking was carried out using H2S, it became Parramatta, while skymarking was dubbed Wanganui.

As with all new methods, teething troubles occurred, mainly due to the precise timing required. The first real success achieved by PFF came during the Barmen-Wuppertal raid on 29/30 May 1943. The target was accurately marked, and the subsequent bombing highly concentrated. How was this done?

BARMEN/WUPPERTAL

A total of 719 aircraft were despatched. Of these, 272 were Lancasters, of which 20 aircraft were Lancaster Is and IIIs of PFF. The attack was spearheaded by 11 Mosquito IVs fitted with Oboe.

Main Force, following on behind, included 31 Lancaster Is and IIIs of No. 8 Pathfinder Group; 76 Lancaster Is and IIIs of No. 1 Group; 16 Hercules-engined Lancaster IIs of No. 3 Group; and 129 Lancaster Is and IIIs of No. 5 Group. Loads consisted of a mixture of high explosives; 4,000lb (1,800kg) cookies in the case of the Lancasters, and incendiaries.

The bombing was heavy and concentrated

Visibility in the target area was poor, but the first Mosquitos marked accurately at 00.47 hours, with red target indicators. They were followed

Above: Incendiary bomb containers are loaded.

by PFF backers-up with green TIs, and PFF 'fire-raisers' with incendiaries. Four of these, equipped with H_2S, also marked with yellow TIs. Main Force aircraft were instructed to aim at the reds if visible; otherwise at the centre of the greens.

The bombing was heavy and concentrated; 611 aircraft claimed to have bombed the primary target. A total of 33 aircraft were lost on this raid. Lancaster losses amounted to seven; barely half the average losses for the raid.

A factor common to all forms of warfare is confusion, and the Pathfinder-led attacks on Germany were no exception. If a Pathfinder put down his TIs in the wrong place,

inevitably a proportion of Main Force would use them as an aim point. The Germans grew very adept at detecting decoys. A third factor was creep-back where crews over a heavily defended target released their bombs early. This resulted in the Main Force bomb pattern extending further back. A raid controller was needed to direct the marking, giving a running commentary on which TIs were to be used for aiming; which was the real target and a decoy.

A possible solution appeared to be that pioneered by Wing Commander Guy Gibson for Operation Chastise, the destruction of the Mohne and Eder dams in the Ruhr. He controlled his force very effectively using VHF voice radio to communicate. Possibly a Master Bomber could control an orthodox raid in the same way. There was only one way to find out; lay on a small-scale experiment.

OPERATION BELLICOSE

The target chosen, Friedrichshafen, called for a high degree of accuracy. It lies on the

---

EXTRACT FROM BOMBER COMMAND NIGHT RAID REPORT No. 340

611 aircraft, out of a force of 719, attacked the Barmen district of Wuppertal with great success. The fire-raising technique was effectively employed, as a complement to ground marking, resulting in the best concentration yet achieved by the Pathfinder Force. Immense damage was caused in the town, covering over 1,000 acres and affecting 113 industrial concerns, as well as totally disrupting the transport system and public utilities.

north shore of the Bodensee, the south shore of which is in Switzerland. In 1943, it was the largest production centre for radar parts for the Third Reich, and its destruction would be a severe blow to the German air defences.

Main Force crews were to orbit the target, with no more than two aircraft at the same altitude. Once a TI landed on the target, the Master Bomber would issue a special signal, and all available aircraft would attack immediately. It was of course possible that the target could quickly become obscured by smoke; in this case the crews were to make their attack run from a certain point, sighting on a second point, but delaying bomb release long enough for the aircraft to cover 6,000ft (1,800m) to the actual target.

This raid required special

training and picked crews. Piloted by Flight Lieutenants Rodley, a survivor of the Augsburg raid, and John Sauvage, and Pilot Officers D.I. Jones and Jimmy Munro, the latter a Canadian, they were flown north to Scampton for two days' intensive training.

For this trial mission the Master Bomber was not a Pathfinder, but the very experienced Group Captain Leonard Slee. His deputy was the Wing Commander G.L. Gomm. There were also two controllers, either of whom could take charge in the event of an emergency. The force took off late in the evening of 20 June 1943 and headed south, crossing the Channel at maximum altitude. Once over France they progressively lost height down to 10,000ft (3,050m) as they passed Orleans, then lower still

to between 2,500 and 3,000ft (750-900m). After crossing the Rhine, they climbed to attack altitude. At about this time, Wing Commander Gomm, of No. 467 (Australian) Squadron, took over as Master Bomber.

Exactly on time, Munro and Jones released a string of flares parallel to, and on either side of, the target. Gomm ordered all aircraft to gain another 5,000ft (1,500m). Realizing that this would make visual identification very difficult, the four Pathfinders stayed at their original altitude.

The Master Bomber ordered all aircraft to attack at once

Sauvage put down a green TI just north of the Zeppelin sheds. He was followed by Rodley, who dropped a green TI accurately. On seeing this, the Master Bomber ordered all aircraft fitted with the Mk XIV bombsight to attack at once. Jones had to abandon one run to

Below: Prototype Lancaster Mk III. Externally indistinguishable from the Mk I, the main difference was American-built Packard Merlins with Hamilton propellers.

Above: Aircraft of No. 50 Squadron at Swinderby. The nearest was struck off charge when it crashed at Thurlby, Lincs, on 19 September 1942.

steady his aircraft. More flares were dropped along the shoreline around the two predesignated points. After the attack, all 59 Lancasters headed for Maison Blanche and Blida airfields in Algeria.

For 'Rod' Rodley, however, it was an eventful trip. Unknown to him, a TI had hung up. When, far out over the Mediterranean he lost height, the barometric fuse operated and the candles ignited. An evil red glow suddenly appeared beneath his Lancaster. Thinking he was under attack from a night fighter, Rodley took evasive action, while Sergeant Duffy, his flight engineer, checked for damage. The bomb bay was a mass of flames, but the cause was obvious. A quick pull on the jettison toggle and the blazing remnants of the TI fell clear, leaving the Lancaster damaged but flyable.

The Master Bomber concept was rated a success. Six of the Lancasters were damaged by anti-aircraft fire, one beyond repair. The 'shuttle' concept of flying on to North Africa was also rated a success, and was later used by both Bomber Command and the USAAF.

As the strategic bombing of the Third Reich continued, PFF methods became ever more sophisticated. At the same time, the proportion of Lancasters to other heavy bomber types grew ever greater. On 23/24 July 1944, a force of 619 heavy bombers was sent against the German naval base at Kiel. Of these, no fewer than 84 per cent were Lancasters.

PATHFINDER PROGRESS

The concept of the Master Bomber was tried and proven. His function was to check on the accuracy of the marking, call by radio for adjustments or back-up where necessary, and, while loitering in the area until the bombing was completed, do everything possible to ensure

that the munitions went down exactly where they were intended to go.

It was not long before the standard aircraft became the fast and agile twin-engined Mosquito. This was the case for the Kiel raid, in which the Master Bomber and his deputy flew two of the 10 Mosquitos

AIRCRAFT IN RAID ON KIEL, 23/24 JULY 1944

Group	Type	No	Missing
8	Mosquito IX	1	–
	Mosquito XVI	6	–
	Mosquito XX	3	–
	Lancaster III	89	1
1	Lancaster I	85	1
	Lancaster III	104	1
6	Lancaster II	14	–
	Lancaster X	28	–
5	Lancaster I	46	1
	Lancaster III	53	–
3	Lancaster I	59	–
	Lancaster II	14	–
	Lancaster III	27	–
4	Halifax III	100	–

Total
10 Mosquitos, 519 Lancasters, 100 Halifaxes.

Top: Detailed models were made by the Central Intelligence Unit. Seen here is Kiel harbour.
Above: Lancaster Mk I of No. 83 Squadron. After a distinguished career with PFF, this aircraft came down in Holland after raiding Essen on 3/4 April 1943.

allocated for primary marking.

'The method employed for the raid on Kiel was controlled Newhaven marking. Blind Illuminators, 21 Lancasters, were to drop red TIs at H-6 (six minutes before zero hour), and white flares if the weather was suitable. If there was more than 6/10ths cloud, they were to retain their white flares, and drop green flares with red stars instead. If their H2S should prove unserviceable, they were to retain their markers and act as Main Force. These were to be followed by the Primary Visual markers, 6 Lancasters, at H-4, who were to drop red and green TIs using the red TIs dropped by the Illuminators as a guide. If they could not identify the target visually they were to retain their markers and act as Main Force. Visual Centerers, 16 Lancasters, distributed throughout the attack, were to aim green TIs with one second overshoot at: 1) the centre of mixed red and green TIs; 2) centre of red TIs; 3) the centre of green TIs; in that order of priority. If no TIs were visible, they were to act as Main Force. The Secondary Blind Markers, 7 Lancasters at H+10 and 4 at

H+11, were to drop red TIs by H2S. If there was more than 6/10ths cloud they were to release skymarking flares green with red stars. If their H2S was unserviceable they also were to act as Main Force. 28 Lancasters of 8 Group were to act as supporters, bombing at H-6 on H2S, or if that was unserviceable, visually or on a good dead reckoning.'

KIEL

The Main Force was scheduled to attack in four very concentrated waves, putting 516 heavy bombers over the target in the space of just 15 minutes. Scattered among them would be 15 ABC (Airborne Cigar) Lancasters of No. 101 Squadron, each carrying an extra crewman whose function was to jam the German night fighter radio frequencies. Bombing instructions were, in order of priority: 1) centre of mixed red and green TIs or red TIs; 2) centre of green TIs; 3) centre of skymarking flares.

During the raid on Kiel, the target was covered with 10/10ths cloud. No contact could be made with the Master Bomber, and his deputy assumed control of proceedings. Marking was considered accurate with Main Force bombing on the glow of TIs and many explosions and fires were reported.

Only four Lancasters were lost on this mission; a mere 0.7. per cent of the total.

PFF led the way to the targets, but Main Force, was the mighty sledgehammer that came crashing down on them.

For all practical purposes Main Force was Bomber Command. Main Force delivered the greatest weight of bombs against the war machine that was the Third Reich, and Main Force took the greatest number of casualties. Nor should it be forgotten that Main Force was the training ground for those who became Pathfinders or who smashed the Ruhr Dams and sank the *Tirpitz*.

As the war continued, the Lancaster progressively became the backbone of Main Force. In numbers of sorties flown and tonnages of bombs delivered, it outstripped all other bombers in service by a large margin.

The strategic bombing of Germany, and to a lesser extent its Axis partner Italy, consisted of a number of what amounted to protracted set-piece battles, interspersed with many highly individual actions. The thousand bomber raids of May and June

1942 had only been achieved by milking training units of aircraft and crews. This tremendous effort could not be sustained. During the months following June 1942, Bomber Command restricted itself to raids of up to 300 aircraft against single targets roughly twice a week, weather permitting.

The number of Lancaster squadrons steadily grew. Prior to October 1942, conversion onto the new type was carried

Top: Crew returning from a raid.
Above: Wing Commander Guy Gibson (right) led No. 106 Squadron to Gdynia, before forming the Dam Busters.
Far Left: The devastated oil refinery at Harburg, just to the south of Hamburg.

out by a specially formed third flight within each squadron. Later, conversion flights were centralized and merged into Heavy Conversion Units.

Special weapons often featured in the Lancaster story. One of these was the huge Capital Ship Bomb, which had a shaped charge designed to cut through armour.

FRIEDRICHSHAFEN, BOMB LOADS

Leader/Deputy Leader	2 x Lancaster III	1 x 4,000lb (1,800kg) 7 x 500lb (227kg)
97 Sqn PFF	2 x Lancaster III	3 x red TI; 3 x green TI 16 x white flares 2 x 500lb (227kg) 2 x red TI 2 x green TI 32 x white flares 2 x 500lb (227kg)
9,49,50,57,61,106 Sqns No. 5 Grp	32 x Lancaster III	1 x 4,000lb (1,800kg) 7 x 500lb (227kg)
44,207,467,619 Sqns No. 5 Grp	Lancaster III fitted with Mk XIV bombsight	14 x 500lb (227kg)
44,207 Sqns, No. 5 Grp	Lancaster III not fitted with Mk XIV bombsight	Full incendiary load

SEARCHLIGHTS

'One of my worst moments of the whole raid was when, during one of my five successful runs over the target, T-Tommy was caught in a cone of searchlights. I fought desperately to lose those probing beams of light which had caught my aircraft in its web. Shrapnel hit the fuselage like hailstones until, by diving at near maximum speed, I escaped into the darkness. Poor Jack Hannah, my wireless operator, stationed at the astrodome on the lookout for enemy fighters, protested as he was tossed about like a pea in a pod.'

*PILOT OFFICER D. I. JONES,
No. 97 SQUADRON*

In August 1942, the German's only aircraft carrier *Graf Zeppelin* and the battle cruiser *Gneisenau* were reported at Gdynia in Poland. A raid was mounted on 27 August by adapted Lancasters of No. 106 Squadron and led by Wing Commander Guy Gibson and Squadron Leader Arthur Richardson.

ANTICLIMAX

The result was, perhaps inevitably, an anticlimax. Visibility was poor, and the

Top: To carry bombs of 8,000lb (3,600kg) or more, Lancaster bomb bay doors were bulged, as seen on this Mk II.

Above: A gaggle of Lancasters at low level. Not the Le Creusot raid, but these in Far Eastern finish show up much better.

defences stronger than expected. Arriving over Gdynia, 106 Squadron was unable to locate *Graf Zeppelin*, but managed to find what was believed to be *Gneisenau*.

Gibson made several runs but the bomb missed the battle cruiser by about 1,200ft (360m).

Early in September, 8,000lb (3,600kg) bombs started to arrive on the squadrons. These needed modifications both to the bomb bay and doors, and Gibson's squadron with its aircraft already adapted for the Capital Ship Bomb, pioneered their use. The following month saw another Bomber Command set-piece attack.

PARTICIPANTS IN OPERATION ROBINSON

Squadron	No. of A/C	Base
No. 9	10*	Waddington
No. 44	9	Waddington
No. 49	10	Scampton
No. 50	12	Skellingthorpe
No. 57	10	Scampton
No. 61	7*	Syerston
No. 97	9	Woodhall Spa
No. 106	12*	Syerston
No. 207	15	Langar

NB. * denotes two aircraft to Montchanin.

OPERATION ROBINSON

Vital targets were not always in Germany. One such was the Schneider armaments factory at south-eastern France. Although covering nearly 300 acres, the need to avoid civil casualties demanded a standard of accuracy that could only be attained in daylight. The nine Lancaster squadrons operational in No. 5 Group began to practise low-level flying early in October.

The lessons of the Augsburg raid had been well learnt. The bombers were scheduled to reach the target just before dusk, making their escape into the darkening sky. This time, however, the inbound route of the raiding force was carefully planned to minimize the possibility of fighter interception.

After take-off, on 17 October, 96 Lancasters from 5 Group assembled over Upper Heyford in Oxfordshire, and from there proceeded to Land's End. Descending to 1,000ft (300m) over the sea to avoid radar detection, they turned south-easterly over the Bay of Biscay. When about 60 miles (95km) from the French coast, they dropped down to 300ft (90m) and turned almost due east.

4,000ft, the minimum release height for the 4,000lb cookies

Unhindered by the German defences, the low-level armada thundered on. The sole incident occurred as a Lancaster of No. 57 Squadron took a partridge through the windscreen. The formation climbed to its attack altitude of 4,000ft (1,200m), the minimum release height for the 4,000lb (1,800kg) cookies that were carried by 15 aircraft. As they climbed, they edged a few degrees southwards in the direction of Le Creusot and took up their attack formation.

Navigation and timing were spot on, and surprise was almost

OVERSEAS LANCASTER SQUADRONS

Sqn	Nationality	First Op	Base
460	Australian	22/23 Nov 42 Stuttgart	Breighton
467	Australian	2/3 Jan 43 Gardening	Bottesford
426	Canadian	17/18 Aug 43 Peenemunde	Linton-on-Ouse
405	Canadian	17/18 Aug 43 Peenemunde	Gransden Lodge
408	Canadian	7/8 Oct 43 Stuttgart	Linton-on-Ouse
432	Canadian	18/19 Nov 43 Sea Search	East Moor
463	Australian	26/27 Nov 43 Berlin	Waddington
75	New Zealand	9/10 April 44 Villeneuve St George	Mepal
300	Polish	18/19 April 44 Rouen	Faldingworth
419	Canadian	27/28 April Friedrichschafen	Middleton St George
428	Canadian	July 44	Middleton St George
431	Canadian	December 44	Croft
434	Canadian	2/3/Jan 45 Nuremburg	Croft
424	Canadian	February 44	Skipton-on-Swale
433	Canadian	1/2 Feb 45 Ludwigshaven	Skipton-on-Swale
427	Canadian	11 March 45 Essen	Leeming
429	Canadian	April 45	Leeming

complete. In an attack lasting just nine minutes, over 200 tonnes of high explosive and incendiaries rained down.

At the same time, six Lancasters attacked a transformer station at Montchanin. They carried ten 500lb (225kg) bombs each, and were briefed to attack from 500ft (150m). The transformer station was wrecked, but two of the pilots were over-enthusiastic and attacked from well below the minimum safe height. One aircraft was damaged and the other crashed, both victims of their own bomb explosions.

One Lancaster forced to turn back with engine failure was intercepted by three Arado Ar 196 floatplanes of the Kriegsmarine. The flight engineer was killed in the attack.

In all, damage to the Lancasters was remarkably light, with just a few holes in some aircraft. Although limited production was resumed at Le Creusot after a period of about three weeks, major repair work was still in progress eight months later.

The battle of El Alamein commenced just five days after the raid on Le Creusot, while Operation Torch, in north-west Africa, was scheduled for 11 November. Lancaster squadrons played an indirect part in these operations by bombarding targets in northern Italy.

Above left: The projection at the bottom of the turret is the Monica aerial; damage was caused by flak.
Left: Star of Wings for Victory Week in Trafalgar Square, this No. 207 Squadron Lancaster was one of the first production aircraft.

Between October and December, 1936 sorties were flown. Italian air defences were ineffective and losses were light. But the long distances involved, plus a double crossing of the Alps, made raiding Italy a tremendous test of endurance for the Lancaster crews.

If the weather was too bad for the Alpine crossing to be attempted, German targets were substituted instead at the last moment.

Lancaster output soon reached the stage where squadrons could start equipping with the type. The first three to do so were No. 460 (Australian) Squadron at Breighton; No. 101 Squadron at Holme-on-Spalding Moor; and No. 103 Squadron at Elsham Wolds.

The conversion of the Australian squadron onto the Lancaster highlighted a trend. Although No. 44 Squadron had been dubbed 'Rhodesia', there were not enough Rhodesians to man it fully. Of the 48 aircrew on the Augsburg raid, only eight were Rhodesians. Two, including Nettleton himself, were South Africans. Two Canadians, two New Zealanders, and a single Australian completed the overseas contingent. The remaining 33 were British.

From the outbreak of war, volunteers from the British Empire, or Commonwealth, as

it is now called, had hastened to the aid of the mother country. A high proportion of Australians, Canadians or New Zealanders in one squadron gave it a uniquely national flavour. No. 460 was the first of many such Lancaster squadrons, but numerically the Canadians took pride of place; No. 6 Group was for all practical purposes an all Canadian Bomber Group.

ELECTRONIC WARFARE

The year of 1943 commenced with raids on Berlin, with the Pathfinders honing their marking techniques on the city. Electronic warfare took on greater significance with the introduction of new jamming and threat detection systems. Of these, Tinsel could be tuned

to transmit engine noise on the German fighter control frequencies; Monica was a tail warning radar; while Boozer could detect German radar emissions. Many other systems followed in the years to come.

Tinsel was initially successful, though the Germans gradually introduced measures to limit its effectiveness. Monica, in contrast, was a minor disaster from the outset. Quite unable to discriminate between friend and foe, it constantly gave false alarms as friendly aircraft came into its search area. The Germans developed a detector codenamed Flensburg which could home on Monica's emissions from long ranges. Naxos-Z was another German detector, designed to home on H2S.

Above right: Lancaster Mk I of No. 106 Squadron damaged by a night fighter during the Battle of the Ruhr in April 1943.
Right: *This Lancaster collided on the ground with an American B-17 Fortress.*

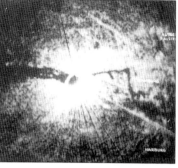

Above: Hamburg showed up well on the H2S screen, when compared to the map on the left. (Alfred Price)

Boozer, was rather better; if the bomber was illuminated by ground radar, a red warning light came on. If fighter radar emissions were detected, an orange light glowed. Once a night fighter gained visual contact its radar was often switched to standby, upon which the warning light went out precisely at the moment of greatest danger.

THE BATTLE OF THE RUHR

The Ruhr was the industrial heart of Germany, invariably heavily cloaked by industrial

WINDOW OVER HAMBURG

Many references to the difficulties caused by Window to the ground and fighter defences were overheard in intercepted wireless traffic. Some enemy aircraft reported interference. One very interesting remark was "it is impossible, too many hostiles". This indicates that the Window echoes, besides producing general interference of the (German) display tube, were also confused with true aircraft echoes.

115 sorties by night fighters were overheard 33 of which mentioned British aircraft. Our crews reported 49 interceptions, but only seven of these developed into attacks. Enemy aircraft frequently seemed unaware of the presence of bombers in their vicinity. Only two instances of fighter damage were reported, and all of the five bombers seen to be shot down in combat were at least 20 miles (32km) away from Hamburg.

BOMBER COMMAND NIGHT RAID REPORT No 383

haze, making targets notoriously difficult to locate. However, with

Below: This 550 Squadron Lancaster survived the war with a tally of over 100 sorties against targets.

the introduction of Oboe it could be attacked accurately for the first time.

The Battle of the Ruhr opened on 5/6 March with a heavy raid on Essen the home of the Krupps steelworks, one of the most important targets in Germany. It was marked by PFF, then bombed by Main Force in three waves. The final wave consisted of 145 Lancasters from 14 squadrons, about half the Main Force total. One-third of the Krupps works was heavily damaged, more than all previous raids on this target combined had achieved.

Raids on Munich, Nuremberg and Stuttgart followed. Just over a week later, Bomber Command returned to Essen. A third raid on Essen took place on 3/4 April, and a fourth on 30 April/1 May. Duisburg had been raided twice. Dortmund and Dusseldorf were hit during May with over 300 Lancasters on each raid. Raids on targets in the Ruhr continued until 14/15 June, culminating in a heavy attack on the steel and coal centre of Oberhausen.

The Battle of the Ruhr conclusively demonstrated Bomber Command's ability to hit targets in this area, while taking only moderate casualties. But the Ruhr was within range of Oboe. The pressing need was to carry the battle deeper into Germany with similar results.

OPERATION GOMORRAH

Hamburg's strategic importance lay in its shipbuilding activities, and the manufacturing of U-boats. Situated close to the coast, and with a large and very easily recognizable river running through it, Hamburg was suitable for locating by H2S.

A new counter-measure codenamed Window was available for the first time. It consisted of bundles of aluminium foil strips, which would each give the appearance of a heavy bomber on German radars, making tracking impossible.

On the night of 24/25 July 1943, 791 bombers set course for Hamburg. Of these, 347, were Lancasters, but they carried nearly three-quarters of the total tonnage of bombs. They

Above: Time exposure of German flak over a defended area.
Right: Flight Lieutenant William Reid VC of No. 61 Squadron. Twice wounded, his aircraft badly damaged and two crewmen dead, he continued the mission and bombed the target.

were monitored by German ground radar until the bomb aimers started to drop bundles of Window down their flare chutes at one minute intervals.

The result was complete chaos for the defenders. The radar screens filled up, giving the appearance of a raid by 11,000 bombers! All semblance of control was lost, and fighters already airborne were ordered to the vicinity. They spent most of their time chasing clouds of Window, while the flak was reduced to firing at random, in the hope of scoring a lucky hit.

Bombing accuracy was marred only by an element of 'creepback' in the later stages, caused by over-eager crews releasing their bombs a fraction too early on the attack run. Only four Lancasters failed to return, but three of these were from the high-flying No. 103 Squadron,

which had gained least protection of all from Window.

FOLLOW-UPS

Daylight raids by the USAAF 8th Air Force were made on 25 and 26 July. Bomber Command returned in force on the night of 27/28, with 787 aircraft, 353 of them Lancasters. A third raid followed on 29/30 July, and the fourth and final one on 2/3 August. The damage assessment report stated: 'The city of Hamburg is now in ruins. The general destruction is on a scale never before seen in a town or city of this size.'

losses started to rise again.

The next heavy raid was on the weapons research centre at Peenemunde, a high-risk mission; Peenemunde was a small target on the Baltic coast, and good visibility was needed for bombing accuracy. A full-moon night was chosen, 17/18 August. Deep penetrations were seldom made at this time of year, as the northern sky was never completely dark. Conditions were therefore ideal for the night fighters.

The course to the target suggested that the bombers were heading for Berlin. Over 200 German fighters converged on the capital. Once bombs started going down on Peenemunde there was no disguising the real

Top: This Heavy Conversion Unit aircraft died in flames following a training accident.
Left: Lancaster Mk I ME703 of No. 576 Squadron survived the Nuremburg raid in March 1944, only to receive a direct flak hit five weeks later.
Below: Chaos in the Juvissy marshalling yards after a raid by 200 Lancasters on 18/19 April 1944.

In this short campaign, some 3,095 sorties were flown, 1,373 of them by Lancasters. In total, more than 8,600 tons of bombs fell on Hamburg. Losses were 86 bombers, 39 of them Lancasters. The German defence system, fire and rescue services were left in complete disarray.

Measures taken by the Germans included a looser form of fighter control, new airborne radar of a different wavelength, emission detectors as described earlier, and saturating the target area with 'cat's eye' single seaters. Before long, bomber

Top: *This Canadian Lancaster visited Berlin on at least seven occasions, with three different squadrons; Nos 432, 426 and 408.*
Above: *Shot down over Berlin, this Lancaster broke up in mid-air and its tail landed in a garden. (Alfred Price)*

target. Those fighters with enough fuel headed north to intercept the final two waves.

Peenemunde was heavily damaged, but the price paid for the raid upon it was high. Losses amounted to 40 aircraft, of which 24 were Lancasters. It is believed that the majority fell to fighters. Diversions and feints became a standard tactic in

Bomber Command's armoury, followed later by simultaneous attacks on multiple targets.

THE BATTLE OF BERLIN

The operations so far described were successful, but Bomber Command also had setbacks. The Battle of Berlin was one such. It commenced on 18/19 November 1943 with an attack by an all-Lancaster force, but on this occasion PFF marking was not up to scratch, and the bombing was scattered. The absence of a Master Bomber did not help matters. Four days later they tried again, this time with better results.

A further 11 heavy raids on the German capital were carried out by the middle of February, interspersed with other targets. In all, 6,209 Lancaster sorties were flown in this period, losing 321 aircraft in action. This represented an unsustainable loss rate of 5.2 per cent, which rose to 8 per cent for a final raid in March.

Peenemunde was heavily damaged, but the price was high

These figures do not include operational attrition. Fog and low cloud over England on 17 December caused the loss of 28 Lancasters, in addition to 25 missing, while two more had collided after take-off. The loss rate for this one mission was an appalling 11.4 per cent.

Berlin was too large an area, too heavily defended, too far inland, and much harder to identify with any precision. And by this time, the advantages of Window were much less as the German defences adapted themselves to it. While extensive damage was caused, the concentrated destruction of Hamburg was not repeated.

NUREMBERG

If the Battle of Berlin was a defeat for Bomber Command, the raid on Nuremberg on 30/31 March 1944 was a disaster. For Bomber Command, the Nuremberg raid was the night when it all went wrong.

Deception attacks on Kassel and Cologne were recognized early, which enabled the defences to concentrate on the

that night, while 13 crashed on their arrival at base. One was written off with battle damage, whilst seventy more aircraft returned with varying degrees of damage.

Most of the losses occurred on the outward leg. Night fighters accounted for 78 aircraft, including 55 Lancasters; two bombers collided and another one was lost to an unknown cause. Of the 440 Lancaster crewmen who failed to return home, only 107 survived. Worst of all was that the raid was an almost complete failure.

Top: *The V-weapons site at Wizernes after a raid by Lancasters of No. 5 Group, 20 July 1944.*
Left: *Repair was a vital part of aircraft replacement.*
Below: *Before and after. A raid on the oil storage depot at Bec d'Ambes on 4 August 1944.*

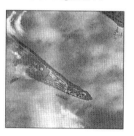

main raid of 781 heavy bombers, of which 569 were Lancasters from 34 different squadrons. The twin-engined night fighters were scrambled, and ordered to assemble over a radio beacon. Unfortunately the course of the bombers took them towards this beacon, running them straight into the trap. Forecast winds were incorrect, and the bomber stream became spread out. Atmospheric conditions were such that long condensation trails formed behind the bombers visible under a half moon. The track of the bombers was visible from miles away.

94 bombers failed to return that night, while 13 crashed on their return

An incredible total of 94 bombers failed to make the return journey from Germany

RETURN TO EUROPE

The outcome of the entire war in Europe hinged on the successful invasion of Normandy. From April 1944 the majority of Lancaster sorties were against targets in France and Belgium, mainly railway centres and airfields, radar stations and coastal gun batteries.

The weeks following D-Day saw road and rail communications, enemy troop concentrations and fuel depots all accorded priority, but as the V-1 and V-2 assault on London had begun, a great deal of effort was diverted to their launching sites.

There was a large-scale return to daylight operations for Bomber Command. Allied air superiority in the area kept up the pressure around the clock. Then, as the Allied armies pushed further inland, heavy attacks were made on German-held airfields in Holland.

During the concluding six months of the war, the Lancaster force grew to an enormous 57 squadrons; over 1,200 aircraft.

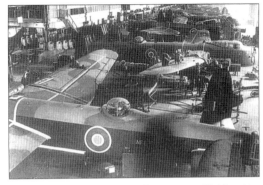

Above: Lancaster assembly line at Baginton. The wartime censor has rather clumsily airbrushed out the aircraft number.

Concentrated attacks on synthetic oil plants were made during the winter of 1944/45, vastly reducing supplies. Dresden, at that time a key road and rail target, was attacked in strength on 13/14 February 1945; Essen by more than 1,000 bombers in daylight on 11 March, and Kiel on 9/10 April. Berlin, once the most heavily defended area in

Germany, was raided five nights later by more than 500 Lancasters, of which only two failed to return. But by this time major targets were in short supply and the majority of raids were on a comparatively small scale, and as the Allied armies pushed into Germany the strategic bombing war gradually drew to a close.

FINAL OPERATIONS

The Lancaster ended the war on more peaceful tasks. Operation Manna saw 17 Lancaster squadrons dropping containers of food to the population of Holland; Operation Exodus involved the repatriation of released British prisoners of war. This was followed by Operation Dodge, the return of 8th Army veterans from the Mediterranean area. It was an honourable finish to a hard-fought campaign.

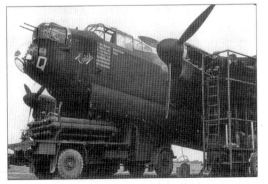

Left: Edith, veteran of 84 sorties during which she destroyed a German fighter, completed a further 14 trips dropping food and repatriating prisoners of war.

BOMBERS VS FIGHTERS

A heavily defended target could put up a storm of light flak, but most bombing was carried out at altitudes beyond its reach. Heavy flak could not be avoided by high flying, but it had a far slower rate of fire than the light automatic guns. Far fewer shells came up at any one time, and they took up to 30 seconds to arrive at typical operational altitudes. Radar-predicted heavy flak was pretty accurate, but one method of avoiding it was to change course and altitude at frequent intervals. Hopefully the shells would then burst in the spot where the bomber would have been had it not evaded.

Pilots felt that the best course was to take no evasive action and to drop the nose and accelerate out of the flak zone. The Lancaster's deadliest enemy was the fighter. As the vast majority of Lancaster sorties were made in darkness, we will concentrate on the night fighter threat.

Countermeasures were used to hinder the defenders but they could not prevent a fighter

Above: Radar-predicted heavy flak guns were mainly deployed along the coast or around cities.
Below left: Searchlights illuminated the bomber for flak or fighters;
Opposite: Two .50 calibre machine guns in the tail gave a mightier punch than the usual four .303 Brownings.

from searching visually. If a night fighter succeeded in entering the bomber stream, it was in a target-rich environment. Even with its radar and radio communications jammed solid, it was often possible for the fighter to make a visual sighting. And once the fighter was in visual contact, an attack usually followed.

Normal Lancaster defensive armament consisted of two machine guns in each of nose and dorsal positions, and four more in the tail, all in power-operated turrets. The guns were Browning .303 calibre, with a high cyclic rate of fire. They could pour out a lot of rounds, but the bullets themselves were small and lacked hitting power. Four types of ammunition were in general use; ball, tracer, armour-piercing and incendiary.

The four guns in the rear turret were usually harmonized on a point at 750ft (225m) for night missions, and on a 7ft 6in (2.29m) square pattern at 1,200ft (365m) by day. The nose and mid-upper turrets were often harmonized 5ft (1.52m) apart at 1,200ft (365m), although it was generally accepted that the maximum effective range of the .303 Browning was 900ft (275m). The main defence at night was the tail and mid-upper turret, in that order.

*Left: This Lancaster example, from
No. 15 Squadron, also carries G-H
radar bombing equipment.
Below: Mk I Lancaster used for trials
of a periscopically sighted ventral
turret in 1942. It was not a success.*

their high rate of fire.

From June 1944, a number of Lancasters were fitted with the Rose Rice tail turret, which mounted two .50 calibre Brownings. While the combination of a much heavier projectile and a slightly higher muzzle velocity gave a rather better effective range, the cyclic rate of fire of this weapon was at most 850 rounds per minute. The standard four-gun Lancaster turret could spew out 306 bullets in a four second burst, compared with just 113 for the Rose Rice turret. However, the weight of fire of the latter was about 50 per cent heavier provided that all bullets struck home.

Few nights were clear enough to allow fighters to make frontal attacks, and it was unlikely that a Lancaster would overhaul a fighter from astern, so the nose turret was of most use in discouraging the ground defences during low-level missions.

Wartime British bomber armament has often been criticized as inadequate, because it was both out-ranged and out-gunned by the German fighter weapons. British bombers were far more heavily defended than those of any other nation except the Americans, and that included their German counterparts. The Heinkel He 111 typically carried a single rifle-calibre machine gun in each of just five positions, with limited fields of fire and no power-operated turrets. At night, German fighters often had to get very close before they could identify the bomber and take aim. This brought them well into the range of the British machine guns, which compensated for their small projectiles by

The primary task of the Lancaster was to deliver bombs and return safely

The primary task of the Lancaster was to deliver bombs on target and return safely. Shooting it down was the cherry on the cake. On dark nights, when the fighters were forced to get in close, the four-gun turret of the Rose Rice, had much to commend it. Few German night fighter pilots would press home an attack while they were taking hits themselves. The final advantage of the standard four-gun turret

LANCASTER, DEFENSIVE GUNS

	.303 calibre	.50 calibre
Browning MG		
Cyclic rate of fire	1,150rpm	750/850rpm
Weight	22lb (10kg)	64lb (29kg)
Muzzle Velocity	2,660ft/sec (811m/sec)	2,750ft/sec 838m/sec)
Projectile Weight	174 grains	710 grains

Above: The nose turret was rarely of use at night, but daylight raids became more frequent. No. 100 Squadron – 128 ops.

was that it had no less than 130 seconds' firing time, compared with a mere 24 seconds for the Rose Rice. This was rarely called for; against enemy fighters 24 seconds' firing time was usually adequate.

From late 1944 Lancasters carried out a surprising number of daylight operations; the heavier gun with its longer range was by far the most preferable. Among the squadrons equipped with the Rose Rice rear turret were Nos 83, 101, 153 and 170.

The other major variation in Lancaster defensive armament was the Glenn Martin 250 mid-upper turret, which also mounted two .50 calibre Brownings. This was carried by the Lancaster B.VII. 150 planes were built but as deliveries of this model did

not commence until April 1945, it was just too late to see action.

GUNSIGHTS

The main gunsight used in Lancaster turrets was the Barr & Stroud G Mk III reflector sight. In use, this showed an illuminated orange circle with a central dot, both focused at infinity. A brightness control adjusted it according to conditions; bright in sunlight, dim at night. The radius of the circle was approximately equal to the wingspan of a single-engined fighter at a range of 1,200ft (365m), while the radius of the circle gave the deflection (the amount of aiming ahead) needed to hit a target with a relative crossing speed of 50mph (80km/hr).

In 1944, the Mk IIc gyroscopic sight entered service as a turret sight. This could actually predict the point of aim, if the

approaching fighter could be tracked for a short while, and its wingspan set on a dial. A gun-laying radar code-named Village Inn was introduced in the final months of the war, which allowed opponents to be engaged from beyond visual range. While potentially devastating, the problem was obtaining positive identification of the radar contact as hostile.

The essence of effective defence against fighters was always to see them first. At night this was far from easy. As a general rule, they came from

ROSE RICE TURRET

2 x .50 Browning MGs
335 rounds per gun
Mk IIIA reflector sight
Traverse +/-94°
Elevation 49°
Depression 59°

Above: Mk I with an experimental arrangement of remote barbettes and the sighting position in the tail.

below, where they were masked by the dark ground and most difficult to see. The bomber would be lined against the sky, even on a starless night. Attacks generally came from astern, with the fighter swimming up from the depths and attacking in a slight climb with its fixed frontal armament. Its target was rarely the fuselage, as if the bombs detonated the resulting explosion could quite easily destroy the night fighter too. Normally the wings, with the vulnerable engines and fuel tanks, were selected.

Later on, the German night fighters used Schrage Musik, cannon pointing upwards at an angle of about 60 degrees, aimed by a reflector sight mounted in the cabin roof. This allowed them to attack from almost directly underneath, and out of sight of the gunners. The fighter had to formate beneath the bomber and take careful aim at the fuel tanks between the engines. A short burst of fire was then usually sufficient.

SCHRAGE MUSIK

The German fighters did not use tracer in a Schrage Musik attack, so Bomber Command was rather slow in identifying it.

If a bomber set out then failed to return there was no one to tell the tale. Only those few aircraft that survived such attacks limped back bearing the tell-tale scars, and gradually the tactic became known.

Methods of dealing with night fighters varied. Often, if one was sighted that was not making any overtly aggressive moves, the policy was to leave it well alone, hoping that the bomber had not been seen. Other crews maintained that an aggressive attitude was best, opening fire even at long range in order to show the fighter the kind of welcome it could expect if it made an attacking move. Sometimes these ploys worked; at other times they didn't.

Flight Lieutenant Tony Weber's Pathfinder crew developed their own unique brand of defence against attack from below. The Lancasters of No. 405 Squadron had had their dorsal turrets removed to improve performance, which left the mid-upper gunner as a spare bod. A small viewing hole was cut in the fuselage floor aft of the bomb bay, fitted with safety straps, oxygen connection for a heated flying suit. This

Below: Canadian-built Mk X, fitted with the small and neat Glenn Martin mid-upper turret.

Above: 'Village Inn' gunlaying radar was fitted to a few tail turrets towards the end of the war.
Left: The most widely used German night fighter was the radar-equipped Messerschmitt Me 110G.

position was then manned by the mid-upper gunner. When a fighter was spotted coming in below, the pilot was warned. He immediately throttled back and lowered 10 degrees of flap, which killed a lot of speed and gave the aircraft greater manoeuvrability. As the Lancaster slowed, the fighter started to overshoot beneath it.

Then, at the critical moment, Weber shoved the yoke fully forward, putting his huge bomber into a dive.

The result was a steep descent right on top of the offending fighter, accompanied by the fervent hope that the German pilot's reflexes were fast enough for him to get out of the way in time. Negative 'g'

made the Merlins cut through fuel starvation, temporarily extinguishing the exhaust flames and probably adding to the German pilot's visual problems. One dose of this nerve-racking treatment usually convinced him to go look for someone who didn't play so rough. No. 405 Squadron later adopted the ventral viewing hole on all its aircraft.

The other, official counter to fighter attack was the corkscrew. Few people (and fighter pilot's are no exception) are any good

Above: The upward slanting cannon installation known as Schräge Musik allowed the night fighters to attack from the blind spot below the Lancaster. (Alfred Price)

at deflection shooting, and the object of the corkscrew was to give the fighter a difficult target rather than a sitting duck.

It consisted of a steep turn of about 30 degrees combined with a dive of about 500ft (150m), followed immediately by a steep turn of about 30 degrees in the opposite direction combined with a climb of about 500ft (150m). These manoeuvres would be repeated as long as the fighter was in an attacking position. In this way, course and altitude could both be maintained, while few German fighter pilots were good enough to follow a

corkscrewing Lancaster and still get into a good firing position.

Instructions for the corkscrew were given by the rear gunner, although the mid-upper gunner or the bomb aimer, from a position in the astrodome, could also act as controller for the engagement. On spotting a fighter moving into position, the man making the sighting would call over the intercom, 'Prepare to corkscrew left [or right]', the rule being to break into the direction of the attack where possible. Then as the fighter moved into firing range, the executive order of 'Go' would be given, launching the bomber into a series of wild gyrations. The controls had to be handled roughly, making the corkscrew violent, if it was to be really effective. The Lancaster

could corkscrew very well even with a 12,000lb (5,400kg) bomb on board, while unladen it was extremely manoeuvrable for such a large machine.

McLean was credited with five German fighters shot down plus one probable

Survival depended on teamwork; total co-operation and trust between pilot and gunners. A classic engagement occurred on 15/16 March 1944, following an abortive raid on an aero engine factory at Metz, near the Franco-German border.

The Lancaster was from No. 617 Squadron, the Dam Busters, and had a mainly Canadian crew. The rear gunner

THE CORKSCREW MANOEUVRE

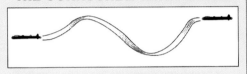

The corkscrew was a manoeuvre designed to make it very difficult for an enemy fighter to gain a firing position.

Above: Some Lancaster squadrons removed their dorsal turrets to improve performance.

was a Scot with original ideas about defensive tactics.

Men are born with differing abilities. Some have a natural flair for ball games; others play the piano outstandingly well. Flight Sergeant T.J. McLean's individual talent was for air-to-air gunnery. Credited with five German fighters shot down plus a probable on a previous tour of operations, he had volunteered to join No. 617 Squadron, widely regarded at that time as a suicide outfit, and had been assigned to Flying Officer Bill Duffy's crew as the tail gunner.

Past experience had convinced Tom McLean that the most effective loading for his guns was 45 per cent tracer and 55 per cent armour piercing, rather than the ball, tracer, incendiary and armour piercing mix laid down in regulations. On this trip he had unofficially arranged for his preferred mix to be loaded for the first time, to his rear turret only. Not even the crew knew about this; the nose turret and the mid-upper, which was manned by Canadian Red Evans, both had standard loadings.

All aircraft were recalled without bombing as the target was under heavy cloud, but on the return trip across France the sky was cloudless, the stars shone brightly, and visibility was exceptionally good.

The first warning came from Monica, the tail warning radar, which picked up a contact to port at a range of about 3,600ft (1,100m). McLean strained his eyes, finally making out a dark

shape which appeared to be four-engined. At first it was assumed to be another returning bomber. Gradually the shape closed, which was unusual, and when it was about 2,700ft (820m) away, McLean realized that it was actually two night fighters in close proximity to one another. Following standard procedure, he told his pilot: 'Prepare to corkscrew port!'

THREE FIGHTERS

A Messerschmitt 109 single-seater fighter was sighted, flying abreast of the Lancaster about 1,500ft (450m) distant with navigation lights burning! The only explanation for this behaviour seemed to be that it was trying to distract the gunners from the fighters astern. At this moment, one of the two broke towards the Lancaster with obviously aggressive intentions. As it closed, McLean gave the order 'Go!' and Duffy commenced a violent corkscrew just as the fighter opened fire at extreme range. The Lancaster was hit, but not seriously, and

Above: German night fighters relied on ground control to position them in the bomber stream.

the German pilot broke away before lining up for another firing pass.

The Me 110 closed right in. Once again the big bomber corkscrewed, spoiling its aim, while McLean poured an angry burst of fire at it, hitting its port engine, then called 'Drop' over the intercom. Immediately, the flight engineer throttled back all four engines and the Lancaster rapidly lost speed, reducing the range faster than the German pilot had expected. On hearing his guns, the flight engineer once more opened the throttles in what was a very well-rehearsed manoeuvre.

On fire, the first Me 110 fell away into the void, and after making sure that the second fighter still remained in its original position, the rear gunner passed the word 'Easy' over the intercom. Upon hearing this, Bill Duffy relaxed the corkscrew manoeuvre.

The second night fighter, moved out to a position almost

abeam of the Lancaster before commencing a curving attack from slightly below it. Again a violent evasive corkscrew, again a torrent of fire from both rear and mid-upper turrets, and the second fighter plunged earthwards, trailing a comet-like fiery tail.

The Me 109 shadowed them, just out of range. A visual search (Monica had been switched off) showed another Me 110 coming up behind, moving from port to starboard, then finally to dead astern.

Duffy spotted some cloud ahead and below, and pushed over into a shallow dive towards it. As he did so, the 110 came in, and the Lancaster went into a hard corkscrew, this time to

starboard. McLean called: 'Drop!' The combination of corkscrew and speed loss spoiled the German pilot's aim completely, and he was met by a barrage of tracer and armour piercing bullets at close range. With pieces flying off, his aircraft entered a flat spin down into the abyss. A red glow lit the cloud layer below.

The second fighter plunged earthwards, trailing a comet-like fiery tail

At this, the Me 109 switched off its lights and turned in for an attack. The tail turret could not be brought to bear, but Red Evans in the mid-upper position returned fire, then, as the Me 109 passed beneath the bomber, quickly traversed his turret to speed it on its way on the far side. It never returned.

At this stage of the war, night fighters were encountered quite frequently. Sometimes, by dint of hard manoeuvring or escaping into cloud, the bomber managed

Below: In March 1944, a Lancaster of No. 617 Squadron accounted for three Me 110 night fighters like these in a single action. (Alfred Price)

to shake them off. At other times, the air gunners managed to beat off the attack.

There are several footnotes to this outstanding action. As noted in the preceding chapter, Monica could be homed in from very long ranges. It was almost certainly this which drew as many as four fighters to a single Lancaster.

The corkscrew saved the lives of hundreds of bomber crewmen

The role of the Me 109 was more mysterious. It seems hardly likely that it was acting as a controller, and it is doubtful that it was acting as a station-keeping aid for the twin-engined fighters; The most probable explanation is that it was a day fighter on a night cross-country that had forgotten to switch off its navigation lights, that just happened to be in the right place at the right time.

Flight Sergeant McLean's ammunition mix had much to commend it, inasmuch as the 'fright factor' of so much tracer, combined with the penetrative power of armour-piercing bullets, was potentially very effective. Some bomber crews preferred to fire no tracer at all on the grounds that this merely demonstrated the inadequate range of the .303 Brownings, thereby encouraging the night fighters to stand off and shoot back. In fact, McLean's idea would only be effective if the fighter could be lured in close, which of course was done.

There can be no doubt that the corkscrew saved the lives of hundreds of bomber crewmen.

RAF LANCASTER SQUADRONS, FORMED NOV 42–DEC 45

Sqn No.	First Op	Base Formed
101	20/21 Nov 42 Turin	Holme-on-Spalding Moor
103	21/22 Nov 42 Gardening	Elsham Wolds
12	3/4 Jan 43 Gardening	Wickenby
156	26/27 Jan 43 Lorient	Warboys
100	4/5 March 43 Gardening	Grimsby
115	20/21 March 43 Gardening	East Wretham
617	16/17 May 43 Dams Raid	Scampton
619	11/12 June 43 Dusseldorf	Woodhall Spa
7	8/9 July 43 Cologne	Oakington
514	3/4 Sept 43 Dusseldorf	Foulsham
166	22/23 Sept 43 Hanover	Kirmington
625	18/19 Oct 43 Hanover	Kelstern
626	10/11 Nov 43 Mondane	Wickenby
550	26/27 Nov 43 Berlin	Grimsby
576	2/3 Dec 43 Berlin	Elsham Wolds
630	18/19 Dec 43 Berlin	East Kirby

RAF LANCASTER SQUADRONS, FORMED JAN 44–MAY 45

Sqn No.	First Op	Base Formed
622	14/15 Jan 44 Brunswick	Mildenhall
15	January 44 not known	Mildenhall
635	22/23 March 44 Frankfurt	Downham Market
35	April 44 not known	Gravely
582	9/10 April 44 Lille	Little Staughton
90	June 44 not known	Tuddenham
149	17 Sept 44 Boulogne	Methwold
218	Sept 44 not known	Methwold
153	7 Oct 44 Emmerich	Kirmington
227	11 Oct 44 Walcheren	Bardney
186	18 Oct 44 Bonn	Tuddenham
170	19/20 Oct 44 Stuttgart	Kelstern
195	26 Oct 44 Leverkusen	Witchford
189	1 Nov 44 Homburg	Bardney
150	2 Nov 44 not known	Kiskerton
138	29 March 44 Hallendorf	Tuddenham

However, to be really effective it had to be violent, as if it was too gently executed, an experienced fighter pilot could simply follow the bomber through the manoeuvre. Properly carried out, it made the bomber a very difficult target, even by day.

In the closing months of the war, Lancasters carried out many daylight raids over Germany. Whereas American heavy bombers flew in tightly packed formations to take advantage of the massed firepower of their heavy machine guns, the reach of the Lancaster guns was less. The combination of fire and movement generally proved an effective defence.

SPECIAL SQUADRONS

As a weapon of war the Lancaster was a bludgeon rather than a rapier. But circumstances alter cases, and when precision weapons were devised for special targets, the Lancaster became a scalpel.

Ruhr industry was dependent on hydroelectric power and water, supplied by several huge dams. The destruction of the largest of these would have a devastating effect on German armaments output. But no ordinary bomb was capable of the task. In the Weybridge offices of Vickers, a quiet genius called Barnes Wallis applied himself to the problem.

The solution he came up with was a large mine, which had to be placed with absolute precision against the inner face of the dams by flying at exactly

Right: Provisioning Lancaster, with modified bomb bay for Upkeep, and dorsal turret removed.
Below: An inert Upkeep falls clear of the dropping aircraft during trials at Reculver.
Left: To mark the 34th anniversary of the raid, a Lancaster reflew the mission in 1977.

220mph (354km/hr) and 60ft (18m), releasing the weapon to an accuracy of less than one fifth of a second. A special squadron was trained specifically for the task. To lead it, Wing Commander Guy Gibson was chosen, and his aircrews were hand-picked from the best that Bomber Command could offer. They were predominantly British, but included 26 Canadians, 12 Australians, two New Zealanders and a single American. It is less widely known that the ground crews and support tradesmen were also hand-picked. Thus was the birth of No. 617 Squadron at Scampton in March 1943.

The mine, codenamed Upkeep, was a large cylindrical weapon weighing 9,250lb (4,200kg), over two-thirds of which was high explosive. Aircraft were taken from squadrons in No. 5 Group. The bomb bay doors were removed and special brackets fitted, together with an electric motor to get Upkeep rotating at 500 revolutions per minute before release. The bomb bay was faired to front and rear of the mine in order to reduce drag and the mid-upper turret was removed. Transformed in this manner, the Mk Is became Type 464 Provisioning Lancasters.

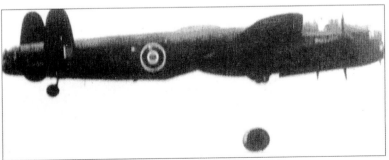

Above: *Dr Barnes Wallis, creator of Upkeep, Tallboy and Grand Slam, pictured with the standard of No. 617 Squadron.*

Other changes were made as they were found necessary. The entire raid was to be flown at low level, so bomb aimers assisted navigation using a specially prepared roller map. The nose turret had to be manned continually, which gave a role to the otherwise redundant mid-upper gunner, and stirrups were fitted to prevent him treading on the bomb aimer's head in moments of excitement.

Achieving the exact height

over water at night proved difficult, but was solved by fitting Aldis lamps in the nose camera port and behind the bomb bay, angled so that the two spots of light touched at exactly 60ft (18m) and offset to starboard where they were easily seen by the navigator, who monitored height on the attack run.

This was the first use of the 'Master Bomber' technique, later to become standard

Standard bombsights could not be used, but the Dann sight, made up from a plywood triangle, an eyepiece and a couple of nails, worked well in practice, while pilots had marks on the windshield to aid them in lining up on a target.

Close control of the operation was vital, and for this Gibson had all Lancasters fitted with fighter-type VHF radios. This was the first use of the 'Master Bomber' technique, later to become standard throughout Bomber Command.

At low level, the Lancasters

might have to fight their way into and out of the target area, while the Mohne Dam at least was known to be defended. Three thousand rounds per gun was carried, giving 157 seconds of firing time. All of it was tracer, to keep the heads of the German gunners down.

OPERATION CHASTISE

The attack on the dams was set for 16/17 May, when good weather was forecast the moon was full, and the water level behind the dams was at its highest. Nineteen Lancasters took off in three waves. The first wave consisted of nine aircraft in three Vics of three, led by Gibson. Its primary targets were the Mohne and Eder Dams. The second wave, of five Lancasters flying individually, took a more northerly route. Their target was the Sorpe Dam, of different construction to the first two and needing a

Below: *Provisioning Lancaster at dispersal, showing the drive belt that rotated Upkeep at 500rpm before release.*

different mode of attack, albeit with the same weapon. The third and final wave of five aircraft also flew individually. Taking off two hours after the others, it was a reserve to be used against the main targets if needed, otherwise to attack secondary dams in the area.

Opposition to the passage of the first wave was moderate, but Bill Astell's Lancaster fell to light flak. The remainder arrived over the Mohne Dam on time. Gibson later wrote, 'In that light it looked squat and heavy and unconquerable; it looked grey and solid in the moonlight, as though it were part of the countryside itself and just as immovable. A structure like a battleship was showering out flak all along its length.'

After circling to make an assessment of the situation, Gibson began his attack run, curving in down-moon, past the hills and low over the water. He had his spotlights on for height and the light flak saw him coming and opened up with everything they had. Bomb Aimer Spam Spafford released the mine and they swept low over the dam. From the air it

looked like a perfect drop, but in fact the mine had fallen short.

Next came Hopgood, whose aircraft caught fire and crashed, while his mine bounced clear; Gibson then ordered Australian Mick Martin to attack. Martin's Lancaster was hit, and its mine was released off course to detonate harmlessly. Dinghy Young made a perfect run and deposited his Upkeep right against the dam wall. Even as Maltby made his run, the parapet crumbled and the dam burst. His mine added to the breach made by Young.

ON TO THE EDER

Martin and Maltby headed for home, while Gibson and Young led the three remaining armed Lancasters to the Eder Dam. Australian David Shannon made three attempts without being able to line up correctly. Henry Maudslay then tried twice, with no luck. On Shannon's fourth attempt his mine exploded against the dam, causing a small breach.

Above: Dams Raid debrief. Standing L to R; Air Chief Marshal Arthur Harris, Air Marshal Cochrane. Seated; intelligence officer, Spafford and Taerum of Gibson's crew.

Maudslay tried once more, but his mine hit the parapet with him just above it. It was assumed that he and his crew died in the explosion, but badly damaged, he had limped some 130 miles (210km) towards home before falling to flak.

Only one armed Lancaster remained, and on the second attempt its pilot, Les Knight, made a perfect run. His mine punched a hole clean through the giant dam wall,

The first aircraft to be lost during Operation Chastise was that of Byers. Les Munro's Lancaster was damaged by flak had to abandon the mission, while Geoff Rice, flying as low as possible, hit the sea and lost his mine. He also was forced to

OPERATION CHASTISE, PARTICIPANTS

Pilot	Letters	A/C No.
First Wave		
Wg Cdr G.P. Gibson	AJ-G	ED 932/G
Flt Lt J. V. Hopgood	AJ-M	ED 925/G
Flt Lt H.B. Martin	AJ-P	ED 909/G
Sqn Ldr H. M. Young	AJ-A	ED 887/G
Flt Lt D.J. H. Maltby	AJ-J	ED 906/G
Flt Lt D.J. Shannon	AJ-L	ED 929/G
Sqn Ldr H.M. Maudslay	AJ-Z	ED 937/G
Flt Lt W. Astell	AJ-B	ED 864/G
Plt Off L.G. Knight	AJ-N	ED 912/G
Second Wave		
Flt Lt J.C. McCarthy	AJ-T	ED 825/G
Flt Lt R.N.G. Barlow	AJ-E	ED 927/G
Flt Lt J. L. Munro	AJ-W	ED 921/G
Plt Off V.W. Byers	AJ-K	ED 934/G
Plt Off G. Rice	AJ-H	ED 936/G
Third and Reserve Wave		
Plt Off W.H.T. Ottley	AJ-C	ED 910/G
Plt Off L.J. Burpee	AJ-S	ED 865/G
Flt Sgt K.S. Brown	AJ-F	ED 918/G
Flt Sgt W.C. Townsend	AJ-O	ED 886/G
Flt Sgt C.T. Anderson	AJ-Y	ED 914/G

NB: McCarthy was originally scheduled to fly ED 923/G, but this aircraft developed a hydraulic leak.

return. Barlow, an Australian, was claimed by flak just inside the German border, and of the ill-fated second wave, only the American, Joe McCarthy, survived. After making nine runs against the Sorpe he dropped his mine on the tenth, but without any visible results.

The final wave fared only slightly better. Burpee, a young Canadian from Gibson's previous squadron, went down over Holland, while Ottley lasted only a little longer. Both fell to light flak. Of the other three, Anderson was the least lucky. Last off, the fates conspired to force him to abandon the mission without attacking.

One Victoria Cross and no fewer than 33 other awards were made

Brown attacked the Sorpe after several attempts, like McCarthy with no visible result, while Townsend, on course for the Mohne Dam, was diverted to the Ennerpe Dam instead. After several brushes with flak, he emerged into an area made unrecognisable by floods from the already breached Mohne and Eder. Finally Townsend arrived at what appeared to be the Ennerpe and dropped his mine, but post-war evidence seems to indicate that he attacked the Bever Dam 5 miles (8km) away.

The entire German air defence system was by now alert to the events. Apart from Maudslay, the only other loss was Dinghy Young. Hit by flak as he recrossed the coast, he went down into the sea. Others,

Above: The Dortmund-Ems Canal, scene of the Dam Busters' worst disaster, was finally breached in 1944. (Alfred Price)
Below: Under the leadership of Group Captain Leonard Cheshire VC, No.617 Squadron became the most accurate heavy bomber squadron of the war.

including McCarthy, Brown and Townsend, had eventful return flights, but recovered safely to Scampton.

Success had been expensive. Eight Lancasters failed to return home; of the 56 men on board, only three survived. Guy Gibson was awarded the Victoria Cross, Britain's highest decoration, and 33 other awards were made to participants in the raid.

The Dams Raid has long passed into legend. No. 617 Squadron had established itself as an elite unit.

A new role was sought for No. 617 Squadron. The modified Lancasters were replaced by standard Mk IIIs, and the crews started intensive high- and low-level training. Wing Commander Guy Gibson was replaced by Squadron Leader George Holden. On 30 August 1943, the squadron was ordered to Coningsby for low-level attacks.

DORTMUND-EMS

The next target was the well defended Dortmund-Ems canal, a strategic artery in the German transport system. 617 squadron was to try, using the new 12,000lb (5,440kg) high-capacity bomb.

Low cloud in the target area caused the first attempt to be recalled, minus Maltby, who went into the sea after hitting someone's slipstream at low level. The next night they tried again. It was a disaster. Heavy mist in the target area foiled all

Above: No. 9 Squadron, pictured with its famous W4964 Johnny Walker, *was something of an elite outfit. Its total of 106 operations took in the Ruhr, Hamburg, Berlin and Peenemunde and Tirpitz.*

attempts to bomb accurately, while the defences claimed five Lancasters, among them those of Holden and Les Knight. The squadron rapidly gained the reputation of being a suicide outfit. Six aircraft, with six more from No. 619 Squadron, went out again the next night to attack the Antheor Viaduct in southern France at low level. This was another failure and the squadron was withdrawn from operations while changes took place.

One was the introduction of the Stabilizing Automatic Bomb Sight, or SABS, introduced by Arthur 'Talking Bomb' Richardson, whom we last saw over Gdynia with Guy Gibson. No. 617 was now to become a medium- and high-level 'sniper' squadron. The other was the arrival of Wing Commander Leonard Cheshire to command on 11 November.

A more exacting test came on the night of 8/9 February

Cheshire was introspective and unconventional, and arguably the most inspirational bomber leader of the war. Always leading from the front, he was described by David Shannon as a pied piper; people followed him gladly. He set out to make the squadron live, breathe and eat bombing accuracy.

Several missions followed against pin point targets, but they were not a great success. Oboe marking was too inaccurate against small targets. Cheshire and Martin worked out between them that only low-level marking in a dive would be good enough, and on 3/4 January 1944, they tried it against a flying bomb site at Freval. By the illumination of flares, they marked from 400ft (120m), and 12,000lb (5,440kg) bombs from the remainder of the formation as they obliterated the target.

A more exacting test came on 8/9 February, by which time No. 617 has moved to Woodhall Spa. The aero engine works at

Limoges were almost totally destroyed, while damage to French houses close by was minimal. Other raids followed with equal success, the only failure during this time being another attempt against the Anthéor Viaduct.

To mark heavily defended targets, a smaller and faster aircraft was needed. The obvious choice was a Mosquito, which Cheshire duly acquired, bringing the low-level marking career of the Lancaster to an end. At the same time, 617 became pathfinders and Main Force leaders to No. 5 Group.

D-DAY DECEPTION

The first of these was Operation Taxable, a deception ploy that was designed to make the Germans think that a vast invasion fleet was moving towards Cap d'Antifer, some 20 miles (30km) north of Le Havre. This was done by 16 Lancasters, flying precise speeds and courses, dropping Window at five-second intervals. Packed with Window bundles,

Above: Lurking in the Norwegian fjords, the German battleship Tirpitz *kept strong British naval forces tied down.*

they maintained the deception for some eight hours until dawn broke to reveal only an empty sea to the expectant Germans.

The second was the introduction of the Tallboy, a new 12,000lb (5,440kg) bomb with exceptionally good ballistic qualities and penetrative power. Like Upkeep, Tallboy was the idea of Dr Barnes Wallis, and only the SABS equipped Dam Busters could bomb accurately enough to make the best use of this new and devastating weapon.

One of the few south-to-north rail routes still open in France at this time passed through a tunnel near Saumur, on the Loire. Shortly after midnight on 8/9 June the squadron arrived, and Cheshire placed two red spot fires in the mouth of the tunnel. Nineteen Tallboy armed Lancasters moved in, plus another six with conventional loads. The result was a series of enormous craters that tore the line to pieces. One Tallboy had

impacted the hillside and bored its way down to explode inside the tunnel almost 60ft (18m) below, completely blocking it.

More precision raids followed; concrete E-boat pens at Le Havre, and V-Weapon sites scattered around the Pas-de-Calais and elsewhere. In July, command of the squadron passed from Cheshire to Wing Commander Willie Tait DSO DFC.

617 VERSUS *TIRPITZ*

The German battleship *Tirpitz* lying in Alten Fjord in Norway, tied down British naval units which would have been better employed elsewhere.

Even from the most northerly of British airfields Alten Fjord was outside Lancaster range. A deal was struck with the Russians, who made Yagodnik,

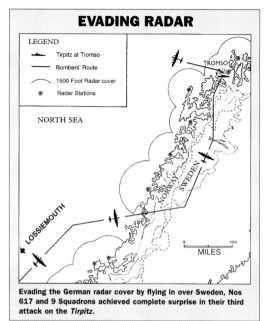

EVADING RADAR

LEGEND

- Tirpitz at Tromso
- Bombers' Route
- 1500 Foot Radar cover
- Radar Stations

NORTH SEA

TROMSO

NORWAY
SWEDEN

LOSSIEMOUTH

MILES

Evading the German radar cover by flying in over Sweden, Nos 617 and 9 Squadrons achieved complete surprise in their third attack on the Tirpitz.

near Arkhangelsk, available as a refuelling stop. For this and subsequent anti-*Tirpitz* operations, No. 617 was joined by No. 9 Squadron, which, although fitted with the Mk XIV vector bombsight, was also something of an elite outfit. Of the 36 Lancasters detailed, 24 carried Tallboys; the others were loaded with 12 Johnny Walker Diving Mines each, an original but ineffective weapon.

The arid nearly ended in disaster when bad weather over Russia forced many Lancasters to land where they could. Six were abandoned in the marshes. On 15 September the attack was

finally mounted, and the German early warning system proved equal to the task and a smokescreen quickly obscured the battleship. A single Tallboy hit was scored, but *Tirpitz* was still afloat. The Kriegsmarine

her south to Tromso for use as a floating German gun battery; she would never sail again, but this was not known either.

Calculations showed that fitting internal fuel tanks in the fuselage of the Lancasters would allow *Tirpitz* to be attacked from Lossiemouth. On 20 October, 40 aircraft of 617 and 9 Squadrons set out on the long haul to Tromso. A combination of poor weather and enemy fighters made this attack a failure, and few crews even so much as saw the battleship.

They achieved complete surprise and scored multiple hits

The final attack on *Tirpitz* was mounted on 12 November, with 31 Lancasters from both squadrons. Approaching from the Swedish side, they achieved complete surprise and scored multiple hits. The *Tirpitz* slowly sank, but the water was too shallow for her to sink completely.

Tait was now replaced by 617's final wartime commander, Group Captain John Fauquier,

Below: 'Twas a famous victory!' Tirpitz *lies in Tromso Fjord, having capsized after multiple bomb hits.*

a Canadian. Tallboys now rained down on the U-boat pens at Bergen, and the Bielefeld Viaduct. The latter proved hard to hit and 54 Tallboys were aimed at it during February 1945 without result. But now Barnes Wallis' 22,000lb (10 tonne) Grand Slam was ready for use.

Only the Lancaster B.I Special could carry Grand Slam. This aircraft had strengthened main gear, nose and dorsal turrets deleted, and the bomb doors removed, plus other minor modifications. The crew was reduced to four.

The first Grand Slam raid took place on 14 March 1945. Five days later, six Grand Slams and 13 Tallboys were hauled to the rail viaduct at Arnsberg, where every bomb fell within a 600ft (180m) radius. To underline the astounding level of the bombing accuracy, when the

bridge at Nienberg was attacked on 22 March the first four aircraft sent in to bomb scored direct hits from a Grand Slam at one end and a Tallboy at the other and lifted the entire centre span into the air, where it was hit straight in the middle by another Tallboy!

The final mission was against Berchtesgaden, Hitler's redoubt

One more bridge was smashed, then the U-boat pens at Farge were attacked. Two Grand Slams went clean through the 23ft (7m) thick reinforced concrete roof and exploded inside, while shock waves from 10 near misses shattered the foundations. 617 Squadron's final mission was against Berchtesgaden, Hitler's southern redoubt, in the final days of the war.

Above: Lancasters of No. 101 Squadron were identifiable by their Air-borne Cigar masts. This one is unloading incendiaries.

There was one other special Lancaster squadron, No. 101, whose aircraft, distinguished externally by three large aerials, carried the top secret ABC (Air-borne Cigar) from October 1943. ABC was a jammer working on the German night fighter frequency, and required an additional member of crew to operate it. Lancasters of No. 101 Squadron carried a full load of bombs and, scattered throughout the bomber stream, accompanied Main Force on nearly every raid. In the later stages of the war, with multi-pronged raids the norm, 101 became the biggest Lancaster squadron of all, with a final complement of 42 aircraft.

THE MESSERSCHMITT
109

Messerschmitt Me 109G-14

1 Starboard navigation light
2 Starboard wingtip
3 Fixed trim tab
4 Starboard Frise-type aileron
5 Flush-riveted stressed wing-skinning
6 Handley Page leading-edge automatic slot
7 Slot control linkage
8 Slot equalizer rod
9 Aileron control linkage
10 Fabric-covered flap section
11 Wheel fairing
12 Port fuselage machine-gun ammunition-feed fairing
13 Port Rheinmetall-Borsig 13mm MG 131 machine-gun
14 Engine accessories
15 Starboard machine-gun trough
16 Daimler Benz DB 605AM 12-cylinder inverted-vee liquid-cooled engine
17 Detachable cowling panel
18 Oil filter access
19 Oil tank
20 Propeller pitch-change mechanism
21 VDM electrically-operated constant-speed propeller
22 Spinner
23 Engine-mounted cannon muzzle

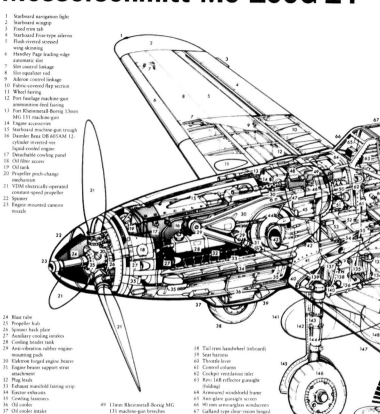

24 Blast tube
25 Propeller hub
26 Spinner back plate
27 Auxiliary cooling intakes
28 Cooling header tank
29 Anti-vibration rubber engine-mounting pads
30 Elektron forged engine bearer
31 Engine bearer support strut attachment
32 Plug leads
33 Exhaust manifold fairing strip
34 Ejector exhausts
35 Cowling fasteners
36 Oil cooler
37 Oil cooler intake
38 Starboard mainwheel
39 Oil cooler outlet flap
40 Wing root fillet
41 Wing/fuselage fairing
42 Firewall/bulkhead
43 Supercharger air intake
44 Supercharger assembly
45 20mm cannon magazine drum
46 13mm machine-gun ammunition feed
47 Engine bearer upper attachment
48 Ammunition feed fairing

49 13mm Rheinmetall-Borsig MG 131 machine-gun breeches
50 Instrument panel
51 20mm Mauser MG 151/20 cannon breech
52 Heelrests
53 Rudder pedals
54 Undercarriage emergency retraction cables
55 Fuselage frame
56 Wing/fuselage fairing
57 Undercarriage emergency retraction headwheel (outboard)

58 Tail trim handwheel (inboard)
59 Seat harness
60 Throttle lever
61 Control column
62 Cockpit ventilation inlet
63 Revi 16B reflector gunsight (folding)
64 Armoured windshield frame
65 Anti-glare gunsight screen
66 90 mm armourglass windscreen
67 Galland-type clear-vision hinged canopy
68 Framed armourglass head/back panel
69 Canopy contoured frame
70 Canopy hinges (starboard)
71 Canopy release catch
72 Pilot's bucket-type seat (8 mm back armour)
73 Underfloor contoured fuel tank (88 Imp gal/400 litres of 87 octane B4)
74 Fuselage frame

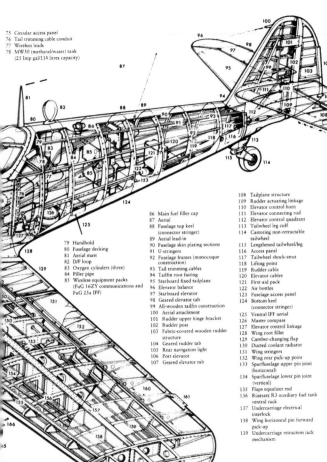

75 Circular access panel
76 Tail trimming cable conduit
77 Wireless leads
78 MW50 (methanol/water) tank (25 Imp gal/114 litres capacity)

79 Handhold
80 Fuselage decking
81 Aerial mast
82 D/F loop
83 Oxygen cylinders (three)
84 Filler pipe
85 Wireless equipment packs (FuG 16ZY communications and FuG 25a IFF)

86 Main fuel filler cap
87 Aerial
88 Fuselage top keel (connector stringer)
89 Aerial lead-in
90 Fuselage skin plating sections
91 U-stringers
92 Fuselage frames (monocoque construction)
93 Tail trimming cables
94 Tailfin root fairing
95 Starboard fixed tailplane
96 Elevator balance
97 Starboard elevator
98 Geared elevator tab
99 All-wooden tailfin construction
100 Aerial attachment
101 Rudder upper hinge bracket
102 Rudder post
103 Fabric-covered wooden rudder structure
104 Geared rudder tab
105 Rear navigation light
106 Port elevator
107 Geared elevator tab

108 Tailplane structure
109 Rudder actuating linkage
110 Elevator control horn
111 Elevator connecting rod
112 Elevator control quadrant
113 Tailwheel leg cuff
114 Castoring non-retractable tailwheel
115 Lengthened tailwheel/leg
116 Access panel
117 Tailwheel shock-strut
118 Lifting point
119 Rudder cable
120 Elevator cables
121 First-aid pack
122 Air bottles
123 Fuselage access panel
124 Bottom keel (connector stringer)
125 Ventral IFF aerial
126 Master compass
127 Elevator control linkage
128 Wing root fillet
129 Camber-changing flap
130 Ducted coolant radiator
131 Wing stringers
132 Wing rear pick-up point
133 Spar/fuselage upper pin joint (horizontal)
134 Spar/fuselage lower pin joint (vertical)
135 Flaps equalizer rod
136 Rüstsatz R3 auxiliary fuel tank ventral rack
137 Undercarriage electrical interlock
138 Wing horizontal pin forward pick-up
139 Undercarriage retraction jack mechanism

140 Undercarriage pivot-bevel
141 Auxiliary fuel tank (Rüstsatz R3) of 66 Imp gal (3000 litre) capacity
142 Mainwheel leg fairing
143 Mainwheel oleo leg
144 Brake lines
145 Mainwheel fairing
146 Port mainwheel
147 Leading-edge skin
148 Port mainwheel well
149 Wing spar
150 Flap actuating linkage
151 Fabric-covered control surfaces
152 Slotted flap structure
153 Leading-edge slot actuating mechanism
154 Slot equalizer rod
155 Handley Page automatic leading-edge slot
156 Wing stringers
157 Spar flange decrease
158 Wing ribs
159 Flush-riveted stressed wing-skinning
160 Metal-framed Frise-type aileron
161 Fixed trim tab
162 Wingtip construction
163 Port navigation light
164 Angled pitot head
165 Rüstsatz R6 optional underwing cannon gondola
166 14-point plug connection
167 Electrical junction box
168 Cannon rear mounting bracket
169 20mm Mauser MG 151 20mm cannon
170 Cannon front mounting bracket
171 Ammunition feed chute
172 Ammunition magazine drum
173 Underwing panel
174 Gondola fairing
175 Cannon barrel

The story of the Messerschmitt 109 began in 1934. Early that year the Air Ministry issued a requirement for an advanced monoplane fighter to replace the Heinkel 51 and Arado 68 biplanes then about to enter service, and invited aircraft companies to submit designs.

The early 1930s saw rapid advances in aviation technology, especially in the design of fighter planes. The new generation of fighters was quite different in shape and in performance from those that had gone before. Out went the fabric-covered strut-braced biplane with its open cockpit and fixed undercarriage. In its place came the sleek low-wing monoplane with an all-metal structure, enclosed cockpit and a retractable undercarriage. These new fighters were much faster than their predecessors in the climb, in the dive and in level flight. Also, in their developed versions, they were more heavily armed.

Chief designer Willi Messerschmitt had no previous experience of designing fighter aircraft

At that time the Bavarian Aircraft Company (Bayerische Flugzeugwerke) was a little-known aircraft firm. It was turning out small batches of planes built under licence for the Luftwaffe. Willi Messerschmitt, the company's brilliant young chief designer, had no previous experience of designing a fighter. He did have great flair and originality and ambition.

Messerschmitt's new fighter used almost every innovation of the period. It was a clean-lined all-metal low-wing monoplane with a retractable undercarriage and an enclosed cockpit. The small wing was fitted with retractable flaps and leading-edge slots. Messerschmitt designed the fighter around the new 610hp Junkers Jumo 210 engine. Work on the airframe advanced more rapidly than that on the power plant, and it was clear that the latter would not be ready in time. Messerschmitt had to look elsewhere for an engine to get his prototype into the air. Ironically, in view of later events, his choice of engine was a 695hp Rolls-Royce Kestrel imported from Great Britain.

Opposite: Ground crewmen reloading the wing and engine-mounted 7.9 mm machine guns of a 'Caesar' of IIIrd Gruppe of Fighter Geschwader 51. Scrupulous cleanliness was essential, any grit or dirt on the rounds was liable to cause a stoppage during firing.
Below: The first prototype Me 109 ground-running its Rolls-Royce Kestrel engine, at about the time of its maiden flight in September 1935. (via Ethell)

MESSERSCHMITT 109 B-1

Type Single-seat interceptor fighter.
Armament Two Rheinmetall-Borsig 7.9mm machine guns mounted on top of the engine and synchronized to fire through the airscrew (500 rounds per gun).
Power Plant One Junkers Jumo 210 Da inverted V-12 liquid cooled engine developing 635 horse power for take off.
Dimensions Span 32ft 4½in (9.87m); length 28ft (8.55m).
Weight Normal operational take off, 4,741lb (2150kg).
Performance Maximum speed 289mph at 13,100ft (465km/hr at 4,000m). Service ceiling 26,900ft (98,200m).

MESSERSCHMITT 109 C-1

Type Single-seat interceptor fighter.
Armament Four Rheinmetall-Borsig MG 17 7.9 mm machine guns. Two synchronized to fire through the airscrew (500 rounds per gun), two mounted in wings (420rpg).
Power Plant Junkers Jumo 210 Ga inverted V-12 liquid cooled engine developing 700 hp for take off. This and subsequent versions were fitted with direct fuel injection engines.
Dimensions Span 32ft 4in (9.87m); length 28ft (8.55m).
Weight Normal operational take off 5,060lb (2,290kg).
Performance Maximum speed 292mph (470km/hr) at 14,770ft (4,500m). Service ceiling 27,570ft (8,400m).

Initially called the Bayerische Flugzeugwerke (Bf) 109, the new fighter made its maiden flight in September 1935. That was one month before the prototype Hurricane and six months before the prototype Spitfire, its two main rivals.

The Arado, Heinkel and Focke Wulf companies also designed for the Luftwaffe. Messerschmitt's design had a maximum speed of 290mph (467km/hr) which was 17mph (27km/hr) faster than any of the rivals and its handling characteristics were also superior.

Below: Line up of early production Me 109 'Bertas', awaiting delivery at the Bayerische Flugzeugwerke factory early in 1937. At this time the aircraft was the most potent fighter in service anywhere in the world. (via Schliephake)

Above: An Me 109 'Caesar' of Fighter Gruppe 152.

INTO PRODUCTION

Following the service trials, the Luftwaffe placed an order for ten more Me 109 prototypes. A second prototype, powered by the Jumo 210A engine, joined the test programme in January 1936. In the autumn of 1936 the Luftwaffe announced that the Me 109 was to be its standard single-engined fighter type. The Me 109B, the 'Berta', was the initial production variant. It was powered by the Jumo 210 engine and carried an armament of three (later four) 7.9 mm machine guns.

In February 1937 production Me 109Bs began emerging from the Augsburg factory. The first Luftwaffe unit to receive the new fighter was IInd Gruppe of Fighter Geschwader 132 based at Jueterbog near Berlin.

Early in 1938 the next major version of the Me 109 appeared, the Me 109C 'Caesar'. This featured detailed improvements and its Jumo 210 engine was fitted with fuel injection. The initial version carried four machine guns, two on top of the engine and one each wing close to the root. The 'Caesar' was built in moderately large numbers and the variant equipped several fighter units.

MESSERSCHMITT 109 D-1

Type Single-seat interceptor fighter.
Armament Two Rheinmetall-Borsig MG 17 7.9 mm machine guns mounted on top of the engine synchronized to fire through the airscrew (500 rounds per gun). One Oerlikon MG FF 20mm cannon mounted under the engine and firing through the spinner (60 rounds).
Power Plant One Daimler Benz DB 600Aa inverted V-12 liquid cooled engine developing 986hp for take off.
Dimensions Span 32ft 4in (9.87m); length 28ft 2in (8.60m).
Weight Normal operational take off, 5,336lb (2,420kg).
Performance Maximum speed 356mph (574km/hr) at 11,490ft (3,500m). Service ceiling 32,800ft (10,000m).

Following hard on the heels of the 'Caesar' came the Me 109D 'Dora'. This was fitted with the new Daimler Benz 600 engine which developed 960 horse power. The more powerful engine gave a much better

The fine performance of the 'Dora' was undermined by difficulties with the DB 600 engine

performance and the 'Dora' could reach a maximum speed of 356mph at 11,400ft (574km/hr at 3,500m). It also had greater fire power, with a 20 mm cannon firing through the propeller spinner and two machine guns mounted on top

MESSERSCHMITT 109 E-1

Type Single-seat general purpose fighter.
Armament Four Rheinmetall-Borsig MG 17 7.9mm machine guns in fuselage and wings. Or two MG17 machine guns and two MG FF cannon. Some aircraft were modified to carry a rack for single 110lb (45kg) bomb.
Power Plant One Daimler Benz DB 601A inverted V-12 liquid cooled engine developing 1,175hp for take off.
Dimensions Span 32ft 4in (9.87m); length 28ft 4in (8.64m).
Weight Normal operational take off, 5,535lb (2,510kg).
Performance Maximum speed 356mph at 13,130ft (573km/hr at 4,000m). Service ceiling 34,450ft (10,500m).

Above: The Heinkel 51 biplane was the main fighter type serving with the Condor Legion during the early stages of the Civil War in Spain. It was outclassed by the Soviet-built fighter types that it came up against.

of the engine cowling. The DB 600 engine suffered serious teething troubles, and the 'Dora' was not popular with pilots. Fewer than two hundred were built before this variant passed out of production.

In September 1938 the so-called Munich Crisis broke, as a result of Adolf Hitler's claim that the Sudetenland area of Czechoslovakia should be incorporated into Germany. It seemed that Great Britain might go to war to help the Czechs retain this territory, but in the end the British prime minister, Neville Chamberlain, acceded to Hitler's demand. Several commentators have said that the move was necessary to

allow Britain time to re-arm. They neglect the fact that the Luftwaffe, too, was in no state to engage in a major conflict. Its fighter force possessed 583 Me 109s of all versions, of which 510 were serviceable. Most of these aircraft were the 'Bertas', with smaller numbers of the later 'Caesar' and 'Dora' variants. Eight fighter Gruppen had equipped, or were in the process of re-equipping, with the Me 109. The rest operated outdated biplane fighter types.

The next version of the Me 109, the first built in really large numbers, was the 'Emil' powered by the new Daimler Benz 601 engine. Based on the DB 600 engine that powered the 'Dora', the new engine was fitted with fuel injection and a more effective supercharger. It was more reliable than the earlier engine. The initial batches of Me 109Es reached the Luftwaffe early in 1939. The main production

version was armed with two 7.9 mm machine guns in the fuselage and two 20 mm cannon in the wings.

MESSERSCHMITT AG

The management of the Bayerische Flugzeugwerke decided to capitalize on the international reputation won by its now-famous chief designer, and so they appointed Willi Messerschmitt to the posts of Chairman and Managing Director, changing the company's name to Messerschmitt AG. The firm's two factories were turning out the fighter in large numbers, yet there were insufficient to meet the needs of the expanding Luftwaffe. Four other aircraft companies, Arado, Erla, Fieseler and Focke Wulf, were producing the Me 109E under licence. Production of the fighter reached 130 per month and it quickly replaced most of the earlier versions.

IN ACTION IN SPAIN

In the summer of 1936 civil war broke out in Spain. General Franco, the Nationalist leader, appealed to Adolf Hitler for help. The Luftwaffe dispatched a force, the Condor Legion, to fight alongside the Nationalists. The Soviet Union had been supplying aircraft to Spain's Republican government. The Luftwaffe pilots found that the Soviet-built Polikarpov I-16 monoplane had a clear edge in performance over their Heinkel 51 biplanes.

To test the new fighter under combat conditions, late in 1936 the Luftwaffe shipped three Me 109 prototypes to Spain. These operated from a primitive airfield near Seville and there were severe problems. Each of the handmade prototypes had components unique to itself, which made it difficult to keep them serviceable. After a few weeks, and without seeing action, the fighters returned to Germany.

Below: The Soviet Polikarpov I-16 was the best fighter in the Nationalist Air Force in Spain. It was clearly superior to the He 51.

THE 109 TRIUMPHS

The trial highlighted the need for better ground support for the Me 109. Several Luftwaffe pilots flew the prototypes in Spain, and they had no doubt that the Me 109 was superior to any of the Soviet-built fighters.

Production Me 109 'Bertas' emerged from the Augsburg factory in February 1937. Sixteen of these machines were loaded, in crates, on a freighter which delivered them to the Condor Legion.

The first unit in Spain to re-equip with the Me 109B was the 2nd Staffel of Fighter Gruppe 88. When it became operational in April 1937 there was a lull in the ground fighting. Then, in July, the Republican forces launched a powerful offensive near Madrid. The Me 109 Staffel joined the battle, escorting Junkers 52 bombers in delivering attacks on Republican troop positions.

The Me 109 proved superior to the Soviet-built I-16. It was faster in level flight and in the dive and had a higher operational ceiling. The I-16 was more manoeuvrable, especially below 10,000ft (3,048m). Republican fighter pilots tried to lure the Messerschmitts into turning fights below 10,000ft, but with little success. German fighter pilots soon learned that their machine's better performance at altitude gave them the advantage of being able to accept or refuse combat, as they chose.

The new German fighter carried radios but the sets gave such poor reception, that many pilots flew with them turned off.

> ### The Me 109 would deliver a series of high-speed diving attacks to break up the enemy

Normally the Me 109s would patrol at altitudes between 16,000ft (4,877m) and 20,000ft (6,096m), which gave them a big height advantage over their opponents. On sighting enemy aircraft, the German formation leader would usually move his force into an attacking

Above: The arrival of the Me 109B in Spain in the spring of 1937 gave German pilots a machine in which they could engage the I-16 with confidence. This example belonged to 2nd Staffel of Fighter Gruppe 88 and wears the markings carried by aircraft of the Condor Legion.

position above the prey.The Messerschmitts then delivered a series of high-speed diving attacks. They repeated the process until the enemy formation broke up, or the German fighters ran low on fuel or ammunition. Provided the Me 109s maintained their high speed and did not get drawn into turning fights, they were almost unbeatable.

Some of the fiercest aerial fighting over Spain took place early in 1938, during the Republican offensive near Teruel. By then both Staffeln of Fighter Gruppe 88 had re-equipped with the Me 109. On 7 February Hauptmann Gotthardt Handrick, the Gruppe commander, was leading his unit during a bomber

escort mission. Over the battle area he sighted a formation of twenty-two Soviet-built Tupolev SB-2 bombers moving in to attack a Nationalist troop position. Seeing no Republican fighters in the area, he led a concerted attack on the enemy bombers. Several of the latter were shot down, and when I-16s finally arrived on the scene they too suffered losses. The Me 109s destroyed ten enemy bombers and two fighters, without loss to themselves.

Leutnant Wilhelm Balthasar delivered a succession of diving attacks on an escorted bomber formation and shot down three bombers and a fighter, all within a space of six minutes.

The Me 109 achieved striking success over Spain, although the number of these fighters sent to fight in the conflict was never large. Up to December 1938 only fifty-five 'Bertas', 'Caesars' and 'Doras' had reached Spain and only thirty-seven were currently on the strength of Fighter Gruppe 88.

However, such was the 109's superiority that these few aircraft had been sufficient to establish air supremacy over the entire country.

In March 1939, after suffering heavy losses, the Republicans were forced to surrender. Following the cessation of hostilities the Condor Legion returned home to Germany, leaving behind some fifty Me 109s for incorporation in General Franco's Air Force.

POISED FOR POLAND

By the summer of 1939 Adolf Hitler judged that he had gained as much as he could in Europe by bluff alone. To advance further, he would have to demonstrate Germany's military might and commit its armed forces. Now his forces were poised to launch an all-out onslaught against Poland. In the next chapter we shall observe how the Me 109 units fared during the early months of the Second World War.

TESTED IN BATTLE

On 1 September 1939 German ground forces invaded Poland, with full support from the Luftwaffe. At that time the Me 109 force was comprised of twenty-four Gruppen and five independent Staffeln, with a total of nearly 1,100 fighters. More than two-thirds of the units flew the 'Emil', the rest operated the older 'Berta', 'Caesar' and 'Dora' versions. Only about one-fifth of the Me 109 force, five of the twenty-four Gruppen operating the type, was earmarked to take part

in the campaign in Poland. The other units remained in western Germany, ready to meet any onslaught from the Royal Air Force and the French Air Force. There was no large-scale Allied reaction and German fighters saw little action. The number of Me 109s assigned to support the attack on Poland proved sufficient to counter the meagre forces at the disposal of the Polish Air Force. The latter possessed only about three hundred combat planes, almost all of them outdated types. The PZL 11, the most modern Polish

fighter type then in service, had a maximum speed of only 242 mph (389 km/hr). It was no match even for the early versions of the Me 109. Two weeks into the campaign the Luftwaffe felt sufficiently confident to move two Me 109 Gruppen from Poland to bolster the air defences in the west. On 28 September the Polish forces laid down their arms and the campaign came to an end.

Left: Instrument panel of an Me 109 'Emil'. The cockpit was small and the outside view restricted, but pilots came to love the machine.

Me 109 FRONT-LINE UNITS

2 SEPTEMBER 1939 - Units marked with asterisk took part in the campaign in Poland.

Aircraft Unit	Aircraft Serviceable/Total	Aircraft Unit	Aircraft Serviceable/Total
Tactical Development Division		Destroyer Geschwader 26	
Tactical Development (Lehr) Geschwader 2		I. Gruppe	46/52B&D
Staff Flight	3/3E*	II. Gruppe	47/48B&D
I.Gruppe	34/36E*	III. Gruppe	44/48B&C
10.Staffel	9/12E		
		Air Fleet 3 (SW Germany)	
Air Fleet 1 (NE Germany)		Fighter Geschwader 51	
Fighter Geschwader 1		I. Gruppe	39/47E
I. Gruppe	54/54E*	Fighter Geschwader 52	
Fighter Geschwader 2		I. Gruppe	34/39E
II. Gruppe	39/42E	Fighter Geschwader 53	
10 Staffel	9/9C	I. Gruppe	39/51E
Fighter Geschwader 3		II. Gruppe	41/43E
Staff Flight		Fighter Geschwader 70	
I. Gruppe	3/3E	I. Gruppe	24/24E
Fighter Geschwader 20		Fighter Geschwader 71	
I. Gruppe	42/48E	I. Gruppe	18/39C&E
Fighter Geschwader 21		Destroyer Geschwader 52	
I. Gruppe	20/21E	I. Gruppe	43/44B
Destroyer Geschwader 1			
I.Gruppe	28/29E*	**Air Fleet 4** (SE Germany)	
Destroyer Geschwader 2		Fighter Geschwader 76	
I. Gruppe	36/36B*	I. Gruppe	45/49E
	40/44D*	Fighter Geschwader 77	
Air Fleet 2 (NW Germany)		I. Gruppe	43/50E
Fighter Geschwader 26		II. Gruppe	36/50E
I. Gruppe	48/48	Destroyer Geschwader 76	
II. Gruppe	44/48E	II. Gruppe	39/40B&C
Staffel	8/10C	Assigned to German Navy	
		Traegergruppe 186	24/24C
		5., 6. Staffel	24/24

This table shows the serviceable and total number of 'Berta'(B), 'Caesar'(C), 'Dora'(D) and 'Emil'(E) versions of the Me 109 in action.

IN ACTION OVER FRANCE

'Relatively few Me 109s were lost in combat and only at the end of the campaign during the Dunkirk evacuation, was there much in the way of fighter-versus-fighter combat. During the campaign in France it was difficult to compare our [Me] 109 with the French Morane or Curtiss fighters, because I never had a dogfight with either of them. I saw only one Morane during the entire campaign and it was disappearing in the distance. Our Geschwader had very little dogfighting experience until the Dunkirk action, where we met the Royal Air Force for the first time in numbers. Our pilots came back with the highest respect for the [new] enemy.'

**OBERLEUTNANT JULIUS NEUMANN,
ME 109 PILOT, FIGHTER GESCHWADER 27**

Above: Me 109 'Emil' of Fighter Geschwader 27. The oversized markings on the wings were to help recognition, after some incidents when aircraft had been engaged in error by 'friendly' forces.

In the west the aerial activity was limited, as each side probed the other's strengths and weaknesses. On 30 September the Royal Air Force learned a hard lesson when five Fairey Battle light bombers flew a daylight armed reconnaissance mission over the Saarbrucken area. Me 109s of Fighter Geschwader 53 intercepted the force and shot down four bombers without loss to themselves. On 18 December 1939 a force of Vickers Wellingtons flew an armed reconnaissance mission

Right: A pilot boards his Me 109 'Emil' for a scramble take off. The aircraft, bears the 'Scalded Cat' insignia of Fighter Geschwader 20, in the summer of 1939.

off the coast close to Wilhelmshaven, intending to attack any German warships. The twenty-four bombers flew in close formation and depended on their combined crossfire to deter fighter attacks. Thirty-four Me 109s, drawn from Fighter Geschwader 26 and 77 and Destroyer Geschwader 1, engaged the bombers, together with sixteen Me 110s. The German fighters shot down twelve of the Wellingtons. Two more bombers crashed on land-

ing. The Wellingtons' gunners shot down only two Me 109s. The RAF made the decision that future attacks on targets in Germany would take place almost exclusively at night.

On 10 May 1940 German forces launched their offensive in the west. There were 1,346 Me 109s serving with the front line units, of which just over a thousand were serviceable. Three-quarters of these aircraft were to support the offensive, while the rest stayed in position to defend targets in Germany. The Luftwaffe established air superiority over the Dutch, Belgian and French Air Forces, and over the Royal Air Force units based in France. Everywhere the Me 109 reigned supreme, with no effective fighter opposition. Without any hindrance from the air or ground the Luftwaffe bombers carried out destructive attacks on airfields ahead of the fast-moving Panzer thrusts.

At the end of May the German advances pushed the battle front to within range of RAF fighter units flying from bases in southern England. Only during the Dunkirk evacuation was there any serious fighter-versus-fighter combat.

THE FIRST PHASE OF THE BATTLE OF BRITAIN

On 13 July a convoy of freighters passed through the Straits of Dover. Half a dozen Junkers 87 'Stuka' dive bombers were attacking the ships when they were engaged by eleven Hurricanes of No. 56 Squadron.

'Unfortunately for them [the Hurricanes], they slid into position directly between the Stukas and our close-escort Messerschmitts. We opened fire, and at once three Hurricanes separated from the formation, two dropping and one gliding down to the water smoking heavily. I saw a Stuka diving in an attempt to reach the French coast, being chased by a single Hurricane. Behind the Hurricane was a 109, and behind that, a second Hurricane, all of the fighters firing at the aircraft in front. I saw the deadly dangerous situation and rushed down. There were five aircraft diving in a line towards the water. The Stuka was badly hit and both crewmen wounded, it crashed on the beach near Wissant. The leading Messerschmitt, flown by Feldwebel John, shot down the first Hurricane into the water. My Hurricane dropped like a stone close to the one that John had shot down.'

MAJOR JOSEF FOEZOE, LEADING ME 109s OF FIGHTER GESCHWADER 51 ESCORTING THE STUKAS

[No. 56 Squadron lost two Hurricanes destroyed and two damaged. On the German side two Ju 87s were seriously damaged but Fighter Geschwader 51 suffered no losses.]

In the course of the evacuation the Luftwaffe learned the same hard lesson as that impressed on the RAF earlier: bombers operating by day without fighter escort could expect heavy losses if they came under attack from well-handled enemy fighters. From then on the Me 109 force would fly an increasingly large proportion of its missions in the fighter escort role.

BATTLE OF BRITAIN

The Battle of Britain was the first major action in which Me 109s confronted similar numbers of enemy fighters of comparable performance and flown by pilots of equal skill.

During the Battle of Britain Me 109 fighter units flew three types of operation. First was the free hunting sweep across enemy territory used to break up defending fighter formations, to clear the sky for a bomber formation coming behind. Second, were the 'intermediate escort' operations where fighters stayed in formation until enemy fighters approached their charges, and only then were they free to break away and go into action. Third, were the close escort operations which occupied the greater part of the fighter force during any large scale attack. German fighter units assigned to this role had to remain with their allotted bomber formation at all times. Frequently the Me 109s would drive the Spitfires or Hurricanes away from the bombers, but had then to break off the pursuit and return to positions close to their allocated bomber unit. The British fighters

Below: Two 'Emils' in factory markings.

Me 109 VERSUS SPITFIRE AND HURRICANE

'I cannot compare the Me 109 with the Spitfire or the Hurricane – I never flew either of those. We were told that there was no better fighter in the world than the 109 and we believed it. Why shouldn't we – it was certainly a very effective fighter. We knew that the Spitfire and the Hurricane were good fighters too and thought they might be closely comparable with our aircraft. So everything depended on the tactics used and how experienced and aggressive the pilots were. Of course, the RAF had some young and inexperienced pilots. But we had the feeling that there was a strong backbone of very well-trained and experienced pilots. The longer-serving RAF pilots had considerable flying experience. We in the Luftwaffe did not have this advantage. Very few of those who fought on our side in the Battle of Britain had more than four years' flying experience. Overall, we felt that we were dealing with an aircraft-pilot combination as good as our own.'

*OBERLEUTNANT JULIUS NEUMANN,
ME 109 PILOT*

Left: *Julius Neumann pictured in the cockpit of the Me 109 at the RAF Museum at Hendon in 1979. He recalled 'Immediately I sat in the cockpit I felt at home. Everything came easily to hand. Had the tank been full and there been enough room in front of me, I should have loved to have been allowed to take it up.'*

Opposite (top left): 'Emils' of Fighter Geschwader 27 at their airfield at Boenninghard near Wesel, shortly before the campaign in the west in May 1940. (Neumann)
(top right): Me 109s of Fighter Geschwader 27 at St Trond in Belgium.
(bottom left): Me 109 'Emils' of IInd Gruppe of Fighter Geschwader 53 preparing to take off from Dinan in western France during the Battle of Britain.
(bottom right): Battle formation of Me 109Es of IInd Gruppe of Fighter Geschwader 27, photographed early in the Battle of Britain when the unit was based at Crepon in western France as part of Air Fleet 3. (Neumann)

would then return to the fray and the frustrating process had to be repeated. From these duels between the two air forces the strengths and weaknesses of 'Emil', compared with the Mark I versions of the Spitfire and the Hurricane, quickly became evident.

At altitudes above 20,000 ft (6,000m) the 'Emil' was slightly faster in level flight and in the climb than the Spitfire. At all altitudes the German fighter was much faster than the Hurricane. Below 15,000 ft (4,600m) the Spitfire was the faster in level flight. Both British

The British Spitfire and the Hurricane could out-turn the Messerschmitt 109

fighter types could out-turn the Me 109 at any altitude. Me 109 pilots found the fuel injection system fitted to the Daimler Benz 601 gave a useful advantage when they had a Spitfire or a Hurricane on their tail. The Messerschmitt pilot would push down the nose of his fighter and 'bunt' away from his pursuer. If an RAF fighter tried to follow

Me 109 FRONT-LINE UNITS
7 SEPTEMBER 1940

Aircraft Unit	Aircraft Serviceable/Total	Aircraft Unit	Aircraft Serviceable/Total
Air Fleet 2 (Holland, Belgium, NE France)		Fighter Geschwader 53	
Fighter Geschwader 1		Staff Flight	2/2
Staff Flight	3/4	II. Gruppe	24/33
Fighter Geschwader 3		III. Gruppe	22/30
Staff Flight	3/3	Fighter Geschwader 54	
I. Gruppe	14/23	Staff Flight	2/4
II. Gruppe	21/24	I. Gruppe	23/28
III. Gruppe	23/25	II. Gruppe	27/35
Geschwader 26		III. Gruppe	23/28
Staff Flight	3/4	Fighter Geschwader 77	
I. Gruppe	20/27	I. Gruppe	40/42
II. Gruppe	28/32	Trials Gruppe 210	17/26
III. Gruppe	26/29		
Fighter Geschwader 27		**Air Fleet 3 (NW France)**	
Staff Flight	4/5	Fighter Geschwader 2	
I. Gruppe	27/33	Staff Flight	2/5
II. Gruppe	33/37	I. Gruppe	24/29
III. Gruppe	27/31	II. Gruppe	18/22
Fighter Geschwader 51		III. Gruppe	19/30
Staff Flight	4/5	Geschwader 53	
I. Gruppe	33/36	I. Gruppe	27/34
Inglevert		Development (Lehr) Geschwader 2	
II. Gruppe	13/22	II. Gruppe	27/32
Inglevert			
III. Gruppe	31/44	**Air Fleet 5 (Norway)**	
Fighter Geschwader 52		Fighter Geschwader 77	
Staff Flight	1/2	II. Gruppe	35/44
I. Gruppe	7/21		
II. Gruppe	23/28	This table shows the serviceable and total number of Me 109s in action on the western front in 1940, leading up to the Battle of Britain.	
III. Gruppe	16/31		

WAR DIARY OF 1ST GRUPPE, FIGHTER GESCHWADER 3

The entry for 15 September 1940, now commemorated as Battle of Britain Day. At the time this unit was part of Air Fleet 2, based at Samer near Boulogne under the command of Hauptmann Hans von Hahn.

On 7 September the unit reported a strength of twenty-three Messerschmitt 109Es of which 14 were serviceable after four weeks of heavy fighting. 1200 [hours, take-off time] Escort (by 12 aircraft) of Do 17s against London. Oblt Keller shot down a Spitfire, Leutnant Rohwer a Hurricane. Fw Wollmer dived into the Channel, the impact was seen by Lt Springer. This crash appears not to have been caused by enemy action. After a long dive Vollmer's machine rolled a quarter turn into a vertical dive and he did not succeed in bailing out. A motor boat detached from a German convoy near Cap Gris Nez and went to the scene of the crash. 1510 [hours] Operation by 9 aircraft to escort He 111s against London.

At 1500h there was almost total cloud cover. Over the Thames estuary and to the north of London there were gaps in the cloud. During the flight in there was contact with Spitfires. The bombers flew in loose formation to the north of London. The Spitfires came from above, fired, and dived away. H von Hahn shot down a Spitfire, Lt Rohwer probably destroyed a Hurricane. During an attack by Spitfires Oblt Reumschuessel became separated from his wing man, Obfw Olejnik, and has not returned [this aircraft crashed near Charing, Kent; the pilot bailed out and was taken prisoner]. Obfw Hessel was heard on the radio, but he failed to return [this aircraft crashed near Tenterden; the pilot bailed out and was taken prisoner]. Obfw Buchholz's aircraft was hit and forced down in the Channel. Oblt Keller made contact with a rescue aircraft nearby, which picked up Buchholz. He had [minor] injuries and was taken to the military hospital at Boulogne. The body of Lt Kloiber has been washed ashore and buried. Lt Meckel and 2 Feldwebels attended the funeral. News has been received from the Red Cross that Oblt Tiedmann, Oblt Rau, Oblt Loidolt, Lt Landry and Obfe Lamskemper have been captured by the British.

Scenes at the airfield at Caffiers near Calais, home of the Me 109 'Emils' of IIIrd Gruppe of Fighter Geschwader 26 during the Battle of Britain. The photos come from the personal album of Gerhard Schoepfel. **Top left:** *Ground crewmen making a sandbag blast pen to protect a fighter on the ground.* **Above left and middle right:** *Aircraft in their camouflaged blast pens.* **Top right:** *Engine change of a fighter in the open.* **Bottom right:** *Officers of IIIrd Gruppe of Fighter Geschwader 26 discussing the next mission. Seated second from left is the unit commander, Major Adolf Garland. To his immediate left is Gerhard Schoenfel.*

above and right: 'Emils' loaded with 550-pound bombs during attacks on England in the closing stages of the Battle of Britain.

this manoeuvre, the negative 'G' shut off the fuel supply from the float carburettor fitted to the Merlin engine. There would be a warning splutter, and unless the RAF pilot restored positive 'G' immediately his engine would stop dead.

RADIUS OF ACTION

Throughout the Battle of Britain, and during its final phases when the capital was the target, the Me 109's limited radius of action was of crucial importance. During that contest the Me 109, the Spitfire and the Hurricane each had an effective radius of action of about 100 miles (160km). For RAF fighters engaged in home defence operations, fighting over air-fields where they could land to refuel, that distance was adequate. However, for Me 109s flying in the bomber escort or support roles deep into enemy territory, it was inadequate. The German fighter pilots could not afford to spend long engaged in combat, their engines running at full throttle and guzzling fuel. If they were close to the limit of their radius of action the Messerschmitts had to break off the action, and head for home. This factor greatly reduced the effectiveness of the German single-engined fighter force.

There is another point to consider. The cliché image of the Battle of Britain is that of a sky full of Spitfires and Hurricanes engaged in one-to-one turning fights with Me 109s. That might make for a spectacular film shot, but it was far from the reality of air combat. Any pilot who fastened his attention too long on one enemy fighter ran the serious risk of setting himself up for a surprise attack by another.

133

PROVIDING CLOSE ESCORT FOR THE BOMBERS

'Sometimes we had to provide close escort for a bomber formation, which I loathed. It gave the bomber crews the feeling they were being protected, and it might have deterred some of the enemy pilots. We needed the advantages of altitude and speed so we could engage the enemy on favourable terms. The British fighters had the initiative of when and how to attack. The Heinkels cruised at about 4,000 m [13,000 ft] at about 300km/hr [190mph]. On close escort we flew at about 370km/hr [230mph], weaving from side to side. We needed to maintain speed, or the Me 109s would have taken too long to accelerate to fighting speed if we were bounced by Spitfires. We had to stay with the bombers until our formation came under attack. When we saw the British fighters approaching we would want to accelerate to engage them. But our commander would call "Everybody stay with the bombers." We handed to the enemy the initiative of when and how they would attack us. Until they did we had to stay close to the bombers, otherwise their people would complain and there would be recriminations when we got back.'

OBERLEUTNANT HANS SCHMOLLER-HALDY, ME 109 PILOT, FIGHTER GESCHWADER 54

Above: At the end of the Battle of Britain the top-scoring Luftwaffe pilot was Major Werner Moelders, commander of Fighter Geschwader 51. On 22 October 1940 he scored his fiftieth aerial victory.

On both sides, the successful fighter pilots stalked their prey like hunters, using the sun and cloud to remain unseen for as long as possible, as they edged into a favourable position before launching an attack. They then dived on their often unsuspecting prey, announcing their presence with a sudden and accurate burst of fire.

Usually the first thing the victim knew of the danger was when his aircraft shuddered under the impact. A textbook example of this type of action appears in the Prologue (see page 139).

From the start of the Battle of Britain one Gruppe operated the Me 109 in the fighter-bomber role, attacking targets in southern England. The fighter carried a bomb load of up to 550 pounds (249kg). In the final part of the Battle, from the end of September, several Me 109 units flew aircraft modified for the fighter-bomber role. The

defending fighters found the fast, high-flying German fighter-bombers difficult targets to engage. As a result the latter suffered minimal losses. The Me 109 carried only a small weight of bombs, and their scattered bombing meant that the attacks had only nuisance value.

REPUTATION INTACT

The Me 109 force emerged from the Battle of Britain with its reputation still intact, although it had suffered losses at the hands of the RAF pilots.

The new variant of the German fighter about to enter service, the Me 109 'Friedrich', would be even better.

Left: Hauptmann Horst Tietzen, the commander of 5th Staffer of Fighter Geschwader 51, with his personal 'Emil' with eighteen victory bars on the tail. On the afternoon of 18 August 1940, when his victory score stood at twenty, he was shot down and killed during an action with Hurricanes of No. 501 Squadron.

THE MOST SERIOUS AND UNPARDONABLE ERROR

'On 23 September our mission was a free hunting sweep in the triangle Ramsgate-Canterbury-Folkestone. With three of my pilots I took off at 10.27 and headed towards Ramsgate in a slow climb to 4,500 m [about 15,000 ft]. The weather was strange, with layers of cloud in which aircraft could easily hide. There were several aircraft about but we never knew if they were British or German. It was uncanny. We flew in wide curves, always changing altitude, never flying straight for long. We had been flying for 60 minutes, I thought that was enough and we were turning for home when I suddenly observed Hurricane squadron between Ramsgate and Dover, twelve aircraft in four "pulks" flying one behind the other. They were about 1,000 m (2,873ft) below us and climbing in wide curves, like a creeping worm. My impression was that it was a Hurricane squadron on a training mission. The Hurricane pilots had no idea that four 109s were above them following each of their movements. The display was so fascinating that we forgot what was going on around us. That is the most serious and unpardonable error a fighter pilot can commit, and catastrophe immediately followed. Four Spitfires, of which we had been unaware due to our carelessness, attacked us out of the sun. They fired at us from behind, roared close over our heads at high speed and disappeared back into the sky. As we broke formation fearing another attack from the Spitfires, I saw a 109 going down in flames on my right. It was Obfw Knipscher, we never heard what happened to him.'

OBERLEUTNANT HANS SCHMOLLER-HALDY ME 109 PILOT, FIGHTER GESCHWADER 54

Top: An 'Emil' crash-landed on a French beach. During the Battle of Britain this fighter was not fitted with drop tanks. Several were lost when they ran out of fuel on their way home following air combats or after encountering strong headwinds.
Above: Me 109E-7s of Fighter Geschwader 1, a unit that spent most of the war operating in the defence of the German homeland. (via Obert)
Right: Major Adolf Galland climbing out of the cockpit of his 'Emil' after a sortie over England during the Battle of Britain.

135

During 1940 the Messerschmitt company improved the Me 109's fighting capability. The new variant was known as the Me 109 'Friedrich'. The most obvious external changes were the more rounded spinner and nose contours, the rounded wing tips and the partially retractable tail wheel. The main production version was fitted with the new Mauser 15mm cannon, one of which fired through the propeller hub. This weapon had nearly twice the firing rate of the older 20mm Oerlikon cannon, and its far higher muzzle velocity made it a much more effective weapon than its predecessor.

The 'Friedrich' was faster than the 'Emil' and it handled better in the air. It was a 'fighter pilot's fighter'. The 'Friedrich' entered service in the spring of 1941. Also at this time the RAF introduced the Mark V Spitfire into its home defence squadrons, a move that restored the balance between the fighter forces of the two sides.

NORTH AFRICA

That balanced existed only over northwest Europe. Until the

MESSSERSCHMITT 109 F-2

Type Single-seat general purpose fighter.
Armament One Mauser 15mm cannon firing through the propeller spinner (200 rounds). Two Rheinmetall-Borsig 7.9mm MGs synchronized to fire through airscrew (500 rounds per gun).
Power Plant One Daimler Benz DB 601N inverted V-12 liquid cooled engine developing 1,200hp for take off.
Dimensions Span 32ft 6in (9.92m); length 29ft 4in (8.94m).
Weight Normal operational take off, 6,174lb (2,800kg).
Performance Max. speed 373mph at 19,700ft (600km/hr at 6,000m). Service ceiling 36,100ft (11,000m).

Top: A brand new Me 109 'Friedrich' in factory markings shows off its distinctive rounded wing form above the Alps.
Above: A 'Friedrich' of Fighter Geschwader 26 returning to its base at Liegescourt in northern France in the summer of 1941. (Schoepfel)
Opposite: Two 'Emils' of Fighter Geschwader 27 on patrol over the North African desert.

Top: 'Friedrich' wearing the personal markings of the commander of IIIrd Gruppe of Fighter Geschwader 2 based in northern France, photographed in 1941.
Above: An Me 109F of Fighter Geschwader 26 outside its camouflaged dispersal hangar in northern France.

spring of 1942 the Spitfire fighter units operated only from bases in Great Britain. Units equipped with the 'Friedrich' were involved in the campaigns in North Africa and the Soviet Union where the new fighter easily out flew the less modern types. For the German fighter pilots this was a 'happy time' when many of them amassed large victory scores.

The leading 'Friedrich' fighter pilot was Leutnant Hans-Joachim Marseille. He gained seven victories during the Battle of Britain, flying the 'Emil'. From

THE ATTACK ON RUSSIA

During the weeks following the invasion of Russia, German fighters ranged far and wide over enemy territory. Close to the ground the Polikarpov I-16, the main Soviet fighter type, was almost as fast as the Me 109F. But the Type 24's radial engine was optimized for low-altitude operations and as height increased its performance fell away steadily; at 20,000ft (6,096m) the I-16 was about 100mph (160km/hr) slower than the German fighter. Although the Soviet fighters were more manoeuvrable than their adversaries, in a fighter-versus-fighter combat that advantage did no more than allow a pilot to avoid being shot down, provided he saw his attacker in good time. For the most part, the Soviet fighter pilots had to dance to their enemies' tune. Typical of the scrappy actions taking place that morning was one near Brest-Litovsk, described by Unteroffizier Reibel of Ist Gruppe of Fighter Geschwader 53: 'I was flying as wing man to Lt Zellot. We flew in the direction of Brest from Labinka. As my leader ordered a turn about, I saw two biplanes in front of us. I immediately reported them and we brought them under attack. When we were about 200m [61ft] from them they both pulled into a tight turn to the right. We pulled up high and then began a new attack, but though we both opened fire it was without success. Soon there were about ten other [enemy] machines in the area. My leader ran in to attack one of the planes while I remained high in order to cover him. Then an I-15 became separated from the others. I prepared to attack it, but had to break away when another enemy machine suddenly appeared 50m [15ft] in front of me. I opened fire with machine guns and the cannon and it burst into flames and spun out of control. Apparently the pilot had baled out. I had to turn away, as I had two [enemy] machines behind me.' Using their superior speed, the two German fighters easily pulled away.

Me 109 'Emils' of Fighter Geschwader 52 pictured at Kabaracie, Rumania, in the spring of 1941 shortly before the attack on the Soviet Union. The 'snake' marking on the rear fuselage indicated that these aircraft belonged to the IIIrd Gruppe.

Top left: Me 109 'Emil' fighter-bomber of Fighter Geschwader 54 over the Eastern Front in 1942.
Middle: Me 109 'Friedrich' of Fighter Geschwader 54 pictured beside a captured Soviet I-16 fighter. The German fighter had a considerable speed advantage over its enemy counterpart, especially at high altitude.
Bottom: Me 109 'Friedrich' of Fighter Geschwader 53, with the unit's 'Ace of Spades' insignia on the cowling, at an airfield in the Leningrad sector on the Eastern Front during the winter of 1941-2.

the start of 1942, in North Africa, his victory total rose rapidly. With no Spitfires yet operating in that area, the 'Friedrich' was superior to the Hurricane and Tomahawk fighters flown by the RAF and its allies. During a remarkable action on 3 June 1942, Marseille shot down six Tomahawks in rapid succession. The action is well documented and the combat is confirmed in the records of the victim unit, No. 5 Squadron South African Air Force. By the time of his death in September 1942, Marseille's tally stood at 158.

Me 109s IN NORTH AFRICA

Opposite page:
1. Hauptmann Karl-Wolfgang Redlich of Ist Gruppe Fighter Geschwader 27 (left, with papers), briefing pilots before taking off from Sicily to fly to North Africa. The 'Emil' in the background is fitted with a dust filter over the engine air intake. (Schroer)
2. Ground running an 'Emil' engine in Sicily, to warm the engine before setting out for North Africa. (Schroer)
3. Me 109 'Emils' of Fighter Geschwader 27 dispersed around the forward landing ground in Libya. The photograph gives a good impression of the primitive conditions under which the unit had to operate. (Schroer)
4. Ground crewmen turning the handle for the inertia starter of the Daimler Benz 601 engine. The handle rotated a heavy flywheel which, when it was turning fast enough, was clutched to the engine to turn it over and start it.
5. 'Emils' of Fighter Geschwader 27 on patrol over the desert.
6. Me 109F of Fighter Geschwader 27 preparing to get airborne. This aircraft is missing its spinner.
7. Hauptmann Hans-Joachim Marseille of Fighter Geschwader 27, the most successful German fighter pilot in North Africa. At the time of his death in September 1942, his victory score was 158.
8. Fighter ace Leutnant Werner Schroer, adjutant of IInd Gruppe of Fighter Geschwader 27, with his personal aircraft. At the end of the war his victory score stood at 114. (Schroer)

The 15mm cannon on the 'Friedrich' was replaced with a fast firing 20mm Mauser cannon. Mounted above the engine cowling, the weapons gave a dense pattern of fire. This was very effective against light bombers. Against the four-engined bombers, it was another matter however.

FIRE POWER

From mid-1942 the Me 109F units operating over western Europe and North Africa encountered the American B-17 Flying Fortress and B-24 Liberator heavy bombers with increasing frequency. On average it needed about twenty hits with 20mm rounds to knock down one of these rugged aircraft. When in formation the heavy bombers put up a powerful defensive cross-fire which forced the fighters to make high-speed firing passes. Only an exceptionally good shot could achieve the required number of

Above: 'Friedrich' of Fighter Geschwader 77 operating on the Leningrad front in 1942. (Pichler via Obert)

hits using a single cannon.

The Friedrich was modified to carry a blister under each wing containing an extra 20mm cannon and ammunition. This trebled the fighter's fire power, but reduced its performance. It was the first sign of a problem that would afflict the Me 109 for the remainder of the war.

That critical shortcoming would become all too evident when the next variant entered production, the 'Gustav'.

THE EASY TIMES IN RUSSIA

Initially the German fighter pilots had an easy time over Russia. In the summer of 1942 Unteroffizier Walther Hagenah was posted to Ist Gruppe of Fighter Geschwader 3 operating the Me 109F. He flew as wing man to Obfw Otto Wessling. Hagenah told this author: 'Wessling was a superb leader who seemed to be able to score hits from ranges as great as 400m [1,312ft]. He would manoeuvre into a position of advantage above his enemy, open fire from long range, hit his enemy and pull away without getting close to his foe. My first weeks as an operational fighter pilot were a disappointment. I was beginning to get discouraged. One day Wessling took me to one side on the ground and said "Now it is time that you made your first victory!" On 12 August 1942 we were on patrol on the central Russian front and he spotted a pair of LAGG-3 fighters. He took us into an attacking position on their tails and down we went. We moved from out of the sun and achieved surprise. He hit one of them from about 400m [1,312ft] and down it went. Then he called me and said "Now you go ahead and hit the other one!" But the second Russian tried to shake us off his tail. Wessling joined in the dogfight, but at the same time telling me what I had to do to get "my" kill. Eventually he succeeded in manoeuvring both me and the Russian fighter into a position where I could open fire at it. I followed Wessling's instructions and fired when he said, hitting the enemy fighter. I was very proud. Wessling was big enough to keep quiet about how I got it.'

During the Second World War the principal fighter types in the major warring nations underwent courses of development to improve their fighting capability. They were fitted with more powerful (and heavier) engines, more effective (and heavier) armament, larger (and heavier) fuel tankage and additional (and heavier) protective armour and equipment.

As the fighter steadily gained weight, the airframe had to be stiffened to restore its original strength factors. That added a further twist to the spiral of increasing weight. Since the fighter's wing area usually remained constant, each increase in weight led to increase in wing loading. And that, inevitably, led to a deterioration in the fighter's handling characteristics. Stalling speeds became higher, control forces heavier, turning performance worsened and, in many cases, the aircraft developed vicious traits.

The Me 109G-2 was 660 pounds heavier than its predecessor, the Me 109F

No fighter design suffered more from this remorseless process than the Me 109. Even at the start of the war, it will be remembered, the Me 109 had already passed through several variants. By the spring of 1942 it had reached the end of its effective development and should then have passed out of production. Messerschmitt's replacement, the Me 209, was still on the drawing board.

At that time the war was still going well for Germany and her leaders confidently expected that the campaign on the Eastern Front would come to a victorious end in the autumn of 1942. Until a replacement fighter type was ready, the Luftwaffe opted to squeeze greater speed from the Me 109 and keep the fighter in full production.

The new variant, the Me 109 'Gustav', was designed around the Daimler Benz 605 engine. In essence this was a DB 601 with the cylinder block rebored to increase the engine's capacity from 33.9 litres to 35.7 litres. The additional capacity gave an extra 175 hp at full throttle, for no significant increase in the

Top: Me 109 'Gustav' of Fighter Geschwader 54 seen at an airfield in Russia.
Above: Me 109 'Gustav' of Fighter Geschwader 53 at an airfield in Sicily in 1943. (via Rigglesford)
Opposite: Pilots of Fighter Geschwader 53 snatching a quick meal beside one of their aircraft. (via Schliephake)

engine's external dimensions. The first major production version, the 'Gustav-2', was 660lb (300kg) or about 10per cent heavier than the earlier 'Friedrich' and its handling characteristics were much worse. During May 1942 a total of 234 Me 109s came off the production lines in Germany and Austria, most of them 'Gustavs'.

MESSERSCHMITT 109 G-2

Type Single-seat general purpose fighter.
Armament One Mauser 20mm cannon firing through the spinner (150 rounds) Two Rheinmetall-Borsig 7.9mm MGs synchronized to fire through the airscrew (500 rounds per gun).
Power Plant One Daimler Benz DB 605A inverted V-12 liquid cooled engine developing 1,475hp for take off.
Dimensions Span 32ft 6in (9.92m); length 29ft 0in (8.85m)
Weight Normal operational take off 6,832lb (3,100kg)
Performance Maximum speed 406mph at 28,535ft (654km/hr at 8,700m) Service ceiling 39,360ft (12,000m).

Soon after the 'Gustav' entered service with Fighter Geschwader 27, Hans-Joachim Marseille lost his life while flying the type. In September 1942 his victory score passed the 150 mark, making him the first fighter ace in history to achieve this total. On the final day of the month he flew a newly-delivered 'Gustav-2' on a bomber escort mission over Egypt. There was no contact with the enemy and the flight was uneventful, until on the return flight the aircraft's engine started to smoke. Then it caught fire. The cockpit filled with fumes and, escorted by his comrades, Marseille stayed with the aircraft until he reached German-held territory. Then he

Marseille jumped from his aircraft but for once luck had deserted him

jumped from the stricken fighter, but his luck had deserted him. As he left the Messerschmitt it appears that his head struck some part of its structure and he was knocked unconscious. His parachute did not open and he was killed on hitting the ground. Subsequent examination of his parachute revealed that it was still in the pack, held

closed by the ripcord which had not been pulled.

Small numbers of 'Gustav-2s' were modified for the tactical reconnaissance role, with the cannon removed and a vertical camera mounted in the rear fuselage. The use of the Me 109 (and also the FW 190) for this purpose became necessary because the increasing enemy fighter opposition

meant that slower reconnaissance types incurred heavy losses. Modified versions of each of the new main variants of the Me 109 would be used for tactical reconnaissance for the remainder of the war.

The next major production version of the fighter, the 'Gustav-6', started to leave the assembly lines in the autumn of 1942. This differed from the G-2 in that it carried two 13mm heavy machine guns on top of the engine cowling, in place of the earlier rifle-calibre weapons. To cover the larger breech mechanism of the 13mm guns, the fighter had two large bulges on the cowling in front of the windscreen.

'WILD BOAR' MESSERSCHMITT 109s

Me 109G-2s operating in the 'Wild Boar' single-engine nightfighter role to counter RAF bomber attacks, summer 1943.

From mid-1943 the Luftwaffe began to employ small numbers of single-engined fighters, including Me 109s, to engage RAF night bombers attacking cities in Germany. Over the target the concentrations of searchlights, the fires on the ground and the Pathfinders' marker flares often combined to illuminate the bombers. The single-seaters patrolling high above the target could then make visual attacks on the raiders. To prevent conflict with the flak defences it was agreed that the latter would engage bombers flying below a certain altitude typically 18,000ft (5,500m). Above that altitude the fighters would engage bombers. The single-engined night fighter tactics bore the apt title 'Wild Boar'. For the remainder of the war these methods were an integral part of the German night air defence system.

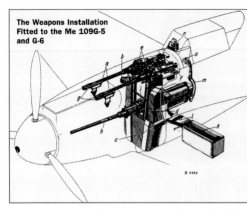

The Weapons Installation Fitted to the Me 109G-5 and G-6

Key:
a. MG 31 13mm heavy machine guns
b. Electrical synchronization unit for firing MG 131s through the airscrew disc
c. Magazine for MG 131 ammunition
d. Empty case chute for port MG 131
e. Mountings for MG 131s
f. Ignition coil, to provide high voltage for electrically fired MG 131 ammunition
g. Mounting brackets for nose fairing
h. MG 151 20mm cannon firing through propeller spinner
i. Front mounting of MG 151
k. Magazine for MG 151 ammunition
l. Feed chute for MG 151 ammunition
m. Control column, with firing button for weapons
n. Revi 16B reflector sight
o. Arming switch for weapons

210mm ROCKETS

The Luftwaffe issued a range of field modification kits to allow units to 'customize' the new fighter for specific operational roles. The R-1 kit, for example, provided an under-fuselage rack to carry a single bomb weighing up to 550lb (249kg). The R-2 kit provided for a tubular launcher under each wing to carry a 210mm rocket, for use against enemy bomber formations or ground targets. The R-4 kit provided a blister mounting for a 30mm heavy cannon and ammunition, one to fit under either wing.

The 'Gustav-6' could carry one or two separate power-boosting systems, to inject a fluid into the supercharger of the DB 605 engine. To boost power at altitudes above 20,000ft (6,096m), the GM-1 system injected nitrous oxide (laughing gas) into the engine. The nitrous oxide was held in liquid form in a heavily lagged pressurized container in the

Above: Diagram from an official Luftwaffe handbook, showing the fuselage armament fitted as standard to Me 109 Gustav-5 and Gustav-6. These fighters had a 20mm Mauser cannon firing through the airscrew hub, and two 13mm Rheinmetall-Borsig heavy machine guns above the engine cowling synchronized to fire through the airscrew. On some later aircraft the engine-mounted cannon was replaced by a Rheinmetall-Borsig 30mm weapon.

Below: The 'Gustav' did not suffer fools gladly. If the pilot opened the throttle too quickly during take-off, the powerful engine torque was liable to lift the fighter off the ground before it attained flying speed. Often the fighter rolled upside down and smashed on the ground under full power, giving the pilot little chance of escape. (Schliephake)

Top: Me 109 'Gustav-2s' of a tactical reconnaissance Gruppe. This version had the nose-mounted cannon removed, and a vertical camera fitted in the fuselage immediately behind the cockpit.

Above: Me 109 'Gustav-2' of Fighter Geschwader 11 at Jever during 1943, fitted with underwing launchers for two 210 mm air-to-air rockets for use against US heavy bomber formations.

on the defensive. More fighters were required and the 'Gustav' was built in ever-greater numbers. In 1943 production of the Me 109 was twice that in the previous year, more than 6,400 'Gustavs' were delivered to the Luftwaffe.

Daylight attacks by US heavy bombers on targets in Germany had grown into deep penetration attacks by several hundred bombers. Several fighter Gruppen were withdrawn from the battle fronts to bolster the defences of the homeland.

In the summer of 1943 Unteroffizier Hans Seyringer was posted to IInd Gruppe of Fighter Geschwader 27, a day fighter unit equipped with the 'Gustav-6'. The young pilot had only about 200 flying hours in his logbook. His recollections give a good impression of what it was like to serve with such a unit.

During bomber-interception missions, fighters usually carried a 66-gal (300l) drop tank under the fuselage. Standard armament fitted to 'Gustavs' on Seyringer's unit was three 20mm cannon and two 13mm machine-guns. Some aircraft also carried two 210mm rocket launchers under the wings.

Aircraft were usually drawn up by Staffeln in line abreast on the ground. The four Staffeln, each with about a dozen 'Gustav-6s', were dispersed separately at 90-degree intervals around the perimeter of the grass airfield. Once the pilots had been brought to cockpit readiness, the order to scramble was given by firing a flare from the control tower. From then on

rear fuselage and the system weighed 670lb (304kg). To boost power at altitudes below 20,000ft, the MW system injected a water/methanol mixture into the engine. The complete MW system weighed 300lb (136kg).

As the 'Gustav-6' entered service Germany's war fortunes deteriorated. On each battle front the Luftwaffe was thrown

Above: A close-up of the rocket installation on a 'Gustav'.
Left: Me 109 'Gustav' of the Finnish Air Force. The type entered that service in March 1943 and remained in use until 1954

it was important to get the Gruppe into the air and assembled into battle formation as rapidly as possible. To achieve this two of the Staffeln on opposite sides of the airfield began simultaneous take-off runs, moving on parallel headings separated by a few hundred yards. As the first two Staffeln passed each other at the centre of the airfield, the other two Staffeln began their take-off runs also heading in opposite directions. After take-off the leader orbited once over the airfield so the individual Staffeln could start to move into position behind him. Then he turned on to his intercept heading and began a slow climb away. Once the formation was fully assembled he increased his rate of climb.

These tactics provided the most rapid means of getting a Gruppe into the air and assembled into formation. There was little small margin for safety if anything went wrong, however. Seyringer recalled a nerve-racking incident when, due to incorrect fitting, a fighter taking off in the opposite direction accidentally loosed off a couple of rockets. The missiles came scorching past Seyringer's Staffel just as the fighters were getting airborne. Their proximity caused considerable consternation but, fortunately for the pilots involved, no damage!

TACTICS

Once the ground controller had brought a fighter Gruppe within visual range of an enemy formation, the Gruppe leader decided on the type of attack to employ. Usually Seyringer's Gruppe attacked bombers from the rear, the fighters flying in four-aircraft units in line abreast

Above: 'Gustav-6' carrying the white fuselage band and wing tips of a unit operating on the Mediterranean front.

Right: Unteroffizier Hans Seyringer of Fighter Geschwader 27, whose experiences are described in the text, pictured with his 'Gustav-6'. With a victory score of four enemy aircraft destroyed, he was shot down and wounded during an engagement with American escort fighters in February 1944. (Seyringer)

or line astern. The fighters split into pairs to make further firing runs. Sometimes Seyringer's Gruppe made head-on attacks, though he did not like this method. He felt that the time spent manoeuvring into position for such an attack was out of proportion to the very short firing pass that resulted.

Until late in 1943 the American escort fighters lacked the range to penetrate deep into Germany. Seyringer's unit had few encounters with them and he thought that was as well, for a heavily laden 'Gustav-6' was no match for a Thunderbolt.

To Hans Seyringer the effect of the fighter's extensive development process on handling was all too evident. To put it simply, the 'Gustav' was too heavy and its engine too powerful for the fighter's small wing and tail surfaces. When carrying a full armament and drop tank the aircraft required careful handling during the take-off. If there was heavy-handedness of the controls the fighter was liable to react viciously. If, for example, the pilot opened the throttle too quickly the powerful engine torque was liable to

lift the fighter off the ground before it attained flying speed. The 'Gustav' would drop its left wing, roll on its back and smash into the ground, giving the pilot little chance of escape.

During 1943 the Luftwaffe tactics to counter the American heavy bomber raids were in a continual state of development. Home defence units used any type of weapon that came to hand. Fighter Geschwader 11 carried out experiments in air-to-air bombing, using time-fused 550lb (249kg) released from above the bomber forma-

DISASTER FOR THE GERMAN DAY FIGHTER FORCE

In the spring of 1944 the American escort fighters were able to reach almost every part of Germany. The new Mustang was superior in performance to the Me 109 and it was usually present in greater numbers. As a result the German day fighter units took increasingly heavy losses. At the end of April 1944 Generalmajor Adolf Galland reported: 'Between January and April 1944 our day fighter arm lost more than 1,000 pilots. They included our best Staffel, Gruppe and Geschwader commanders. The time has come when our force is within sight of collapse.' Now the German pilots had to fight for their very survival, and one by one even the best of them were being picked off. Gone were the days when the aces could 'play' enemy planes to allow their less experienced colleagues to get easy kills, as over Russia a couple of years earlier. One of those who died in action with the American fighters in April 1944 was Leutnant Otto Wessling, then credited with 83 victories, who had set up Walther Hagenah's first 'kill' described earlier.

tion. If the bombs did not destroy the enemy planes, they might damage some of them sufficiently to force them to leave their formation. There were serious problems with this method. Carrying a bomb in place of a drop tank, the 'Gustav' had a short radius of action. Also it proved difficult to vector the heavily laden fighter into position above a high-flying bomber formation. Since there was no effective proximity fuse then available, the problem of getting the bomb to detonate as it passed the target aircraft defied

MESSERSCHMITT 109 G–2 VERSUS HAWKER TEMPEST

At the beginning of 1944 a captured Me 109 'Gustav-2' was flown in a comparative trial against the latest RAF fighter type, the Hawker Tempest Mark V. These extracts from the official report show that the German fighter was outclassed in almost every respect. **Maximum Speed:** The Tempest possesses an advantage of 40-50mph [64-80km/hr] at heights below 20,000 feet [5,850m] but at heights in excess of 20,000 feet [6,096m] the advantage possessed by the Tempest rapidly diminishes. **Climb:** The climb of the Me 109 is superior to that of the Tempest at all heights but this advantage is not pronounced at heights below 5,000 feet [1,520m]. When both the aircraft commence a dive at the same speed and are put into climbing attitude, the Tempest is slightly superior, but providing the Tempest possesses the initial advantage in speed, it has no difficulty in holding it providing the speed is kept in excess of 250mph [400km/hr]. **Dive:** Comparative dives between these aircraft show that the Tempest will pull away from the Me 109. This is not so marked in the early stages of the dive, but in a prolonged descent the Tempest is greatly superior. **Turning Circle:** It was found that in this aspect of manoeuvrability the Tempest was slightly superior to the Me 109. **Rate of Roll:** At speeds below 350 IAS [mph indicated, 564km/hr] there is practically nothing to choose between the two aircraft, but when this speed is exceeded the Tempest can out-manoeuvre the Me 109 by making a quick change of bank and direction. **Conclusions:** In the attack the Tempest can always follow the Me 109, except in a slow steep climb. In the combat area the Tempest should maintain a high speed, and in defence may do anything except attempt a climb at low speed.

Comparative trials revealed that the Hawker Tempest Mark V, which entered service in the RAF early in 1944, was superior to the Me 109 'Gustav-2' in almost every respect.

solution. Most of the bombs detonated well clear of their intended victims, and after a month or so the unit abandoned this form of attack.

During the spring of 1944, following the introduction of new and larger drop tanks, the American escort fighters were able to reach almost every part of Germany. The new Mustang fighters were superior in performance to the defending Me 109s, Me 110s, Me 410s and FW 190s. Moreover the escort fighters operated in large numbers and as a result the German fighter units took heavy losses.

HOME DEFENCE

By now the greater part of the Luftwaffe fighter force was committed in the defence of the homeland. And it was losing pilots faster than the German flying training schools could provide replacements. The Luftwaffe was being bled white. The only possibility of reversing this trend was with the large-scale deployment of the Messerschmitt 262 jet fighter.

Below: Me 109G-6s of IIIrd Gruppe Fighter Geschwader 27 waiting at readiness at Wiesbaden-Erbenheim in 1944. The broad red band around the rear fuselage indicated that the aircraft belonged to a Reich air defence unit. (Schroer)

Above: Damaged Me 109 'Gustav' trailing glycol smoke, after being hit in the cooling system during an engagement with a US escort fighter.

Yet this type was still not ready to enter mass production.

Although the 'Gustav' was now well beyond its effective development life, new sub-types continued to appear. By optimizing it for a narrow range of combat roles, the fighter might survive in action. Thus the 'Gustav-10', was built specifically to engage in high altitude fighter-versus-fighter combat. These aircraft carried the new Daimler Benz 605D engine with an enlarged supercharger and the GM-1 power boosting. Their armament was reduced to one 20mm cannon and two 13mm machine guns. They were assigned to units to provide top cover for heavily armed fighters delivering attacks on bomber for-mations. Small numbers of 'Gustav-l0s' were modified for the tactical reconnaissance role with the two heavy machine guns removed and a fixed vertical camera mounted in the rear fuselage.

A DESPERATE TIME

In the spring of 1944 the German aircraft industry underwent a major reorganization. The Luftwaffe needed every modern fighter it could lay its hands on. Under the new

IN ACTION DURING THE
FINAL MONTHS OF THE WAR

'Leutnant Hans-Ulrich Flade flew the Me 109 'Gustav' and the 'Kurfürst' with IInd Gruppe of Fighter Geschwader 27 early in 1945. In previous months the production of these fighters had reached an all-time high, and if an aircraft was damaged it was usually simpler to get a new fighter than repair the old one: 'We simply went to the depot nearby, where they had hundreds of brand-new 109s – G-10s, G–14s and even the very latest K models. There was no proper organization any more; the depot staff just said: "There are the aircraft, take what you want and go away." But getting fuel, that was more difficult. Flade's Gruppe had a strength of about twenty pilots, but it was losing these at a rate of two or three each day. Morale on the unit was low. 'Each morning we pilots had breakfast together, and the replacements would come in. The older pilots regarded the newcomers as though they had only days to live – and with reason, for the standard of fighter conversion training was now so low that most of the new pilots flew only two or three missions before they were shot down. I remember many conversations along these lines – not exactly a cheerful subject for a young man who had just joined his first operational unit!' The Gruppe operated in the top-cover role, to keep the American escort fighters off the backs of other German fighters making for the bombers. 'We followed the old rules: dive as a pair or a four out of the sun, make a quick attack to break up their formation and make them drop their tanks, then climb out of danger and assess the situation. If conditions were favourable, we would go down for a second attack. Always the escorts were so numerous that it would have been foolish to get into a dog-fight.'

Top: The Me 109G-14 featured a larger rudder and a redesigned cockpit canopy to give better vision to the sides and the rear. This example belonged to IIIrd Gruppe of Fighter Geschwader 3, a unit that flew escort missions for more heavily armoured fighters delivering attacks on US heavy bomber formations. (Romm)

Above: Me 109 'Kurfürst', the final version of the fighter to go into production in Germany before the end of the war. As well as the revised tail surfaces and redesigned canopy fitted to the late production 'Gustavs', this variant featured a more powerful Daimler Benz 605 engine and carried two 15 mm cannons mounted on top of the engine.

Luftwaffe procurement plan, almost the entire capacity of the industry was turned over to the manufacture of fighter-type aircraft. At the same time, to render the industry less vulnerable to air attack, a large part of the aircraft construction and assembly work was dispersed into small factories and workshops dotted throughout the country.

Once the new system was in place, production of the Me 109 rose in leaps and bounds, despite the heavy and continual raids on German cities and industrial centres. For the Me 109 September 1944 was the peak month, with the Luftwaffe taking delivery of 1,605 new aircraft. That year 14,212 examples of this type of aircraft were delivered, more than twice as many as in the previous year which had itself been a record. At this stage of the war the units equipped with Me 109s always had plenty of aircraft, although there were shortages of trained pilots and fuel as the tide turned against the German forces.

Above and left: The unusual 'Mistel' weapon, a Me 109F mounted rigidly on top of a Junkers 88 bomber that had the cabin removed and a large warhead fitted In its place. The Me 109 pilot aligned the bomber on the target, then fired explosive bolts to separate his aircraft so he could make his escape.

Despite the poor handling qualities of the Me 109 'Gustav', work continued in attempts to squeeze yet more speed and combat capability out of the basic design. The final variant of the Me 109 to enter large-scale production was the 'Kurfurst', deliveries of which began at the end of September 1944. The initial production sub-type, the 'Kurfurst 2', had a pair of 15 mm cannon in place of the 13 mm weapons mounted above the engine. The 'Kurfurst-4' was a high altitude fighter with a pressurized cabin. The 'Kurfurst-6' was a specialized bomber-destroyer version, with a 30 mm high-velocity cannon firing through the airscrew spinner.

The final sub-type to enter production before the end of the war was the 'Kurfurst-14', which was powered by a DB 605L engine with a two-stage supercharger. This aircraft was the fastest Me 109 of them all, with a maximum speed of 452mph at 19,700 ft (728km/hr at 6,000m).

During the early months of 1945 the Allied ground forces were thrusting into Germany from both the east and the west. As the factories building components and assemblies for the Me 109 came under threat from these forces, they were blown up to prevent capture. Also at this time attacks on the German road, rail and canal systems made it difficult to deliver air-

craft components to the assembly plants. However, despite these obstacles, the Me 109 continued to be turned out in large numbers until the very end of the war.

In the final four months of the conflict the Luftwaffe took delivery of nearly three thousand Me 109s. It is estimated that several hundred more of these aircraft were probably completed, but they never reached the units for which they were intended, remaining in the factories where they had been assembled.

The precise number of Me 109s built will never be known with certainty, but without doubt it can be stated that the figure exceeded 33,000. So, to the type's other 'firsts' can be added the distinction that no other fighter design, anywhere else in the world, was produced in greater numbers.

THE BOEING B-17
FLYING FORTRESS

1 Rudder construction
2 rudder tab
3 Rudder tab actuation
4 Tail gunner's station
5 Gunsight
6 Twin .50in (12.7mm) machine-guns
7 Tail cone
8 Tail gunner's seat
9 Ammunition troughs
10 Elevator trim tab
11 Starboard elevator
12 Tailplane structure
13 Tailplane front spar
14 Tailplane/fuselage attachment

15 Control cables
16 Elevator control mechanism
17 Rudder control linkage
18 Rudder post
19 Rudder centre hinge
20 Fin structure
21 Rudder upper hinge
22 Fin skinning

23 Aerial attachment
24 Aerials
25 Fin leading-edge de-icing boot
26 Port elevator
27 Port tailplane
28 Tailplane leading-edge de-icing boot
29 Dorsal fin structure
30 Fuselage frame
31 Tailwheel actuation
32 Toilet
33 Tailwheel (retracted) fairing
34 Fully-swivelling retractable tailwheel
35 Crew entry door
36 Control cables

37 Starboard waist hatch
38 Starboard waist .50in (12.7mm) machine gun
39 Gun support frame
40 Ammunition box
41 Ventral aerial
42 Waist gunners' positions
43 Port waist .50in (12.7mm) machine gun
44 Ceiling control cable runs
45 Dorsal aerial mast
46 Ball turret stanchion support
47 Ball turret stanchion
48 Ball turret actuation mechanism
49 Support frame
50 Ball turret roof
51 Twin .50in (12.7mm) machine guns
52 Ventral ball turret
53 Wingroot fillet

54 Bulkhead
55 Radio operator's compartment
56 Camera access hatch
57 Radio compartment windows (port and starboard)
58 Ammunition boxes
59 Single .30in (7.62mm) dorsal machine gun
60 Radio compartment roof glazing
61 Radio compartment/ bomb bay bulkhead
62 Fire extinguisher
63 Radio operator's station (port side)
64 Handrail links
65 Bulkhead step
66 Wing rear spar/ fuselage attachment
67 Wingroot profile
68 Bomb-bay central catwalk

69 Vertical bomb stowage racks (starboard installation shown)
70 Horizontal bomb stowage (port side shown)
71 Dinghy stowage
72 Twin .50in (12.7mm) machine guns
73 Dorsal turret
74 Wing flaps
75 Cooling air slots
76 Aileron tab (port only)
77 Port aileron

78 Port navigation light
79 Wing skinning
80 Wing leading edge de-icing boot
81 Port landing light

82 Wing corrugated inner skin
83 Port out wing fuel tank (nine inter-rib cells)
84 No. 1 engine nacelle

85 Cooling gills
86 Three-blade propellers
87 No. 2 engine nacelle
88 Wing leading-edge de-icing boot

89 Port mid-wing (self-sealing) fuel tanks
90 Flight deck upper glazing
91 Flight deck/bomb-bay bulkhead
92 Oxygen cylinders
93 Co-pilot's seat
94 Co-pilot's control column

95 Headrest/armour
96 Compass installation
97 Pilot's seat
98 Windscreen
99 Central control console pedestal
100 Side windows
101 Navigation equipment
102 Navigator's compartment upper window (subsequently replaced by ceiling astrodome)
103 Navigator's table
104 Side gun mounting

Boeing B-17 Flying Fortress

105 Enlarged cheek windows (flush)
106 Ammunition box
107 Bombardier's panel
108 Norden bombsight installation
109 Plexiglass frameless nose-cone
110 Single .50in (12.7mm) machine gun
111 Optically-flat bomb-aiming panel
112 Pitot head fairing (port and starboard)
113 D/F loop bullet fairing
114 Port mainwheel
115 Flight deck underfloor control linkage
116 Wingroot/fuselage fairing
117 Wing front spar/fuselage attachment

118 Battery access panels (wingroot leading-edge)
119 No. 3 engine nacelle spar bulkhead
120 Intercooler pressure duct
121 Mainwheel well
122 Oil tank (nacelle inboard wall)
123 Nacelle structure
124 Exhaust
125 Retracted mainwheel (semi-recessed)
126 Firewall
127 Cooling gills
128 Exhaust collector ring assembly

129 Three-blade propellers
130 Undercarriage retraction struts
131 Starboard mainwheel
132 Axle
133 Mainwheel oleo leg
134 Propeller reduction gear casing
135 1,000hp Wright R-1829-65 radial engine

136 Exhaust collector ring
137 Engine upper bearers
138 Firewall
139 Engine lower bearers
140 Intercooler assembly
141 Oil tank (nacelle outboard wall)

142 Supercharger
143 Intake
144 Supercharger waste-gate
145 Starboard landing light
146 Supercharger intake
147 Intercooler intake
148 Ducting
149 No. 4 engine nacelle spar bulkhead
150 Oil radiator intake
151 Main spar web structure
152 Mid-wing fuel tank rib cut-outs
153 Auxiliary mid spar
154 Rear spar

155 Landing flap profile
156 Cooling air slots
157 Starboard outer wing fuel tank (nine inter-rib cells)
158 Flap structure
159 Starboard aileron
160 Outboard wing ribs
161 Spar assembly
162 Wing leading-edge de-icing boot
163 Aileron control linkage
164 Wing corrugated inner skin
165 Wingtip structure
166 Starboard navigation light

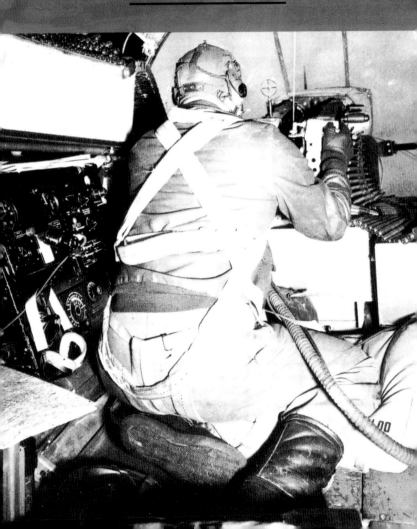

The Boeing Airplane Company was versatile, surviving the lean years after the First World War, and the world recession, by building a wide variety of aircraft: fighters, seaplanes, mail planes, transports and even, a twin-engined bomber, the B-9A. The vast experience gained on these projects stood it in good stead when, in May 1934, the USAAC mooted the idea of a really big bomber.

The standard USAAC bomber at that time was the Martin B-10 and only just entering service. The B-10 was state of the art, an all-metal cantilever construction monoplane with retractable main gears, enclosed crew positions, including a gun turret in the nose, and an internal bomb bay. Its two 775hp Wright Cyclone radial engines were fitted with variable pitch propellers, itself a considerable innovation, and gave it a maximum speed of 213mph (343km/hr); fast enough to make interception by the fighters of that era extremely problematical. At cruising speed it could haul a bomb load of just over one ton out to a target 300 miles (480km) away.

At that time, the United States had retreated into near-isolationism, and was only concerned with its own defensive needs. Neither of the adjoining countries, Canada and Mexico, was regarded as potentially hostile and the Atlantic and Pacific

Left: Nose gun position, showing the ring and bead sight. The semi-kneeling position allows the gunner to move more freely.

Oceans appeared to rule out the possibility of air attack across them. The perceived threat was of enemy fleets approaching the coast; not only of the continental USA, but of Alaska and Hawaii also. The proposed counter to this was a very long-range bomber.

THE BIG BOMBER

The operational requirements specified exceeded all other attempts. They called for a wingspan of 150ft (46m); a maximum weight of 60,000lb (27,200kg); a still air range of 5,000 miles (8,050km) and a bomb load of 2,000lb (900kg). The project was called XBLR-1 (Experimental Bomber, Long Range, No. 1), later abbreviated to Project A. Basically it was a technology demonstrator to determine precisely what was possible. Both Boeing and the Glenn Martin company were invited to submit proposals by 15 June, just one month later.

On 28 June, Boeing received a contract for the design and construction of a single aircraft. This brought problems in its train, caused by the sheer size of the machine. Special jigs had to be made, and it was built in sections in two different plants. By

---

XB-15, BOEING MODEL 294

DIMENSIONS
Wingspan: 149ft 0in (45.41m)
Length: 87ft 7in (26.69m)
Height: 18ft 1in (5.51m)
Wing area: 2,780sq.ft (258.27m²)

WEIGHTS
Empty: 43,000lb (19,505kg)
Max. loaded: 70,706lb (32,072kg)
Bomb load: 8,000lb (3,629kg)

ENGINES
4 x P & W R-1830-11 Twin Wasp radials rated at 850hp each.

PERFORMANCE
Max. speed: 200mph (322km/hr)
Cruise speed: 152mph (245km/hr)
Service ceiling: 18,900ft (5,760m)
Max. range: 5,130 miles (8,254km)
Endurance: 24 hours

XB-15

With nothing to give it scale, the sleek lines of the Boeing Model 294, military designation XB-15, belie its enormous size. Compared to the standard bomber in service with the USAAC at that time, it was double the size and nearly four times heavier, and was expected to carry a similar bomb load seven times further. The huge wings were so deep that crawlways in them enabled mechanics to make adjustments to the engines in flight. With round-the-clock endurance, it needed extra crew and sleeping and cooking accommodation. Its influence on the design of the smaller B-17 is obvious. (Bruce Robertson)

Above: 'Grandpappy', as the XB-15 was known, had a larger wingspan than the B-29 Superfortress. Over an 18-month period it carried more than 100,000lb (45,000kg) of cargo and 5,350 passengers without incident.

the time it was complete, more than two-thirds of a million man-hours had been expended on the Boeing Model 294, while the USAAC had redesignated it the XB-15.

The XB-15 suffered from galloping weight, and maximum weight increased by nearly one-fifth, leaving it underpowered. It was to have been powered by four Allison in-line engines each rated at 1,150hp, but it finally emerged with four Pratt & Whitney Twin Wasp radials of a mere 850hp each.

The wings contained crawl-ways for crewmen to reach the engines in flight to make minor adjustments. Two crews were necessary, and bunk space and a small galley with cooking facilities was provided. Two petrol-driven generators were installed, providing power for all the electrical systems. There was also an automatic pilot, de-icing and fire protection system, plus large flaps to reduce take-off and landing speeds. Defence against air attack consisted of four .30 and two .50 calibre machine guns, in nose, dorsal, ventral and two side blister positions. First flight

took place at Boeing Field, Seattle, on 15 October 1937. It was clearly evident that the power of the four Pratt & Whitney Twin Wasp radials was insufficient to provide the required level of performance. But, the XB-15, quickly dubbed 'Grandpappy', handled well enough by the standards of the era. Accepted by the USAAC in March 1938, it served through most of the Second World War as the XC-105 troop and cargo-carrier, and was extensively used as a flying test bed.

Mass-producing an aircraft such as the XB-15 would be a tremendous drain on resources, both technical and financial. If it could be shown to be a resounding success, then it might be worth the effort. But flight trials were still three years in the future, and it was not practicable to wait so long. The USAAC hedged its bets and thought smaller.

RETHINKING

Less than eight weeks after the contract for the XB-15 was placed, a new requirement was issued in the form of Circular 35-26. What was wanted was a 'multi-engined', which in those days usually meant twin-engined, bomber.

The specification was issued with firm requirements that had to be met, combined with a 'wish list' of 'nice to have' parameters. The proposed new aircraft would carry a bomb load of 2,000lb (900kg) and have a maximum range of at least 1,020 miles (1,640km) and possibly 2,200 miles (3,540km). Maximum speed was to be at least 200mph (322km/hr) but preferably 250mph (402km/hr), and a cruising speed of 170mph (274km/hr) or 220mph (354km/hr). Finally, the service ceiling fluctuated from a low of 20,000ft (6,100m) to a high of 25,000ft (7,600m).

Below: Minus engine cowlings and with nose shrouded, Model 299 is prepared for its press debut on 16 July 1935. The Seattle Daily Times report of the event called it a '15-ton flying fortress', which was later adopted by Boeing. (G.S.Williams)

A flying prototype had to be ready in just 12 months, but in August 1935 no development funding was available. A feature was that the maker of the aircraft selected would receive a contract to build no fewer than 220 bombers, later cut back to 185. This was quite a substantial order for the time, which made Boeing very keen to compete.

While it was expecting the contenders to be twin-engined, the USAAC had no objection to four. This would normally have been surprising but the service knew what it was about. The order placed would be for either 185 twin-engined bombers, or 65 four-engined types.

While the lesser number may have appeared less attractive Boeing's decision to use four engines was made to enhance flight performance. Work on the Boeing Model 299, as it became, was conducted under conditions of semi-flight performance, thereby greatly increasing their chance of success. Prior to this

time, four engines were traditionally used to improve take-off.

Work on the Boeing Model 299, as it became, was conducted under conditions of semi-secrecy. Technology was taken from the XB-15, and the earlier Model 247. The former provided the wing design, scaled down and given tubular truss spars, while the latter influenced the shape of the fuselage. The tail surfaces of all three showed a strong family resemblance.

The urgency of getting the Model 299 ready in time caused it to race ahead of the XB-15, and it was rolled out and shown to the public on 16 July, only 11 months after the go-ahead had been given.

15-TON FLYING FORTRESS

The *Seattle Daily Times* carried a feature the next day together with a photograph bearing the caption '15-ton Flying Fortress'. This caught the imagination of Boeing's man-

BOEING MODEL 299

DIMENSIONS
Wingspan: 103ft 9in (31.62m)
Length: 68ft 9in (20.95m)
Height: 18ft 4in (5.59m)
Wing area: 1,420sq.ft (131.96m²)

WEIGHTS
Maximum: 32,432lb (14,711 kg)
Bomb load: 4,800lb (2,175kg)

ENGINES
4 x Pratt & Whitney R-1690-E Hornet radials, each rated at 750hp.

PERFORMANCE
Max. speed: 236mph (380km/hr)
Cruise speed: 140mph (225mph)
Service ceiling: 24,620ft (7,500m)
Max. range: 3,010 miles (4,840km)

agement, and they duly registered the name. It was very suitable for an aircraft which, like the XB-15, was intended for maritime reconnaissance and anti-shipping roles.

On the ground, the Model 299 was impressive. In polished aluminium and with colourful USAAC wing and tail markings, the sleek, cigar-shaped fuselage looked exactly right. The four radial engines spoke of power, while four streamlined blisters, concealed machine guns.

The maiden flight of the Model 299 took place on the morning of 28 July. All went smoothly. Several more flights followed before the prototype was delivered to the USAAC at Wright Field, Ohio, for official evaluation. The non-stop journey of 2,100 miles (3,380km) took just over nine hours, giving an average speed of 233mph (375km/hr), which in 1935 was quite exceptional.

Y1B-17

One of the major differences between the prototype and the Y1B-17 was a redesigned single strut main gear leg. This had several effects. It saved weight and complexity, and made changing a wheel or a tyre a far simpler operation. Many other changes had been made, but many were still to come. Also clearly visible from this angle is the turbo-supercharger exhaust above the engine nacelle, the efflux from which interfered with the slipstream and caused buffeting. This aircraft is the sole Y1B-17A. (Roger Besecker)

The two other contenders for the contract were Glenn Martin's B-12, and Douglas' DB-1, which was based on the DC-2 airliner, forerunner of the immortal DC-3 Dakota. Against these the Model 299 demonstrated a clear performance advantage, which made it appear certain that it would be the winner. But on the morning of 30 October, the Model 299 stalled and crashed just off the end of the Wright Field runway. It was totally destroyed, and with it died Leslie Tower, and USAAC test pilot Major Ployer Hill. The cause was human error. Control locks, fitted to prevent the moving surfaces from being flapped around by wind while on the ground, had not been released prior to take-off. Once in the air, Model 299 had become uncontrollable.

At the time that the disaster occurred, the final stage of testing, consisting of evaluation flights by service crewmen, had still to take place. With the Model 299 out of the competition, the DB-1 was declared the winner. It entered service as the B-18 Bolo, and after just a few years was to vanish quietly.

The short while that Boeing Model 299 had been evaluated at Wright Field had been long enough to convince many people of its worth. On 12 January 1936 a contract was issued for 14 aircraft, one of which was a static test bed. A new designation was issued, YB-17, the Y prefix denoting pre-production machines, which included modifications that had been found to be desirable during the trials of the prototype.

The main modification was the use of the Wright R-1820-39 Cyclone engine, rated at 850hp. Fabric-covered flaps replaced the original metal items, and the main gears were given single legs in lieu of the original doubles. This made wheel changing a much simpler process. Other changes affected the fuel system, instrument layout, de-icing and oxygen systems. In November of that year, the designation changed once more to become Y1B-17, but this reflected funding arrangements rather than hardware changes. The first Y1B-17 flew on 2 December 1936. Problems were encountered on only its third flight. Engine overheating caused the flight to be cut short; then on touch-down the aircraft tipped onto its nose, fortunately without any injury to the crew.

The brakes had overheated on take-off, then on being retracted while still too hot had seized up solid. A feature of this model was that the panelled transparent nose was able to rotate through a complete circle, allowing the machine gun installed a wide field of fire.

INTO SERVICE

The first delivery to an active service unit was made on 1 March 1937, at Langley Field, Virginia. A further 11 followed, making the 2nd Bombardment Group the first four-engined bomber outfit in the USAAC. The thirteenth Y1B-17 remained at Wright Field for development work.

It was planned to have two B-17 Groups, one on the east coast, the other on the west. A further 50 B-17s were ordered

Above: Y1B-17 of the 2nd BG, which was charged with the operational evaluation of the type.

Below: Part of the 2nd BG over New York City on its way to Buenos Aires in February 1938.

Above: *The 38th Reconnaissance Squadron was unusual in that it operated Y1B-17s in other than the strategic bombing role.*

Above: *The Fortress was tough; All American of the 97th BG returned to base despite being nearly cut in half in a collision with a German fighter. (Boeing)*

for 1938, plus 11 more for development work. Meanwhile the 2nd Bombardment Group was to develop operational techniques for the new bomber. During this work, several records were broken, while the high spot was a goodwill visit to Buenos Aires in February 1938 by a formation of six aircraft. The 5,000 mile (8,050km) flight from Miami was made in just two stages, the big bombers calling at Lima, the capital of Peru, en route.

It was during this period that interservice rivalry reared its ugly head. The US Navy had always regarded itself as the defender of the American coastline, and now observed the activities of the 2nd Bombardment Group with suspicion. Their chance came in May 1938, when three Fortresses of the 2nd Bombardment Group carried out a practice interception of the Italian liner *Rex*.

What really upset the Navy was that the liner was more than 700 miles (1,100km) out in the Atlantic at the time, and the exploit received a lot of publicity. They reacted by accusing the USAAC of poaching on their patch; successfully, it would seem, because from then on, the 2nd Bombardment Group was restricted to within a limit of 100 miles (160km) of the coast! This was followed by a directive from the Secretary of State for War that in 1940 the USAAC was to procure only tactical bombers.

This was reversed by the Munich crisis in September, when it was planned to make a significant increase in air striking power. Meanwhile, the 2nd Bombardment Group had flown a total of 9,293 hours without a single serious accident, and had developed suitable navigation methods and tactics.

The development machines provided valuable data, none more so than one that flew into a thunderstorm, where it was exposed to structural stresses far greater than those planned for the ground test article. The Y1B-17 ended in a spin, from which it recovered, remarkably for such a large aircraft. The evidence of structural integrity made the static test machine redundant, and it was assigned to flight trials with turbo-superchargers fitted as the Y1B-17A.

First flight was made on 20 November. The exhaust from the turbo-superchargers was initially expelled above the engine nacelles, but this caused buffeting. A redesign brought the exhaust below the wing, which cured the problem.

TRIALS COMPLETED

The increase in performance was dramatic. Maximum speed increased to 311mph (500km/hr), while service ceiling went to 38,000ft (11,600m). These figures were of course for a lightly loaded aircraft; a full load of fuel and bombs reduced these figures significantly. The Y1B-17A set a record by carrying 11,000lb (5,000kg) over a distance of 620 miles (1,000km) at an average speed of 238mph (383km/hr). A typical operational capability was 2,400lb (1,100kg) of bombs for 1,500 miles (2,400km).

With operational trials completed, Y1B-17s became B-17s, while the single Y1B-17A became the B-17A. The initial

Left: *Nose cupola 'more appropriately located in an amusement park than in a war aeroplane' was the comment of Air Commodore Arthur Harris RAF on inspecting the Y1B-17.*

B-17B

Only 39 B-17Bs were built. They were very similar in external appearance to the Y1B-17, the main changes being turbo-supercharged Wright Cyclone engines as standard, giving a significant performance increment, a larger, redesigned rudder for greater lateral stability at high altitudes, and a revised transparent nose with an optically flat panel in front of the bombsight. Many other changes took place under the skin. It was a step in the right direction.

production batch of Fortresses was ordered. These started life as Boeing Model 299Es, but the performances demonstrated by the B-17A resulted in the adoption of turbo-supercharged engines, among other things. They then became 299Ms or, in USAAC service, B-17Bs.

The maiden flight of a B-17B came on 27 June 1939. Externally it looked very similar to its predecessor. Engines apart, the main differences were a larger and reshaped rudder and a new nose transparency with an optically flat panel for bomb aiming replacing the previous ventral window.

Internally, crew positions were revised as a result of 2nd Bombardment Group experience; the pneumatic brakes were supplanted by a hydraulic system, and the top-secret Norden bombsight was fitted. This last was to become notorious, less for its alleged accuracy than for the tight security measures that surrounded it. It was

installed, still under wraps, in the aircraft shortly before take-off, and removed again right after landing, always with an armed guard in attendance.

All 39 B-17Bs were delivered between 29 July 1939 and 30 March 1940, and this variant became the first to equip an

operational Air Corps outfit. But even before the first arrived, work was in hand on an improved variant, of which 38 were ordered in 1939. This was the Model 299H, or B-17C.

This new aircraft featured several modifications, many of them influenced by the twin demands of greater survivability and improved performance. Externally, the greatest changes made were to the defensive gun positions. The lateral blisters had been found to provide an inadequate field of fire, and in any case caused unnecessary drag. They were consequently replaced by teardrop-shaped transparencies flush with the cylindrical fuselage, with pintle-mounted machine guns which gave a wider field of fire. The ventral blister gun was supplanted by a longer and more solid 'bathtub'. The dorsal blister was removed, and replaced by a sliding transparency faired to

Y1B-17

The waist gun blisters of the Y1 B-17 were innovative but not very practical. They were an attempt to provide the greater field of fire of a turret while minimizing aerodynamic drag. In service it was found that while they gave a reasonable arc of fire, elevation and depression were very limited, while drag was considerable, and disturbance of the slipstream adversely affected the tailplane and elevators. As protection against attacks from astern they were ineffective, as even at maximum traverse they left a considerable arc uncovered, while the tailplane shielded a significant area.

The B-17C was the first Flying Fortress to see action. Among other changes it did away with the stylish but aerodynamically and defensively unsound gun blisters. The waist positions were made flush, although the original teardrop-shaped opening was retained so as to minimize structural changes. The ventral position was replaced by a much more solid bathtub, while the dorsal blister was omitted altogether and replaced by a sliding transparent fairing. The revised and enlarged rudder first introduced on the B-17B is seen to advantage here on this B-17C, in RAF service as the Fortress I.

B-17C DATA

DIMENSIONS
Wingspan: 103ft 9in (31.62m)
Length: 67ft 11in (20.70m)
Height: 15ft 5in (4.70m)
Wing area: 1,420sq.ft (131.96m²)

WEIGHTS
Empty: 31,150lb (14,130kg)
Max. loaded: 49,650lb (22,520kg)
Bomb load: 4,800lb (2,180kg)

ENGINES
4 x Wright Cyclone R-1820-65 turbo-supercharged radials each rated at 1,200hp.

PERFORMANCE
Max. speed: 320mph (515km/hr)
Cruise speed: 232mph (373km/hr)
Service ceiling: 36,000ft (11,000m)
Normal range: 2,100 miles (3,380km)
Climb rate: 1,300ft/min (6.60m/sec)

were Wright Cyclone R-1820-65 radials each rated at 1,200hp, driving constant speed, fully-feathering three-bladed propellers.

THE B-17C

The first flight of a B-17C took place on 21 July 1940, by which time the Second World War had been running for ten months. While the ground war in Western Europe remained static until May 1940, British, French and German bombers had all been active. Much early combat

the contours of the fuselage. Finally, the central nose gun was replaced by two gun mountings in side windows.

Other changes included armour protection for the crew and self-sealing fuel tanks. All-up weight increased to 49,650lb (22,500kg), and the engines

experience, particularly that of the Royal Air Force, which set great store by heavily armed strategic bombers, had filtered back across the Atlantic, influencing American thinking.

This resulted in the B-17D, of which 42 were ordered. The USAAC recognized the need for greater defensive fire power and for increased survivability. The dorsal and ventral gun positions were modified to accept twin .50 calibre machine guns, while more armour was added. Cowl flaps were introduced on the engine nacelles, the bomb racks were redesigned, with a new release mechanism, and 24 volt electrics replaced the original 12 volt system. Deliveries of the B-17D began in February 1941, and the order was completed by the end of April. B-17Cs in USAAC service were also modified to D standard. But at the end of the day, the Dog was still an interim type.

Below: The B-17E featured a complete redesign of the entire rear fuselage and tail unit to make room for a tail turret. (Frank F. Smith)

By an irony of fate, the Flying Fortress did not make its combat debut in either its designed role of coastal defence, or even in the service of its country of origin. Instead it went to war as a high-altitude bomber with the Royal Air Force.

The Fortress got off to an unpromising start. With war looming, a British Purchasing Commission visited the United States in 1938 with the task of investigating the possibility of acquiring American aircraft. With it was Air Commodore Arthur Harris, later to become famous as Commander-in-Chief of RAF Bomber Command between 1942 and 1945. He also inspected a Y1B-17 of the 2nd Bombardment

Above: Boeing got the serial letters wrong on the batch of Fortress Is for the RAF; they should be AN, not AM. On the left is Air Chief Marshal Sir Hugh Dowding, the former head of RAF Fighter Command during the Battle of Britain. (Bruce Robertson)

Group at Langley Field. Harris was scathing on the subject of its gun armament, and concluded that it was far too vulnerable against any modern fighter. His comment on the nose cupola was that it was 'more appropriately located in an amusement park than in a war aeroplane'.

At the time, this was of course fair comment. But Boeing and the USAAC were aware of these and other shortcomings, and were making every effort to correct them. By the end of 1940, the single most glaring deficiency was the lack of a power-operated gun turret.

By this time, the RAF had discovered through hard experience that daylight raids on targets in the Third Reich, where

Left: As the Japanese swept across the Pacific, the Panama Canal took on a new importance. B–17s spent many weary hours patrolling the area. This is a B–17E with the early ventral turret. (USAF)

Below: A Messerschmitt Me 109 can just be seen in front of B–17F Virgin's Delight of the 91st BG, performing the Split–S breakaway manoeuvre. (USAF)

ME 109E

The Messerschmitt Me 109E was the standard German interceptor during 1940 and most of 1941, and thus was the fighter that the Fortress I had to defeat. Powered by a Daimler-Benz 601 liquid-cooled engine, it could reach a maximum speed of 354mph (570km/hr) at 12,500ft (3,800m). While its service ceiling was marginally better than that of the Fortress I, speed, rate of climb and manoeuvrability were all greatly reduced at extreme altitudes.

THE BOEING B-17 FLYING FORTRESS

Above: Belly landing! A B-17 of the 379th BG touches down tail-first at Kimbolton. The ball turret has been jettisoned and all looks good. This group flew more sorties and dropped a greater weight of bombs than any other. (Bill Smith)

strong fighter opposition might be encountered, were likely to incur unacceptable losses.

The standard German day fighter of the period was the Messerschmitt Me 109E. It would take something over 30 minutes for the fighters to reach 30,000ft (9,150m). And once they did get there, both their maximum speed and their manoeuvrability would be greatly reduced.

WAS HEIGHT THE KEY?

In the space of 30 minutes, a bomber cruising at 180mph (290km/hr) would cover a distance of 90 miles (145km). At that time there was little information about the German early warning system, but unless this could provide significantly more than half an hour's notice of impending attack, the chances were that the bombers would be able to do their work before the fighters arrived. And even if adequate early warning was available, ground control would need to be very precise in order to position the fighters correctly

for an interception.

Flying at such extreme altitudes appeared to offer bombers relative immunity from fighter interception, and almost total immunity from flak. A trio of British four-engined heavy bombers was entering service at about this time, but they were unable to reach such a high perch. The Flying Fortress had sufficient altitude capability, and of course this was coupled with the much-vaunted accuracy of the top-secret Norden bombsight.

TRIALS AND TRIBULATIONS

Initial British approaches for the Fortress were made in the summer of 1940, but not until the end of the year was the request approved, when 20 B-17Cs were released. Unfortunately these were not fitted with self-sealing fuel tanks, and had to be returned to Boeing for these to be installed. The delay thus caused was considerable, and not until April 1941 were the first four aircraft ready for delivery.

The first B-17C, known in RAF service as the Fortress I, arrived at Watton in Norfolk on 14 April. Others followed, and by the end of the third week, 14 had been delivered. Certain modifications were needed; standard British radio and signals equipment, identification

FORTRESS 1

Fortress I of No. 90 Squadron, RAF Bomber Command, the specially formed unit which pioneered very high altitude bombing, and with which the Flying Fortress made its combat debut. This aircraft, AN 530, F for Freddie, had an eventful career. It arrived in England on 10 July 1941; just too late to take part in the initial raid on Wilhelmshaven but, as one of the more reliable aircraft, it was selected for the abortive Berlin raid on 23 July. On 2 August it fought off attacks by three Me 109Fs of 3/JG 52, shooting down Feldwebel Wilhelm Summerer and damaging the other two. It was later transferred to No. 220 Squadron of Coastal Command and struck off charge in September 1943. (Bruce Robertson)

lights etc, and all guns except the one in the nose were replaced by .50 Brownings. Most important of all was the bombsight. The Norden was still top secret and had not been released; however RAF Fortresses were to have the Sperry Mk 0-1. This was duly installed, together with a Sperry autopilot system which, coupled to the sight, allowed the bomb aimer to make flat turns while lining up on target.

The recipient of the Fortress I was No. 90 Squadron, which was faced with the initial task of selecting men physically capable of standing up to the extremely demanding high-altitude operational environment. This was far from easy; nearly two-thirds of applicants failed the medical.

As soon as sufficient personnel had been accepted and crewmen had been converted onto type, high-altitude training was initiated. This revealed a number of problems.

The USAAC considered the optimum bombing altitude to be 20,000ft (6,100m), whereas the RAF proposed operating the Fortress I at least 50 per cent higher, and probably even more, in temperatures of -40° Celsius or even lower.

PROBLEMS

Two related factors caused unexpected problems; the first was the low temperature and atmospheric pressure encountered at 30,000ft (9,150m) and above; the second was the delta temperature and atmospheric pressure; the difference between ground level and high altitude. These played havoc with

the engines and other systems.

The former caused many Cyclones (but not all) to throw oil from the crankcase breather pipes. The turbo-superchargers became unduly sensitive to ham-fisted control movements, surging at the least provocation, with the turbine blower breaking up in consequence. Heated window panels were needed to keep them clear of frost, while the autopilot/bombsight coupling caused violent yaws if the gyros had not been synchronized beforehand. The extreme changes in temperature and pressure during the course of a standard mission caused engine exhaust flanges to fracture, and was responsible for hydraulic leaks which allowed air to infiltrate the system.

Watton was a grass field not really suitable for such heavy machines, and pending the completion of a new airfield at Polebrook, with hard runways and taxiways, No. 90 Squadron moved to Great Massingham. It was during a flight from here,

Above: The 305th BG which, under the command of Curtis LeMay, did so much to get the tactics right. Station-keeping in the formation ahead appears to leave much to be desired. (USAF)

shortly before the projected move to Polebrook, that the first serious accident occurred.

In June a Fortress I on a training flight over Yorkshire failed to climb above a thunderhead, and entered it. The giant bomber was pounded by huge hailstones, while a thick layer of ice built up on the wings. This destroyed the lift, forcing the bomber into a death-dive. As it tumbled from the sky, the forces exerted on the unlucky machine wrenched off a wing then tore the fuselage in half. The only survivor was Flight Lieutenant Steward, a medical officer from the Royal Aircraft Establishment at Farnborough, who managed to parachute to safety. Lieutenant Bradley, an American B-17 pilot, was the first airman of the USAAF to die on active service.

Above: Damaged over Bremen, this 100th BG Fortress made a spectacular crashlanding when a propeller came off after touch-down. Over 800 holes were counted from the radio room aft. *(John Kidd)*

FIRST ACTION

The essentials for a very high altitude bombing mission were clear weather and near-perfect visibility. If the target area cannot be identified from many miles away, and the actual target cannot be clearly seen from nearly 6 miles (9km) up, there is little point in even starting out. These conditions were met on 8 July, and three Fortresses were despatched from Polebrook. The crews, led by the squadron commander, Wing Commander MacDougall, were perhaps not as well trained as they might have been, but political pressure was exerted by those eager to see how the big bird would acquit itself in action.

The target was Wilhelmshaven. The three Fortress Is were to fly there in loose formation, closing up only if fighters were encountered. They would bomb the naval base individually from 30,000ft (9,150m) with four American-type 1,100lb (500kg) bombs,

then, climb away from the target area to make the task of interception even more difficult.

As Robbie Burns once observed, 'The best laid plans of mice and men gang oft agley!' He might have added aviators. On the climb-out from base, all four engines of one Fortress started throwing oil, which streamed back and froze on the tail surfaces. This set up intense vibration, forcing its pilot to abandon the main mission and seek a target of opportunity.

The other two pressed on. They reached Wilhelmshaven and attacked with no intervention from the defences, but two bombs on the leading aircraft failed to release due to a frozen solenoid. This was the first of many failures caused by extreme

cold and high humidity. On trials the Americans had not gone so high, nor was there much humidity over the bombing ranges in Nevada or Utah. Humidity in particular bedevilled Fortress operations for the next two years. But even the bombs that did drop missed their targets. It was concluded that the physical problems encountered at high altitude in unpressurized aircraft were greater than had been thought, and made bombing accuracy very hard to achieve.

After the Fortresses left the target area, two black specks were sighted climbing towards them by Tom Danby, a beam gunner in the squadron commander's aircraft. Fighters! The Fortresses lifted their noses and climbed laboriously, but to no avail. The Messerschmitt Me 109s easily drew level with Danby's aircraft. Danby lined up his sight and took first pressure on the trigger. As he did so, his pilot commenced a gentle turn towards the direction of attack. This forced the German

Below: Pillars of dark smoke denote hits on an oil refinery by the preceding wave, as more bombers bore in to attack. *(USAF)*

Above: Fortress I, formerly of No. 90 Squadron, seen here in the colours of No. 220 Squadron Coastal Command, escorting a convoy across the Atlantic. (Alfred Price)

pilot to tighten his turn, but as he did so, his wings lost their grip on the rarified air and he literally fell out of the sky! No shooting was done by either side, which was probably just as well because there was more than a fair chance that the guns of the Fortress were frozen up.

The next raid was a complete fiasco. On 23 July, three Fortresses set out to attack Berlin in daylight. Over Denmark they started leaving long white contrails, pointers in the sky that led the fighters straight to them. Far below, the crewmen could see menacing black specks, frantically grabbing for height but as yet nowhere near them. Over Denmark, the three Fortresses turned southwards towards

Below: Nineteen B-17Fs served with RAF Coastal Command as the Fortress II. This aircraft was written off in the Azores in 1944 after a taxiing accident. (Bruce Robertson)

Berlin, only to be faced with a solid wall of cloud. With no chance of locating their targets through it, they turned back, frozen and frustrated.

Other raids followed. On 24 July Brest was attacked, and hits were claimed on the battle cruisers *Scharnhorst* and *Gneisenau*. Emden was raided two days later. On 2 August a Fortress was attacked north of Texel at only 22,000ft (6,700m) by three Me 109Fs, which made seven passes at the bomber, hitting it, but not seriously. One German fighter was shot down into the sea, a second was damaged and force-landed, while the third suffered some minor damage from the Fortress's return fire.

The first high-altitude fighter engagement that took place was a much more deadly affair. The same crew was caught at 32,000ft (9,750m) over Brest by seven Messerschmitts on 16 August and subjected to 26 attacks in quick succession. The pilot put the bomber into a shallow dive for maximum

speed, taking evasive action against each attack. Eventually he escaped into cloud, but not before two crewmen had been killed and another two wounded. The Fortress crashed on landing and burned. Then a four-aircraft attack against the German pocket battleship *Admiral Scheer* at Oslo on 8 September also encountered fighters. One bomber was shot down, another went missing without trace. The third returned too badly damaged to be repairable. At high altitude the Fortress I was proving too vulnerable in daylight, the bomb load was too small and the bombing too inaccurate.

The final Fortress operational mission from Polebrook was flown on 25 September, bringing the total to 48 sorties, 26 of which were aborted. At this point, four aircraft were detached to Egypt, from where they carried out maritime reconnaissance missions over the Mediterranean, and night attacks on Tobruk and other North African targets. It was found that the heat and dust of the desert reduced performance and service ability, and the two survivors of this period were sent to India, where they were eventually handed over to the USAAF.

Back at Polebrook, experimental high altitude flights

Above: Action replay of the Pearl Harbour attack, as a 'Japanese Zero' swoops down on a landing Fortress at the annual air show at Oshkosh. The B-17 is specially modified to put one main gear and the tail wheel down to simulate battle damage. (Eric Lundahl)

continued for a while. By this time the oil throwing and freezing-up of the guns had largely been cured. The remaining Fortress Is were transferred to No. 220 Squadron of Coastal Command.

PACIFIC CRUCIBLE

By December 1941, the USAAF had about 150 Flying Fortresses, flying reconnaissance missions. Most were based in the continental USA, but some flew anti-submarine patrols from Newfoundland.

The 19th Bombardment Group was based at Hickam Field, right next door to Pearl Harbour on Oahu in the Hawaiian Islands. In the Philippines, at that time an American Protectorate, were 35 B-17Cs and Ds of the 7th Bombardment Group, based at Clark Field. Both Groups were about to be reinforced, and a dozen aircraft were in transit to them. When the Japanese carrier aircraft made a surprise strike against the American fleet at Pearl Harbour on the 7th of the

month, the attack finally brought America into the war.

At Hickam Field, the 19th Bombardment Group was caught on the ground by the Japanese attack, and all 12 aircraft were destroyed. The reinforcements for the 7th and 19th Bombardment Groups arrived at the height of the raid; low on fuel and unarmed, they were unable to defend themselves. Four were destroyed and all the others damaged.

The Japanese turned their attention to the Philippines, destroying 14 B-17s of the 19th Bombardment Group on the ground at Clark Field. A single squadron from this group had been deployed to Del Monte, 200 miles (320km) further south, so some of the group escaped this attack unscathed.

The surviving Fortresses of the 19th were employed against the Japanese invasion force, with little success, for ships at sea proved elusive targets.

Fighter opposition was provided by the Mitsubishi A6M2 Zero, and two encounters with Fortresses took place in the first few days of fighting. On 10 December, a Japanese landing force of one light cruiser, six destroyers and four transports, was off-loading at Vigan on Luzon. At an altitude of 18,000ft (5,500m) above them flew 27 covering Zeros, one of them piloted by Saburo Sakai, later to become the top surviving Japanese fighter ace (62 kills).

Six B-17Ds of the 14th Bombardment Squadron were sent against the invaders. They bombed from 25,000ft (7,600m), and succeeded in doing little

ZERO ATTACK
'This was our first experience with the B-17, and the airplane's size caused us to misjudge our firing distance. The bomber's speed, for which we had made no allowance, threw our range finders off. All through the attack the Fortress kept up a steady stream of fire at us from its gun positions. Fortunately the accuracy of the enemy gunners was no better than our own.'
SABURO SAKAI, ZERO PILOT.

damage. One of their number, was spotted after the attack, and seven avenging Zeros set off in hot pursuit.

The Zeros were slower than their European counterparts, and had additional height to gain. Not until 100 miles (160km) further on did they catch the speeding bomber. Before they could gain a firing position, three other Zeros appeared ahead and attacked from above, but with absolutely no effect.

At last the pursuers caught up, making pass after pass, again with no apparent effect. The chase lasted a further 50 miles (80km), taking them over the US base at Clark Field. Sakai then took a hand. With two other fighters in attendance he closed right in, braving the

ZERO FIGHTER
The Mitsubishi Zero was optimized for dogfighting rather than bomber interception. Japanese engines of the time lacked power, and to maximize manoeuvrability and performance by reducing weight, the Zero had no armour plating, no self-sealing fuel tanks, and often no radio. It was therefore very vulnerable to return fire.

Above: General MacArthur's personal transport, Bataan, had reclining seats and hot and cold running water installed. (USAF)

Below: This E-model became a personal transport for General George Kenney. (USAF)

defensive fire. Fuel streamed back from the ruptured tanks, its gunners ceased firing, and fire broke out in the fuselage. The crew baled out, but the pilot did not manage to escape. It was the first Flying Fortress to fall to Japanese fighters in the Pacific.

Four days later, a battle against even heavier odds ended differently. On 14 December, a B-17D of the 19th Bombardment Group became separated from its formation. When he was just about to bomb a Japanese freighter from low altitude, he found himself bounced by 18 Zeros.

The Japanese fighters made attack after attack, knocking out the left outboard motor, the radio and the oxygen system, shooting off the tail wheel, riddling the fuselage, holing the fuel tanks, damaging the control runs and killing one crewman. The Fortress gunners fought back desperately, claiming three fighters shot down, but their guns either jammed or ran out of ammunition. It looked like the end of the road, but the remaining Japanese fighters had also run out of ammunition.

This was perhaps less surprising than it may seem. Zeros carried a mere five seconds-worth of ammunition for their 20mm cannon, while their rifle-calibre machine guns were virtually useless against a Fortress. The B-17D sustained over 1,000 hits and still kept flying, although it was eventually wrecked in the forced landing on Mindanao.

THE B-17 ENTERS SERVICE

The Japanese overran the Philippines by the end of December, and the handful of Fortresses were pulled back to Darwin in Northern Australia. From there it was about 1,500 miles (2,400km) to targets in the southern Philippines, which meant that the bomb load that could be carried was exceedingly small; less than two tons in many cases. The B-17s were sent to Java. There were so few of them, but they were the only aircraft available with the necessary range to reach Japanese bridgeheads in Borneo and elsewhere, and even then they needed to stage through those Allied airfields which had not yet fallen.

By now the improved B-17E was entering service, and more than 50 of these were sent to reinforce the theatre, although Japanese successes forced them to come via Africa and India. Attrition was heavy; nearly two-thirds of the available Fortresses were lost in the first three months of the Pacific War. During this period, Fortresses claimed to have sunk three warships, including the battleship *Haruna*, and eight transports, in the course of some 350 sorties. Japanese records showed that only two transports probably succumbed to air attack by Fortresses.

After two months operating out of airfields on Java the Allies had to evacuate in the face of Japanese advances, and once more the surviving Fortresses found themselves back in Australia. But by this time, very few of the original B-17Cs and Ds were left, and their replacement, the B-17E, was a very different bird indeed.

When in December 1941 the USA entered the war, both the RAF and the USAAF were agreed on one thing: for the immediate future, the Third Reich could only be effectively attacked from the air. The primary disagreement was as to how. As a result of hard experience, the RAF had, with a few notable exceptions, abandoned daylight raids in favour of the cover of darkness, and argued strongly that the Americans should join them in this.

The USAAF, however, was not convinced. The British night crews were unable to land their bombs within 5 miles (8km) of their targets. It consisted of little more than exporting bombs to 'somewhere in Germany'. Area bombing, which was to devastate German cities in the next three years, had not yet matured. The truth was that while night

Above: 8th AF commander General Jimmy Doolittle talks to a weather reconnaissance crew on their return. Second from left is Flying Officer Eldridge, an RAF weather observer. (USAF)

Left: Fortresses of the 381st BG leave contrails emblazoned across the sky, while two fighters hurtle across them high above. (USAF)
Below: Typical European weather made navigation, target finding and accurate bombing far more difficult than the USAAF expected. B-17F Meat Hound of the 306th BG in cloudy skies. (USAF)

attacks tied down valuable German resources in the shape of flak and night fighters, they were at that time doing little real damage.

The USAAF view was that precision attacks on industrial targets would be far more effective, and these could only be carried out in daylight. Daylight made accurate navigation much easier, and also the precise identification of industrial complexes. The American Norden tachometric bomb sight was inherently far more accurate than the British Mk XIV vector

sight. On the bombing range in peacetime in clear visibility, releasing from an altitude of 10,000ft (3,050m), circular error probability (the radius within which the best 50 per cent of bombs fall) was about 300ft (90m) for the Norden and 775ft (235m) for the Mk XIV.

In combat, heavy and accurate flak would force the bombers to climb to much greater altitudes. Not only did circular error probability increase significantly with height, but shrapnel rattling against the wings and fuselage was a distraction to the bombardier. European weather

Above: Airfields for the USAAF bombers were hastily prepared. An open-air bomb dump at Framlingham, with tented accommodation. (USAF).

conditions bore no similarity to those of California. All these factors conspired against the highly accurate Norden bombsight. But there was no substitute for practical experience, and the USAAF decided to press ahead and see for itself.

The ultra-high altitude bombing pioneered by the RAF in late 1941 was not repeated. Instead the American heavy bombers attacked in close for-

mation from rather lower levels, relying on their defensive armament to beat off the German fighters. The new and better protected B-17E and F were coming on stream, and the vulnerability against attack from astern had been reduced.

But before operations could start, there was much to be done. RAF Bomber Command was expanding fast, and new airfields sprang up like mushrooms across England. More airfields were needed for their American allies, and providing these took time.

THE FIRST BOMB GROUP

Nor was the USAAF ready initially. The basic unit was the Bombardment Group (BG), which consisted of a headquarters and three squadrons, quickly increased to four, each of which had an establishment of 8–10 aircraft. The demand for personnel, training and aircraft initially outstripped supply. It was

B–17 UNITS THAT BECAME OPERATIONAL IN ENGLAND 1942

Group No.	Squadrons	Base	First Mission	Notes
97	340, 341, 342, 414	Polebrook	17 Aug 42	to North Africa Nov 42
32	301, 352, 353, 419	Chelveston	5 Sept 42	to North Africa Nov 42
92	325, 326, 327, 407	Alconbury	Sept 42	training unit after four missions, returned to ops May 43 with YB–40
306	367, 368, 368, 423	Thurleigh	9 Oct 42	Last mission 19 Apr 42
91	322, 323, 324, 401	Bassingbourn	7 Nov 42	Last mission 25 Apr 42
303	358, 359, 369, 427	Molesworth	17 Nov 42	Last mission 25 Apr 45
305	364, 365, 366, 422	Grafton Underwood	17 Nov 42	Last mission 25 Apr 45

months before the first USAAF Bombardment Group (Heavy) was able to take off and point its Fortresses eastwards, across the cold grey Atlantic.

The first unit to arrive in England was the 97th BG, equipped with B-17Es; it was followed by other units with the newer B-17F. The recently formed US 8th Air Force had received its first weapons. Intensive training followed, and a period of acclimatization to European weather conditions.

The first mission was flown by the 97th BG, which was based at Polebrook, on 17 August 1942. Twelve B-17Es raided the Sotteville mar-shalling yards at Rouen, strongly escorted by four RAF Spitfire squadrons. Visibility was good and about half the bombs land-ed in the target area. Two bombers were slightly damaged by flak. It was a promising debut and all seemed set fair for the 8th AF, with the 301st SBG in pre-combat training and the

Above: Fortresses on Iceland, 21 July 1942.

Below: A Fortress breaks up and goes down over northern France after being hit on the way to the target. (USAF)

Above: Two B-17F Fortresses of the 91st BG arrive in England late in 1942. In the foreground are a Hurricane (left) and a Fairchild Argus (right) of the RAF. (Merle Olmsted)

92nd BG arriving. Due shortly were the 306th, 91st, 303rd and 305th BGs.

The 97th was given no time to rest. Two dozen B-17Es bombed Abbeville airfield on 19 August during the Dieppe Raid, and the next day 12 aircraft attacked the Amiens marshalling yards, again with a Spitfire escort. All the bombers returned unscathed on both occasions, having seen little of German fighters.

Shallow penetrations over enemy territory continued for the rest of the month; sometimes the bombing was accurate, at others it was less so. In September the 301st and 92nd BGs became operational, and joined the fray. Then on 6 September, the Luftwaffe reacted strongly, penetrated the escorting fighters and shot down two of the 20 B-17s. The loss of 10 per cent of the raiding force came as a nasty shock.

In November, just as the B-17 force was getting into its stride, the 97th and 301st BGs were transferred to the 12th Air Force in North Africa, while the 92nd BG became a B-17 'finishing school', and did not return to action until September of the following year. This left only the 306th BG in the front line, although it was joined during the month by the 91st, 303rd and 305th BGs. The latter two units flew their first mission on 17 November.

It was not an auspicious start. The target was the U-boat base at St Nazaire, but it was obscured by heavy cloud. Those that managed to bomb were met with fierce flak, though they all returned. The 303rd had no such luck. They completely failed to find the target, and brought their bombs home. On the following day, the 303rd managed to bomb St Nazaire. The problem was that the briefed target was La Pallice, over 100 miles (160km) away! This was the very thing that daylight raiding was supposed to avoid. Then, four days later, only 11 out of 76 bombers

despatched were able to find Lorient.

The final months of 1942 were very much a proving period for the B-17 units. Methods and tactics were in a continual state of flux. Formations were changed in an attempt to use the heavy defensive armament to its best advantage, while allowing concentrated bombing. The leader in this field was Colonel Curtis LeMay, commanding the 305th BG at Chelveston. One of the problems to be overcome was that of bomb aiming. It was impossible to keep a tight formation yet still have every aircraft aim individually, without risking multiple mid-air collisions. Having sorted out his optimum formation, LeMay solved the aiming problem by having everyone drop when they saw the leader's bombs go down. Against all but pinpoint targets it was good enough, and it ensured concentration. As 1942 drew to a close, the 8th had neither raided Germany nor attempted a deep penetration so far. But this was not far off.

1943
THE TEMPO INCREASES

The Casablanca Directive, signed on 21 January 1943, listed target types in order of priority. They were: U-boat construction; aircraft construction; transport; fuel; other industries. Six days later, the 8th AF put this into practice as 67 B-17s set off to raid the U-boat construction yards at Vegesack, the first German target scheduled.

As was so often the case, the primary target was socked in by

REVISED 18–AIRCRAFT GROUP DEC 1942

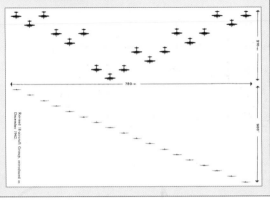

The revised 18-aircraft Bomb Group formation, introduced in December 1942. The requirements were threefold; a concentrated bomb pattern which called for a narrow frontage; concentration of defensive firepower, which called for close formation, and freedom from masking the defensive guns, which demanded vertical staggering of aircraft. Formations changed throughout the course of the war, culminating in 1945 with a 36-aircraft BG occupying a frontage of 1,170ft (356m), with four nine-aircraft squadrons staggered through 1,150ft (350m) vertically.

cloud, and the secondary, which was Wilhelmshaven, was attacked instead, although with poor results. Fortunately the flak was ineffective, and the FW 190 pilots of JG.1, lacking experience in estimating range against anything as large as a B-17, failed to press home their attacks. Three bombers were shot down for 22 German fighters claimed, which seemed a good rate of exchange.

Appalling weather foiled planned raids on Germany over the next few months, while the Luftwaffe fighters polished their tactics and became ever more effective. Although much of the early bombing effort was directed against the U-boats, it quickly became apparent that measures against the fighters were badly needed. In the largest raid so far, 115 B-17s took off on 17 April, their target the Focke-Wulf factory at Bremen.

Fighters arrived in force as the bombing run commenced, and wave after wave of them attacked from head-on. The leading wing, consisting of the 91st and 306th BGs, suffered the worst of the onslaught. In the former the entire low squadron went down, while the latter lost 10 out of 16 aircraft. Total losses for the mission were 16; one to flak, the rest to fighters. This amounted to 14 per cent of the entire force, while another 48 bombers returned with varying degrees of damage. This rate of attrition could not be sustained. The one apparent bright spot was the claim for 63 German fighters destroyed, but this turned out to be misleading.

GUNNER CLAIMS

Overclaiming has always been a feature of air warfare, and arises from confusion caused by the rapidity of events. This was

Right: A tight 'ladder' of bombs goes down from a B-17F of the 96th BG. In the background are other groups in ragged formations, while flak bursts stain the sky. (Boeing via Alfred Price)

54-AIRCRAFT COMBAT WING FORMATION INTRODUCED MARCH 1943

The 54-aircraft Combat Wing, consisting of three Bomb Groups each of 18 aircraft, was introduced in March 1943. Its aims were basically those of the Bomb Group formation; bombing concentration and defensive security. At first it occupied a box of sky some 1⅓ miles (2km) wide, 1,800ft (550m) from front to rear, and 2,900ft (880m) vertically. This proved unwieldy, and it was condensed into just over ½ mile (900m) wide, 1,275ft (390m) front to rear, and 2,700ft (820m) vertically.

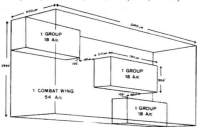

inevitable. Several dozen gunners blazed away at one fighter; if it went down they all claimed it in good faith. Figures for the period allowed 450 claims for fighters destroyed to be upheld, but the true figure was in all probability fewer than 50. Total bomber losses for the same period amounted to 103. The false picture gave rise to unfounded optimism in the USAAF.

Escort fighters were in desperate short supply. The British Spitfire was too short-legged for the task; the Republic P-47 Thunderbolt was a little better, but not by much, while the twin-engined Lockheed P-38 Lightning was no match for the Focke-Wulfs and Messerschmitts in a dogfight. It was at this point that the 92nd BG returned to operations, bringing with them the YB-40

gunship, of which so much was hoped. As related previously, these were a failure and were withdrawn from service in September of that year.

On 22 June came the deepest penetration yet when 235 Fortresses raided the synthetic rubber plant at Huls, in the Ruhr. To minimize fighter opposition, a feint course was flown to deceive the German fighter controllers, while both the RAF and USAAF mounted diversionary operations. This worked in part, but one of the

Right: Not all losses were due to enemy action. A B-17F of the 91st BG sheds its tailplane without realizing that another aircraft has strayed almost directly beneath it. The first bomb strikes the tailplane without detonating, bending it down. In the final picture the Fortress goes down out of control; the victim of poor lookout and less than perfect station-keeping. (Boeing)

diversionary forces suffered heavily. The main force landed just under 25 per cent of their bombs on target, which was a good result for the time. The plant was out of action for a month and production reduced for five months thereafter. Sixteen Fortresses of the main force failed to return, a more acceptable 6.8 per cent, one of them a YB-40 hit by flak, but no fewer than 170 were damaged.

The weather improved in late July, and a series of heavy raids was made by forces of 250–300 bombers. The deeper penetrations were often combined with raids on targets in occupied Europe by medium bombers, splitting the defender's strength. On 28 July, bombers returning from Oschersleben beset by German fighters were

Left: Lockheed P-38 Lightnings escorting Fortresses of the 381st BG late in 1943. (USAF)
Below: Flames streaming from the starboard wing and separated from its formation, a Fortress is remorselessly hunted down by a FW 190 after raiding the aircraft plant at Oschersleben. (USAF)

met at the Dutch border by more than 100 P-47s equipped with new drop tanks to extend their radius of action. These shot down nine of their assailants in short order. It was the shape of things to come.

SCHWEINFURT

It was 17 August 1943, the anniversary of the raid on Rouen, and the event was celebrated with the most ambitious deep penetration yet. Early that morning, 147 Fortresses took

off to attack the Messerschmitt works at Regensburg, escorted by Thunderbolts as far as the German border. Shortly after, another 230 B-17s would take off, bound for the ball-bearing factories at Schweinfurt. These had no escort, as the German fighters would be on the ground refuelling and rearming. At least, that was how it was planned. In the event the second wave was delayed by fog, and got away hours later.

The German fighters waited

for the Thunderbolts to turn back before launching their attack on the first wave. Then dozens of single and twin-engined fighters pounced. For the next 90 minutes they tore into the bombers, concentrating on the rearmost bombardment wing, which lost 13 Fortresses. Four more went down from the two leading wings. Only as the target hove in sight did the attacks cease. Visibility was excellent, and the bombing, led by Curtis LeMay, was accurate. The force then veered to the southwest, crossed Italy, and landed in North Africa, the first of the so-called 'shuttle' missions. On arrival, 24 B-17s were missing; one had crash-landed in Italy; two more, badly damaged, had sought sanctuary in Switzerland, while four had ditched in the Mediterranean out of fuel. Refuelled and rearmed, the German fighters waited in vain for the return flight.

They were however rewarded by the arrival of the second wave, now three hours behind schedule. This time they concentrated on the leading bombardment wing. Twenty-one bombers were shot down by fighters on the way to Schweinfurt and one more was lost to flak over the target. The second wave did not head for North Africa; instead it returned to England, losing 14 more en route. Schweinfurt was

Above: Aircraft of the 381st BG lined up on the runway at Ridgewell prior to a mission. (USAF)

heavily hit, although accuracy was less than had been achieved at Regensburg.

Losses on this two-pronged raid were 60 Fortresses lost on the day, or 16 per cent. But worse was to come. When the remnants of the first wave returned from Tunisia, it was without 55 bombers too badly damaged to make the return flight. In all, the raid cost 118 aircraft, an unacceptable attrition rate of 31 per cent. American gunners had claimed an incredible 288 fighters destroyed, later reduced to 148. Actual German fighter losses were just 25. Nor was the damage on the ground particularly rewarding. Production resumed a few days later, and was normal after a few weeks.

BOMBING THROUGH THE WEATHER

The weeks that followed the Schweinfurt raid were quiet, with shallow penetrations only, as losses were made good. The B-17G started arriving in

Right: A Messerschmitt 110 curves away after attacking Fortresses of the 91st BG. (USAF)

England at about this time, ready for its combat debut. The 8th did not sally forth in force again until 6 September, when 338 Fortresses set out for Stuttgart. This time the main enemy was the weather. Heavy cloud covered much of Western Europe. Stuttgart was socked in and few so much as saw it; formation cohesion was lost. German fighters attacked in force over the target area, and again near Paris on the return flight. The result was a disaster. Eleven B-17s were lost to fighters; a round dozen had come down in the Channel out of fuel; at least two more crashed on landing, while five lost or damaged machines set down in Switzerland. All this with hardly a bomb anywhere near the target.

The weather was kind to Germany over the following weeks, and the remainder of the month passed with raids on French and Belgian objectives. On 15 September two 1,000lb

(450kg) bombs were carried on racks externally for the first time, one of the rare occasions on which this was done. Meanwhile, measures to overcome the worst effects of cloud were in hand.

In August 1943, the 482nd Bomb Group was formed at Alconbury, as the 8th Air Force's sole Pathfinder unit. It was made up of two B-17 and one B-24 squadrons equipped with British gadgets. The first was Gee, a comparatively short-ranged navigational device. The second was Oboe which, using signals from English ground stations, allowed fairly accurate blind bombing. The third was H2S, a primitive (by modern standards) ground mapping radar, later slightly improved to become H2X. The former was carried in a bathtub under the chin, the latter initially in a retractable dome in the same position, although production aircraft had this fitted in place of the ball turret. All Pathfinder aircraft carried smoke markers. Dropped above a solid undercast on radar indications alone, these left a distinctive trail above the clouds obscuring the target, providing a point at which successive waves of bombers could aim.

Pathfinding with H2S was pioneered on 27 September with an attack on Emden. The

leading Wing dropped with the Pathfinder aircraft; the second Wing dropped on the smoke markers, while the third was able to find a gap in the cloud and bombed visually. Post-strike reconnaissance showed that only the Pathfinder-led units had hit Emden; the visual bombers were miles adrift. A blind bombing leader was to become a standard part of most 8th AAF raids. First the technique had to be refined, and sufficient crews trained.

In 1943, the life expectancy of a Fortress was 11 missions; a tour of duty was 25 missions. When a crewman completed his tour, he was statistically dead twice over! Carpet, a gunlaying radar jammer, gradually entered service, and this equipment decreased the effectiveness of the flak. While flak destroyed only a small proportion of the bombers, it was responsible for most of those which returned damaged, while forcing them to bomb from ever higher altitudes, with a reduction in accuracy. Carpet was a British invention that saved many American lives.

The following month saw a return to Schweinfurt on the 14th by 291 Fortresses. The defending fighters held back until the bombers passed Aachen, when their escorts turned back. They then struck, in a way described by American official historians as 'unprecedented in its magnitude, in the cleverness with which it was

planned, and in the severity with which it was executed'.

SCHWEINFURT AGAIN!

By the time that Schweinfurt was reached, 28 bombers had gone down and others were badly damaged. The bombing was heavy and accurate, and only one aircraft was lost to flak in the target area. But now they had to run the fighter gauntlet once more on the homeward leg. Again they were assailed from all sides, and when they reached the relative safety of the escorts, all cohesion was lost.

Three ball-bearing factories had been hard hit, but once again the price was high. Sixty Fortresses were lost; five more crashed on reaching England, and 12 were written off with battle damage; over 26 per cent of the total. A further 121 were damaged but repairable. Barely one in three returned unscathed, and these figures might have been worse had the RAF not

sent fighters with long-range tanks to the aid of the hard pressed American escorts.

The defenders had taken the measure of the Fortresses. They used 21cm rockets to break up the closely packed bomber formations, then attacked en masse from head-on. The B-17 was able to sustain severe damage and keep flying, and it normally took several attacks on one machine to bring it down. The essential thing, from the German point of view, was to isolate it so that it could be picked off at leisure.

The second Schweinfurt raid underlined that unescorted bombers, no matter how well armed, could not fly daylight missions against determined fighter opposition without incurring unacceptable losses. Long-range escort fighters were needed desperately.

Using drop tanks, P-47s were able to penetrate a little way into Germany; P-38s a bit further. Then in December came the answer to the problem. The P-51 Mustang was a happy marriage of an American airframe and a British engine. Using drop tanks it could range deep into Germany and go all the way to most targets.

BIG WEEK AND BERLIN

Operations continued following the Schweinfurt raid, but poor weather meant that many of them were radar bombing missions led by Pathfinders. Few visual attacks could be made, and in January 1944 the 8th concentrated on V-1 launch sites in the Pas-de-Calais. Not until late February did the bombers really get into their stride again, as the clouds parted, giving clear skies over Germany.

Big Week, the period from 20 to 25 February, saw a concerted attempt by the Allies to cripple the German aircraft industry. At last with escort fighters able to accompany them, the bomb raided Focke-Wulf plants at Tuetow and Oschersleben; Messerschmitt factories at Augsburg, Regensburg, Gotha, Brunswick, Furth and Erla/Leipzig; the Junkers works at Bernberg, Aschersleben and Halberstadt; and Heinkel's facility at Rostock. German production losses were estimated at 1,000 aircraft. Total bomber losses, B-17s and B-24s, amounted to 226. Fighter escort losses during Big Week amounted to 28, but the low figure of bomber loss underlined their worth.

On 4 March, the bombers set off to Berlin, the only major German target not yet attacked in daylight. The weather turned sour, and the recall signal was issued, but one combat wing of 29 Fortresses failed to receive it and carried on. Realizing this,

B-17 UNITS THAT BECAME OPERATIONAL IN ENGLAND 1943

Group No.	Squadrons	Base	First Mission	Notes
94	331, 332, 333, 410	Bassingbourn	13 May 43	Last mission 21 Apr 45
95	334, 335, 336, 412	Alconbury	13 May 43	Last mission 20 Apr 45
96	337, 338, 339, 413	Grafton Underwood	14 May 43	Last mission 21 Apr 45
351	508, 509, 510, 511	Polebrook	14 May 43	Last mission 20 Apr 45. Clarke Gable, film star, flew with this group.
379	524, 525, 526, 527	Kimbolton	29 May 43	Last mission 21 Apr 45; flew most sorties, dropped greatest bomb tonnage.
381	532, 533, 534, 535	Ridgewell	22 Jun 43	Last mission 25 Apr 45
384	544, 545, 546, 547	Grafton Underwood	22 Jun 43	Last mission 25 Apr 45, dropped last 8th AF bombs of war.
100	349, 350, 351, 418	Podington	25 Jun 43	Last mission 20 Apr 45
385	548, 549, 550, 551	Gt Ashfield	17 Jul 43	Last mission 20 Apr 45,
388	560, 561, 562, 563	Knettishall	17 Jul 43	Last mission 20 Apr 45 flew 19 Aphrodite missions.
389	568, 569, 570, 571	Framlingham	27 Sep 43	Last mission 20 Apr 45
482	812, 813, 3rd sqn flew B-24s	Alconbury	27 Sep 43	Last mission 22 Mar 44, pioneer Pathfinder unit, also operational research.
410	612, 613, 614, 615	Deenethorpe	26 Nov 43	Last mission Apr 45
447	708, 709, 710, 711	Rattlesden	24 Dec 43	Last mission 21 Apr 45

Top: H₂X ground mapping radar, fitted in a retractable dome in the nose compartment, allowed blind bombing through cloud. This was an experimental installation.

Above: Radar-equipped pathfinder of the 401st BG, showing the retractable radome fitted in place of the ball turret. (Ralph Trout)

Right: Heavily armed Messerschmitt Me 410 commences its firing pass on a B-17F of the 390th BG.

ball-bearing factory in the Erkner suburb and against the Bosch factory at Klein Machnow, plus 249 Liberators which were to attack the Daimler-Benz engine works. Fighter cover was provided by 691 Thunderbolts, Lightnings and Mustangs, some of the latter

RAF, working in relays. The distance to Berlin ensured that no deceptive course changes could be used.

Assembling a massive armada in its correct order meant that it was under radar observation ong before it left the English coast. In the occupied countries and in Germany, fighter units were brought to readiness; on this day they were to meet numbers with numbers.

The bomber stream was 94 miles (150km) long, as it thundered eastwards at 180mph (290km/hr), but some four hours after the first bomber had taken off, it had become disorganized. The head of the stream, well protected by Thunderbolts, had inadvertently veered southwards. The 13th Combat Wing was running behind schedule, and had lost visual contact with the aircraft in front. Not realizing this, it continued on the correct course, thus forming an offset in the formation.

The first German fighters

headquarters allowed part of the escort to continue also. Fighters were encountered as the bombers neared the target, but they pressed on, releasing their loads on a Pathfinder's marker. They were intercepted on the homeward leg, but the Mustang escorts fought to protect them, losing 23 of their number. Five Fortresses failed to return, a surprisingly small loss under the circumstances.

Two days later the 8th tried again. The force consisted of 561 Fortresses, tasked against a

Above: Long-range escort fighters wheel protectively above B-17F Fortresses of the 390th BG. They tipped the balance against the defenders decisively. (USAF)
Right: Flying Fortresses over the German capital. The low squadron is barely in the contrail belt. (USAF)

attacked over Haselunne, just east of the Dutch border, to meet the 13th CW head-on. Only eight Thunderbolts were on hand to greet 107 Me 109s and FW 190s, and this was not enough to hold them off. The German fighters flashed between the bombers, guns blazing, and narrowly avoided collisions with them. Damaged Fortresses dropped out of formation in all directions. Black smoke from burning aircraft stained the clear sky; white parachutes blossomed below.

Calls for help brought more P-47s from all directions; these took some of the pressure off,

but there were simply not enough of them. The German fighters regrouped for another head-on attack. In all the battle lasted 45 minutes.

Meanwhile the front of the bomber stream was faring almost as badly. Attempting to get back on course, it crossed several flak zones before meeting up with another huge German fighter formation. The escorting Mustangs were in the

right place, but failed to avert the blow completely. More bombers went down, although the German interceptors paid a heavy price for their success.

At last the bombers reached Berlin, only to run into the most vicious flak that most of them had ever seen. Partial cloud foiled the bomb runs on two of the primary three targets but widespread damage was caused in the city. The return flight was

Above: Target Berlin! Tempelhof airfield can be seen near the right wingtip of this 452nd BG Fortress as it fines up on its primary target. (USAF)

marked by skirmishes with small numbers of German fighters, which were generally held at bay by the escorts. There was however one exception. Forty-four German fighters managed to assemble near the Dutch border; they cost the 388th BG six Fortresses.

Losses on the Berlin raid amounted to 73, of which 56 were Fortresses. Of these, three reached Sweden in a damaged state, while four were struck off charge in England. Fighters accounted for 45, fighters and flak for four; flak alone for six, while one fell to unknown causes. This was the largest bomber loss ever suffered in one raid by the 8th Air Force. However, it was not enough to stop the 8th. Over the next three days, two raids of similar strength were visited upon the German capital, and a third on 22 March.

With the invasion of Europe looming, priorities switched. Attacks against communica-tions centres intensified, while tremendous efforts were made to

Peenemunde was heavily damaged, but the price was high

reduce the German oil industry. On 12 May 935 heavy bombers raided oil plants at Bruex, Bohlen, Leuna, Lutzendorf and Zwickau. Meanwhile 15th Air Force was raiding the Romanian oil fields at Ploesti. Raid followed raid, and aviation fuel production slumped from 175,000 tons in April to 52,000 tons in June; 35,000 tons in July, and a mere 7,000 tons in September. This caused a tremendous reduction of German fighter effectiveness.

Below: A large hole through her fin making control difficult, Boche Buster of the 401st BG breaks formation to seek safety in neutral Sweden, 7 October 1944. (Bert Hocking)

FORTRESSES THROUGH THE BERLIN FLAK

'A dark puffy veil that hung like a pall of death covered the capital city. It was the heaviest flak I had ever seen. It seemed to swallow up the bomber formations as they entered it. One ship blew up and three others dropped away from their formations . . It didn't seem that anything could fly through that. But there they were, Flying Fortresses sailing proudly away from the scene of devastation.'

LT LOWELL WATTS, 388TH BG

THE FINAL ROUND

By October 1944 the bombing campaign against the Third Reich had sapped the strength of the German day fighter arm. Lack of aircraft was not the cause; plants in Germany maintained production at record levels, and the depots were full of replacements.

The critical shortage was of trained pilots. The German fighter units had suffered swingeing losses. Experienced men were irreplaceable; novices rarely lasted long. Then, as the fuel shortage bit ever harder, training was curtailed, and the quality of replacement pilots dropped still more. Even the ever-shrinking band of old stagers sometimes found themselves grounded for lack of fuel. From this time on, only on rare occasions were they able to put up serious opposition to the American armadas. Fortress operations over Germany became safer and in the closing months of the war, it was possible to fly a full tour and never

encounter a German fighter in the air! The flak defences were strengthened, and losses began to exceed those of the fighters. This reduction in risk was acknowledged by the USAAF, who increased the number of sorties in a tour of operations from 25 to 30, and eventually to 35.

While in the early months the loss rate of Fortresses was horrendous, a few survived to complete more than 100 missions. Others were no longer sufficiently reliable for operations, although still flyable. One use for some of these was as assembly ships. Positioning hundreds of bombers into the correct order was not easy. One solution was to paint war-weary aircraft in bright colours and strange patterns. These unmistakeable psychedelic monsters were then launched and took up their assigned place in the assembly area, where their assigned formations took station on them. When all was in order, they returned to base.

APHRODITE

B-17s were also used as radio-controlled flying bombs. Stripped of all unnecessary equipment, these were packed with 20,000lb (9,000kg) of Torpex high explosive. For Project Aphrodite, these were flown off by a two-man crew, who parachuted to safety near the English coast. Control was then handed over to a specially equipped 'mother' aircraft, which remotely guided the flying bomb to its target. The hazardous Aphrodite missions were flown by the 388th BG from Fersfield, an isolated airfield in the wilds of Norfolk, but the difficulties of accurately guiding them onto their targets, plus a couple of unfortunate accidents, ensured that only a handful of missions were flown.

Left: The 91st BG unloads over Berlin on smoke markers dropped by lead aircraft in February 1945. The nearest aircraft is a late model B-17G, with the taller dorsal turret. (USAF)

B-17 UNITS THAT BECAME OPERATIONAL IN ENGLAND 1944

Group No.	Squadrons	Base	First Mission	Notes
	803	Oulton	5 Jun 44	Countermeasures Squadron Largely replaced by 2 B-24s, Aug 44
486	832, 833, 834, 835	Sudbury	1 Aug 44	Last mission 21 Apr 45
487	836, 837, 838, 839	Lavenham	1 Aug 44	Last mission 21 Apr 45
490	848, 849, 850, 851	Eye	27 Aug 44	Last mission 20 Apr 45
493	860, 861, 862, 863	Debach	8 Sep 44	Last mission 20 Apr 45
25 (R)	652 Sqn	Watton	Nov 44	Composite unit, weather recon.
34	4, 7, 18, 391	Mendlesham	17 Sep 44	No losses to enemy fighters

Other experiments carried out from Fersfield involved Batty, a system using a television-guided bomb. Rather ahead of its time, Batty was beset with technical difficulties, and achieved little.

Some idea of the reduction of defensive effectiveness was given on 22 February 1945, when 1,411 heavy bombers attacked communication centres all over the Third Reich from the low altitude of 10,000ft (3,050m), chosen to achieve bombing accuracy against small targets. Losses were remarkably low. One B-17 was lost to a Me 262 jet fighter, while four more went down to flak, which damaged a further

Right: B-17F Talisman, *seen here at Port Moresby in 1943, was one of the last B-17s to operate in the Pacific theatre. (USAF)*

Left: The 30mm cannon of the Messerschmitt Me 262 jet fighter packed a tremendous punch. This Fortress was lucky to survive. (USAF via Alfred Price)

Below left: In the final months of the war flak was the main hazard. On 10 April 1945, Wee Willie of the 91st BG went down on its 124th sortie. (USAF via Alfred Price)

85 aircraft. Just to show it was no fluke, 1,193 heavies went out on the following day, losing only two of their number. This pattern continued.

The British Lancaster routinely carried bombs of up to 12,000lb (5,400kg), but Fortress (and Liberator) bays could not accommodate a bomb larger than 2,000lb (900kg). The Disney bomb was introduced to correct this shortcoming. Weighing 4,500lb (2,000kg), it used rocket propulsion to pierce 20ft (6m) of reinforced concrete.

Nine B-17s of the 92 BG each carried four Disney bombs on underwing racks to the U-boat pens at Ijmuiden on 14 March 1945. Only one hit was scored, and a further raid was mounted, but soon the Allied advance overran the area, making further attacks unnecessary.

Just four days later, the 8th mounted its final major attack on Berlin with 1,327 heavy bombers. They were met by an estimated 40-50 Me 262 jet

fighters, which accounted for a mere eight Fortresses. The remaining 16 bombers which failed to return, plus a further 16 which force-landed in Russian-held territory, all fell to flak. The loss rate of three percent, while heavy for 1945, was a far cry from the first Berlin raid just over a year earlier.

By now worthwhile targets were becoming few and far between, and on 16 April, General Spaatz stated that the strategic air war was over; from then on only tactical targets remained. The final 8th AF bombs of the war were dropped on the Skoda Armament Works at Pilsen on 25 April 1945, by a B-17 of the 384th BG.

As by far the majority of Fortress operations in the Second World War were flown by the US 8th Army Air Force based in England, it was only to be expected that the narrative would mainly concern itself with these. But the B-17 served well and faithfully with other air forces and in other theatres.

We have already touched on the early years of the Pacific War. While those Fortresses there at the start gave sterling service, backed up by the reinforcements, this period was essentially tactical. There was little scope for strategic bombing until the Japanese advance had been

B-17 OPERATIONAL STATISTICS 8TH AF

BG No.	Missions	Sorties	Bombs	A/c Missing	Sort/Miss (tons)
303	364	10,721	24,918	165	64.98
306	342	9,614	22,575	171	56.22
91	340	9,591	22,142	197	48.68
305	337	9,231	22,363	154	59.94
379	330	10,492	26,460	141	74.41
94	324	8,884	18,925	153	58.06
95	320	8,903	19,769	157	56.70
96	320	8,924	19,277	189	47.21
384	314	9,348	22,415	159	58.79
351	311	8,600	20,357	124	69.35
92	308	8,663	20,829	154	56.25
100	306	8,630	19,257	177	48.78
388	306	8,051	18,162	142	56.70
390	300	8,725	19,059	144	60.59
381	296	9,035	22,160	131	68.97
385	296	8,264	18,494	129	64.06
447	257	7,605	17,103	97	78.40
410	255	7,430	17,778	95	78.21
452	250	7,279	16,467	110	66.17
457	237	7,068	16,916	83	85.16
398	195	6,419	15,781	58	110.67
97	14	247	395	4	61.75
301	8	104	186	1	104.00
TOTALS	**6,034**	**181,828**	**422,788**	**2,935**	**av61.95**

halted, which did not occur until mid 1942. While the Fortresses helped to hold the ring, there was little more they could do. Vulnerable to fighters at medium and low altitudes, they yet lacked the precision to hit either small fixed targets or moving ships from high altitude.

This was all too clearly demonstrated at the decisive Battle of Midway in June 1942, when 19 B-17s were based on the island. During the four days of battle, they flew over 80 sorties in the course of seven missions. They first attacked the invasion force; the main Japanese carrier force twice; two cruisers; a solitary destroyer; and finally an American submarine under the impression that it was a Japanese cruiser. They claimed hits on two battleships or heavy cruisers; two transports; three aircraft carriers, and finally

'sank' the 'cruiser'. During this flurry of activity, two B-17s were lost. In actual fact there was not even a near-miss. The sunk 'cruiser' had of course crash-dived to safety.

This is not to denigrate the efforts of the Army fliers, but it does provide an illustration of the difficulties; first of hitting moving targets from a level bomber, secondly of distinguishing bomb hits from other signs of battle, and thirdly of ship recognition by aviators, all from 3 miles (5km) up!

When at last the situation stabilized and the Japanese were forced onto the defensive, high-altitude bombing came once more into its own. However, the distances in the Pacific were so vast that the longer-ranged Liberator was preferred to the Fortress, which from mid 1943 had vanished from the scene. A few aircraft went to India, but the same factors applied.

In any case, the days of the Flying Fortress were numbered; a specification for an ultra long-range bomber was issued in 1942. The B-29 Superfortress was far larger than its predecessor, better armed, longer ranged, and could carry a much bigger

Below: The Boeing B-29 Superfortress commenced operations in the Far East in June 1944, as B-17 production was being run down.

293845

Above: Tail gunners rarely carried cameras, which makes this view of B-17Gs of 15th AF setting out from their Italian base the more interesting.

bombload as well as bigger bombs. B-29 bases in the Marianas Islands became operational from October 1944, and from then on, Japanese targets were under constant attack, culminating in the nuclear raids on Hiroshima and Nagasaki which brought the war in the Pacific to an abrupt close. B-17 production peaked in March 1944, but was thereafter run down in favour of the B-29 Superfortress.

MEDITERRANEAN THEATRE

Two B-17 groups were detached from the 8th AF in November 1942 and transferred to the newly formed 12th AF, commencing operations from Maison Blanche in Algeria on the 16th of that month. They were joined in the spring of 1943 by the 2nd and 99th BGs, and carried out raids on targets in the western Mediterranean area.

Once German resistance in North Africa had ceased, they moved forward to raid Sicily, softening it up for invasion.

Distances in Europe were generally shorter; fighter escort,

often from bases on Malta, was usually available; and the German and Italian flak and fighter defences far weaker. The weather was better, and usually the primary target was bombed from high altitude. The Fortresses then flew in very low over the sea, under the enemy radar coverage, before pulling up to a moderate altitude to bomb.

When bases on the Italian mainland became available, a new command, 15th AF, was formed. While a considerable portion of heavy bomber strength in Italy consisted of Liberators, the Fortress strength was increased with the arrival of more B-17 BGs, although Fortress numbers never exceeded one fifth of the B-17 strength of the 8th AF. As the Axis forces were driven back in 1944, so 15th AF joined in the campaign against oil targets with raids on Ploesti in Romania.

Shuttle missions were not an 8th AF prerogative. On 2 June 1944, 130 B-17s of 15th AF bombed communications targets in Hungary before continuing to Russian airfields near Kiev. Two days later they attacked targets in Romania from the Kiev area, before once more raiding Romania while returning to Italy.

ROYAL AIR FORCE

Reference has already been made to Fortresses in RAF Coastal and Bomber Command service. In the former they were mainly used on anti-submarine patrols, operating from stations as diverse as Chivenor in Devon, Benbecula in the

Hebrides, and the Azores, from where they helped to close the infamous mid-Atlantic Gap. The Azores, some 900 miles (1,450km) east of Lisbon, are part of Portugal, and Portugal was neutral during the Second World War. Permission to use Lajes airfield on the island of Terceira was granted when Britain invoked a Treaty of Alliance dating back to 1386!

European weather comes mainly from the southwest, and other Coastal units were Meteorological Reconnaissance squadrons, whose aircraft also ranged far out into the Atlantic, recording weather conditions which would allow the accurate forecasting so necessary for planning bombing raids.

Finally two squadrons equipped with Fortress IIIs (B-17Gs) flew with the No. 100 group of Bomber Command from Tempsford and Oulton, packed with black boxes on electronic countermeasures sorties.

BLACK CROSSED BOEINGS

There was however a third major combatant which operated the B-

Below: Coastal Command Fortress IIs and IIa's of No. 220 Squadron at Lajes in the Azores, December 1943, from where they played a sterling role in containing the U-boat menace. (Bruce Robertson)

17. The Luftwaffe was naturally very interested in this new opponent, which was frequently encountered in the autumn skies of 1942. What were its strengths and weaknesses? Shot-down Fortresses were eagerly examined and deductions made. Then, with Christmas approaching, the Germans received a present when a fairly intact B-17F made a wheels-down landing in northern France. It was taken to the flight test centre at Rechlin where all its secrets were laid bare, after which it was used for fighter affiliation trials. Nine months after its capture, it was sent to I/KG.200, a unit engaged in clandestine operations. Over the next 15 months it was joined by two more B-17s, and they were given the fictitious designation Dornier Do 200.

The black-crossed Fortresses task was the dropping of agents behind Allied lines. The area covered by these operations was vast, from Ireland in the west to Trans-Jordan in the east and Algeria in the south. Just one of these aircraft survived the war, and was recaptured at Altenburg in April 1945.

ODDBALLS

During and shortly after the war, many Fortresses were converted for uses other than bombing. Transport was an obvious choice, although the circular fuselage cross-section did not particularly lend itself to this.

Four Fortresses were evaluated as transports. One, fitted with side windows and 38 seats, became the XC-108; this was later used in the Pacific by General MacArthur as a personal transport. The second was fitted with a large side-loading cargo door to become the XC-108A. The third was fitted out as an executive transport as the YC-108, while the fourth was converted to a fuel tanker as the XC-108B. None entered production. More numerous was the CB-17, a conversion of war-weary bombers to the transport role.

Yet another wartime conversion was the F-9. This was a long-range reconnaissance machine based on the B–17F, which carried both vertical and oblique cameras. Depending on the equipment carried, these became F-9As, Bs and Cs.

At the end of the war, the USAAF converted B-17Gs to the search and rescue role as the B-17H. This was fitted with a sea search radar under the chin, and a para-droppable lifeboat under the belly. The US Navy also had its own uses for the type; fitted with an APS-20 search radar it became a pioneer airborne early warning aircraft, with the designation PB-1W.

Above: Dornier Do 200. A captured B-17 wearing Luftwaffe markings at Orly Airport, Paris, in December 1942. (Roger F. Besecker)

The PB-1W also carried out maritime reconnaissance and anti-submarine missions. Yet another user was the US Coast Guard with the PB-1G, a long-range air-sea rescue machine, which was occasionally used for iceberg reconnaissance sorties. But despite these conversions, there were far too many Fortresses. The vast majority were scrapped.

RAF SQUADRONS OPERATING FORTRESSES

BOMBER COMMAND
No. 90, high-altitude bombers, Fortress I Nos 214 & 223, electronic countermeasures, No. 100 Group, Fortress III

COASTAL COMMAND
Nos 206 & 220, anti-submarine, Fortress I, II, IIa and III, Nos 59 & 86, anti-submarine, Fortress III Nos 251, 517, 519 & 521, meteorological, Fortress III

POST-WAR B-17 DESIGNATIONS

Transports	CB-17G
	VB-17G
Reconnaissance	FB-17F
	FB-17G
	RB-17F
	RB-17G
AEW/Maritime Reconnaissance	1PB-1W
Air/Sea Rescue	PB-1G
	SB-17G
Target Drone	MB-17G
	QB-17G
	QB-17L
	QB-17N
	QB-17P
Drone Remote Controller	CQ-4
	DB-17G
	DB-17P
Engine Test Bed	EB-17G
	XPB-1W
Pilot Trainer	TB-17G

Above: *Waist gun positions in a B-17F, June 1943, showing the gun mounting and ammunition feeds.*